OXFORD LIBRARY OF
AFRICAN LITERATURE

General Editors

E.E.EVANS-PRITCHARD
G. LIENHARDT
W. WHITELEY

Oxford Library of African Literature

A SELECTION OF AFRICAN PROSE
I. Traditional Oral Texts
II. Written Prose
Compiled by W. H. WHITELEY
(*Two Volumes*)
(Not for sale in the U.S.A. or Canada)

THE HEROIC RECITATIONS OF THE
BAHIMA OF ANKOLE
H. F. MORRIS

SOMALI POETRY
An Introduction
B. W. ANDRZEJEWSKI *and* I. M. LEWIS

PRAISE POEMS OF TSWANA CHIEFS
I. SCHAPERA

THE GLORIOUS VICTORIES OF 'ĀMDA ŞEYON
KING OF ETHIOPIA
G. W. B. HUNTINGFORD

A SELECTION OF HAUSA STORIES
H. A. S. JOHNSTON

THE CONTENT AND FORM OF YORUBA IJALA
S. A. BABALQLA

AKAMBA STORIES
JOHN MBITI

LIMBA STORIES AND STORYTELLING
RUTH FINNEGAN

IZIBONGO
Zulu Praise Poems
TREVOR COPE

THE MEDICINE MAN
HASANI BIN ISMAIL and P. A. LIENHARDT

I. A Zande Homestead

THE ZANDE TRICKSTER

EDITED BY

E. E. EVANS-PRITCHARD

*Professor of Social Anthropology
and Fellow of All Souls College
in the University of Oxford*

OXFORD
AT THE CLARENDON PRESS
1967

Oxford University Press, Ely House, London W. 1

GLASGOW NEW YORK TORONTO MELBOURNE WELLINGTON
CAPE TOWN SALISBURY IBADAN NAIROBI LUSAKA ADDIS ABABA
BOMBAY CALCUTTA MADRAS KARACHI LAHORE DACCA
KUALA LUMPUR HONG KONG TOKYO

PRINTED IN GREAT BRITAIN
AT THE UNIVERSITY PRESS, OXFORD
BY VIVIAN RIDLER
PRINTER TO THE UNIVERSITY

PREFACE

THE Azande people of Central Africa have a body of folk-tales about a man called Ture. In a very broad way of speaking all their folk-tales can be spoken of as *sangba ture*, Ture tales,[1] but in the selection presented here only those are included in which Ture is the central character, so that they may be seen as variations of a single theme.

Chapter I gives a brief account of the Azande. There is a considerable literature about this people, but the general reader, who, I trust, will enjoy these tales, will require some introductory guidance if he is to understand them, not having read that literature nor having had the experience of living with the Azande, and this I have tried to provide. A short select bibliography is appended for the benefit of those who might wish to read more about them.

Chapter II gives an account of when, how, and where the tales were collected, and also in it there are comments on some of their main characteristics; not that I consider myself competent to make any very original analysis of them. Indeed, I scarcely make an attempt at one. So far as the purpose of this book is concerned, to present an example of African imaginative thought, my own view is that they are best read simply as tales, without my trying to get between the reader and the read with elaborate structural and sociological interpretations.

Chapter III contains the stories themselves, with occasional footnotes where the significance of a word or sentence requires them. The final chapter, IV, gives some different versions of the tales, so that the reader may understand better how much each tale is a construction of the teller.

In Appendix I a tale, in which Ture is not mentioned, is given in Zande, so that it may be seen what the tales look like in that language. Zande is a very complicated language and therefore a difficult tongue to master—but, here again, grammars and dictionaries listed in that appendix are available for all who wish to consult them. This is not a linguistic study—that may

[1] As among the Akan-Ashanti (R. S. Rattray, *Akan-Ashanti Folk-Tales*, 1930), tales in which the spider does not appear are still called *Anansesem*, spider stories.

come later. I should say, however, that there are different ways of writing Zande, with regard to spelling, diacritical marks, and word-division; and, without entering into the question, which sometimes in the recording of African languages engenders some heat, state baldly that this is my way of writing Zande. In Appendix II, I give an index to the tales as printed in journals and other publications.

A second volume of Zande texts, dealing with historical events, institutions, customs, and conversational pieces, is in course of preparation.

I had hoped to obtain from Zande friends some more of the Ture tales and also other texts, and to settle some points arising in the translation of them. The serious political situation in the Southern Sudan has denied me this opportunity.

CONTENTS

LIST OF PLATES   x

ACKNOWLEDGEMENTS   xi

I. THE SOCIAL AND CULTURAL BACK-GROUND   1

II. INTRODUCTION TO THE TALES   15

III. THE TALES

1. How Ture got food from the sky   37
2. How Ture released the water   38
3. How Ture spread fire over the earth   39
4. Ture and Nanzagbe's termites   40
5. First account of Ture and Depago   43
6. The honouring of Ture's son in the place of Ture   44
7. Ture's wife and the great bird Nzanginzanginzi   48
8. Ture and Depago again   50
9. How Ture cheated the Prince Man-killer   52
10. How Ture fought with Nzangirinza   54
11. First account of Ture and One-leg   55
12. How Ture lacked termites because of dancing   58
13. Eye-bees and Big-ears   59
14. The running of Ture and One-leg   61
15. Ture and the woman's dogs   63
16. Ture and Thunder's eggs   67
17. The shooting of guinea-fowl by Ture and the Orphan   71
18. How Ture swept around the grave of ghosts   73
19. How Ture chased the Weaver-birds into the bush   75
20. How Ture lacked termites because of fear   76
21. How little Monkey consumed Ture's porridge   77

22. How Ture lacked termites because of laziness 79
23. Tortoise and the termites of Wagtails's sons 81
24. Ture and Bat and Duiker and bread-fruit 84
25. Ture's terror at a fire-hunt 87
26. How Ture struck the ground-fruit for salt in vain 90
27. How Mbiangu saved Ture from death by fire 91
28. How Ture killed Big-tooth for bread-fruit 93
29. Ture and Cicada 95
30. Ture and Red Duiker 97
31. How Ture's page got the better of him by trickery 99
32. Ture's war with Gburenze and his sister 100
33. Ture and Nzuangba 106
34. Ture and Man-killer again 108
35. Ture, Frog, and the river Baku 109
36. Ture and a man's fish 111
37. How Ture brought out his intestines 111
38. Ture's sons and the *kpengbere* elephant 113
39. How Ture used his eyes as fish bait 117
40. Ture and how it began with an egg 119
41. Ture's fight with a man and his sister 124
42. Ture and Yangaimo's feathers 126
43. Ture, the youth, the old woman, and the ripe fruit 128
44. How Ture burnt Leopard all over 130
45. Ture and Duwainga 133
46. Ture and Eye-bee 135
47. Ture and Bakureako 135
48. How Firefly cheated Ture 137
49. How Ture killed his father 139
50. The fathers of Ture, who were Bambasi and Bangirimo 141
51. Ture and his mother-in-law 144
52. Ture, Nanzagbe, and the toad 146
53. Ture and Civet Cat 149
54. Ture, his mushrooms, and Death 150

Contents

55. Ture, Leopard, and Cricetus — 152
56. Ture and Bativogo — 153
57. How Ture was saved by his dogs — 155
58. Ture and Leopard's fruit — 156
59. Ture and Kpikoro — 160
60. Ture and the Orphan — 162
61. Ture and Nguali — 163
62. Ture's failure with his termites — 165
63. Ture and Wilimbia — 168
64. Ture and the two brothers — 168
65. Ture and the old hoe — 170
66. How Ture saved a child who fled from Man-eater — 171
67. Ture and the hypocritical mother-in-law — 177
68. Ture and Bangbangate — 180
69. Ture and Bakumeme — 183
70. Two sisters — 184

IV. SOME DIFFERENT VERSIONS

A to D. How Ture released the water — 185
E to G. Ture's sons and the *kpengbere* elephant — 190
H. A man and his daughters Ingo and Kpoko — 205
I & J. Ture and Yangaimo's feathers — 209
K to M. Ture and the woman's dogs — 213
N. How Firefly cheated Ture, and Ture and Nanzagbe's termites — 223

APPENDIXES

I. Vernacular version of Tale 70, 'Two sisters', with line-by-line translation — 225
    Forward — 225
    Two sisters — 225
II. Index of Ture stories in print — 235

LIST OF PLATES

I. A Zande Homestead — *Frontispiece*

II. *a.* A Termite Mound — *facing page* 48
   b. Witch-doctors

III. *a.* Gong and Drum — „ 96
   b. This could be Ture

ACKNOWLEDGEMENTS

THESE are made to the authors and publishers of books and to the editors of journals in which these tales first appeared. They are listed in Appendix II. I express my thanks also to those who have read the tales in manuscript: my co-editors of the Library of African Literature, my colleagues at the Institute of Social Anthropology at Oxford, Mr. A. Tyson of All Souls College, and Mrs. E. Ettlinger. I am indebted to the Azande, mentioned in the text, for writing many of the stories, and also, in some cases, for translating them. I thank All Souls College for financial assistance in the publication of some of the texts in the vernacular.

ACKNOWLEDGMENTS

CHAPTER I

THE SOCIAL AND CULTURAL
BACKGROUND

(1) READ just as pieces of oral literature these tales require very little general background of Zande social institutions, for they are seldom referred to in them, even by allusion. The plots are placed in homely commonplace activities, eating and drinking, cooking, collecting termites, hunting animals, fishing, gathering honey and wild fruits and yams and mushrooms, salt-making, the wearing of barkcloth, the use of magic, and so on. But, treated in a scholarly and analytical way, what the tales omit to mention, what sectors of the Zande social life they pay little or no attention to, may be as significant as what they speak of. Therefore a sketch of their way of life in general is presented, though with particular reference to what is related in the tales.

(2) The Azande live plumb in the centre of Africa on the Nile–Congo divide. As their country is very extensive, natural conditions are not the same in all parts, those of them to the north occupying savannah forest while those to the south live in tropical rain forest. In this book I speak only of those of the north-east (the Sudan), whom I know best and where most of the tales were recorded. I want to make it clear also that when I say the Azande do this or that I am sometimes using what we like to call the 'ethnographic present', that is to say, what I observed them doing or what we know used to be their custom. It is over forty years since I first visited them, and doubtless many changes have taken place, but I cannot give an account of them, because I have not revisited their country since 1930. They are well represented—one might almost say famous—in the literature of Central Africa, usually under the name 'Niam Niam'. Nevertheless, no one seems to know how many Azande there are, or were; estimates have varied between 750,000 and 2 or 3 million, or even more.

(3) The Azande of the Sudan live for the most part in undulating

savannah forest, threaded by innumerable small streams running into a few large rivers flowing northwards into the Nile. But though this vegetation belt is called savannah forest it is best described as bush or scrub, for trees have a stunted appearance and are sparsely distributed. They are unlike what we ordinarily have in mind when we think of forests, except along the streams, where the trees grow high and dense in fringing forest—what has been named 'gallery' forest. The country is covered with grass, which during the rains is so high and dense as to discourage anyone from leaving the paths that constant use keeps clear of vegetation. During the dry season, when little or no rain falls, from the end of November to March, the grass withers and the bush is fired, the undulating shape of the country then being revealed, all black with charred grass and brushwood. Here and there are ironstone or granitic outcrops, mentioned in the tales, either bare or covered with a carpet of dwarf grasses and in the rains holding pools of water. Because it is more convenient for them, Azande prefer to make their homes at the side of streams; but owing to the prevalence near water of tsetse carrying trypanosomes fatal to man, the administration of the Anglo-Egyptian Sudan compelled them to settle away from streams and along roads, where they could also more easily be subject to inspection—a movement which was taking place during my sojourn among them.

(4) Historical records about the Azande go back to about a century ago, the period of the first explorations of the valley of the upper Nile, in the observations of the Italians Piaggia and Casati and the Russo-Germans Schweinfurth and Junker; but oral traditions taken down by some of these early explorers, and by others who came after them as administrators and missionaries, take us back another century or so, and there is no reason to doubt their essential accuracy.

It would appear that the Ambomu people, led by their Avongara rulers, moved from what was then their homeland in the valleys of the Mbomu and Shinko rivers and later became Afrique Équatoriale Française (now the Central African Republic) and in the course of their migrations conquered and occupied a vast territory in the north-eastern part of the country that became the Belgian Congo (now the Republic of the Congo) and the south-western part of what became the Anglo-Egyptian Sudan (now the Republic of the Sudan). In the course of these migrations, wars, and settlements, they absorbed politically and assimilated culturally a number of foreign peoples, some of whom, however, retained their languages and distinctive customs into the present century and some even to the present day. The resultant politico-cultural amalgam is what we know as the Azande people, that is to say, a people of very mixed ethnic origins who have accepted Vongara rule, as the Ambomu had done, and either completely or in the main have adopted Avongara-Ambomu language and custom, though, as is commonly the case, the conquerors also acquired cultural traits from the conquered and made them their own.

(5) Zande history is almost entirely a history of war. War was waged incessantly against neighbouring peoples during the period of expansion, from probably about the middle of the eighteenth century, till it slowed down a century later, and to these wars were added dynastic struggles over the spoils, war of kingdom against kingdom. From about 1860 Arab caravans seeking slaves and ivory began to penetrate Zandeland and to add to the confusion, which was further increased by the Egyptian Government's attempt to establish control; the overthrow of that Government by the Derwishes, who also tried to gain control, made for further disturbance. Then, at the same time, and ostensibly to drive out the Derwishes, but also to grab as much of Africa as 'they could, there arrived on the scene French, Belgian, and British (Anglo-Egyptian) forces, who imposed their rule on the Azande, dividing their country between them so that they came under three different European administrations. The kingdom of Gbudwe, where I conducted most of my research, was the last to lose its independence, in 1905, when Gbudwe was killed by an English patrol. Since the European Powers have departed the Azande have still been under three different, but now African, administrations.

(6) Zande political institutions have developed in and by these many decades of turmoil. We do not know how the royal clan, or family, of the Avongara came to gain leadership of the Ambomu people but Azande agree that they greatly increased

their power and prestige during the migratory wars, and we do know that eventually they founded six dynasties, all descended from King Ngura, who lived seven or eight generations ago. These dynasties ruled over autonomous kingdoms, some fifteen of them in about 1880 (the number varied from time to time). Kingdom was separated from kingdom by a wide stretch of unoccupied bush. Each kingdom occupied some thousands of square miles and probably contained a population of from 50,000 to 100,000 inhabitants (one can only make a rough estimate, almost a guess). The density can scarcely have been more than ten to the square mile, perhaps less.

A kingdom was divided (and this seems to have been the same in all kingdoms) into provinces ruled in the name of the king by governors appointed by him, who were for the most part his sons; when he died these sons became independent rulers and sometimes fought each other to enlarge their heritage and for control of the central province the king had administered in person. In Gbudwe's kingdom there were twenty-six of these provinces towards the end of his reign. When a prince became independent on the death of his father he was a monarch in his own right, and planted out his sons as governors of provinces as his father had done. Delegation of authority to provincial governors was inevitable. The size of a kingdom and the fact that communication was by foot meant that a king could not exercise direct control over more than a portion of it. Each province was a kingdom in minature, its governor having the same authority in it as the king had in his, and each was organized on the same pattern. The governor's court was in the centre and he delegated authority to deputies in charge of districts.

A king and his governors had similar functions. All important legal cases came to them for judgement and their verdicts in them were final. They had command in war, their subjects being enrolled in military companies of married and unmarried men, the latter having barracks at court, where some of the young warriors would usually be stationed. The upkeep of the court, the maintenance of its officials and retainers, and provision for clients of one sort or another, depended on tribute paid by the subjects in labour and food.

(7) Before they were herded into settlements along roads Azande

lived in isolated homesteads separated from each other by stretches of bush, each homestead being the abode of a family. Sometimes a homestead straggled, each wife having her huts, granary, courtyard (a cleared space in front of the huts), and permanent garden apart from the others; sometimes the homestead was circular or oval, the huts and granaries of the wives ranged round a common courtyard with a ridge of earth and rubbish edging it. Beyond the homestead were the cultivations, under crop or fallow, and in the surrounding bush the family had their private water supply, their termite mounds with their mushroom beds, their supply of firewood, and clay, wood, and straw for building. Each family thus had its little estate, rather like farms in our own country, and there was nothing corresponding to what we think of as a village. Winding paths ran from one homestead to the next and close neighbours were usually blood or affinal kin. But there were no local communities based on kinship. In so far as we can speak of local communities at all, it would have to be in political terms, in reference to those homesteads which came under a deputy of the governor of the province in which they were situated.

The Zande family might well be described as patriarchal. Wives had a decidedly inferior position in the home and were treated more as servants than as partners, though in this matter appearance could lead one astray, because in spite of apparent subservience, if a husband neglected or ill-treated his wives they could, especially if there was only one wife, make life very uncomfortable for him. This is illustrated in these Trickster tales. When Ture, the hero of them, enrages his wives beyond forbearance they retaliate. In spite of all his bravado he is afraid of them, and could even be said to be hen-pecked. Since no statistics are available it can only be said in a general way that polygamy was common, older men often having several wives, and kings and princes dozens of them. In the old days a man paid at least twenty spears for a bride, and these were not easily acquired. The fact that older men and those higher in rank, being wealthier, were able to marry several wives made it difficult for young men to marry; and, the penalty for adultery being heavy, sometimes severe mutilation, homosexuality was common. Youths were entirely dependent on their fathers in the matter of marriage, or on the generosity of a prince whom they served at court. A father was therefore very much master of his home and family and had many sanctions to support his authority. A daughter was supposed to consent to a marriage. In practice her father chose her husband (very often from birth), and he was likely to be swayed by considerations of wealth and social influence. Ture of the tales, with his three wives, is a prototype of, and a kind of skit on, the Zande *bakumba*, a middle-aged man of substance.

As among all non-industrial peoples, kin relations outside the family were, and are, important, but among the Azande it was only close relations—near uncles and aunts and first cousins—from whom a man might expect much help. The only kin relationship mentioned in the tales is the *ando*, maternal uncle, to whom Azande turn in adversity, and whose possessions they may, if they are not too greedy, steal with impunity— unless the uncle is a cross-grained person. A man is born into his father's clan, and there are hundreds of these (totemic) clans throughout Zandeland. They are widely dispersed, having no common territory and engaging in no corporate action. Consequently, beyond an obligation of hospitality, ties of clanship count for little. When Ture appeals for help to his maternal uncles the term would seem to mean members of his mother's clan rather than his mother's own brothers, for he could not otherwise have tricked them. The importance of in-law relations, involving respect and reserve and tension on both sides, is very evident in some of the tales.

(8) A word often used in the tales with a pronominal suffix is *bakure*. Strictly speaking this means 'blood-brother', but it is sometimes used in a rather loose sense for 'friend'. Zande men, because they are friends or wish for security or for some economic advantage, make blood-brotherhood between them by consuming each other's blood. A blood-brother may not refuse any reasonable help asked for by his partner, and the obligation extends, though less forcibly, to members of his clan. It is believed that should a man refuse such aid his partner's blood will kill him, and perhaps his near kin of the same clan as well. The expression 'blood-brother', now well established in ethnographical writings, is unfortunate, at any rate for the Azande, for it suggests that the ceremony by which the pact is sealed makes

the partners of one blood, as natural kin are, whereas the tie is of quite a different sort. The partners swallow each other's blood while a long spell is uttered, citing the obligations each will bear towards his partner, and calling on the blood inside the partner to avenge failure to carry them out. The procedure is of a typical magical order, the blood being treated as a 'medicine' through which, as with other magical substances, the spell operates.

(9) Today Zande economy is predominantly agricultural. There are indications that the cultivation of crops was not so extensive even a century ago. The staple food crop in the Sudan is eleusine or finger millet, but other cultivated plants also have a considerable part in a Zande's diet: maize, manioc, ground-nuts, sweet potatoes, sesame and other oil-bearing plants, bananas, peas and beans, gourds, and yams. Also cultivated are tobacco and a Ficus from the inner bark of which bark-cloth, which they drape around their loins, is manufactured. There is decisive evidence that some of the more important of these plants are a fairly recent addition to Zande economy, because they originate on the American continent—maize, manioc, ground-nuts, sweet potatoes, and tobacco—and could not therefore have reached the Azande before the seventeenth, and possibly not till the eighteenth or nineteenth, centuries. Preparation of the ground, sowing, and weeding, and for the most part harvesting, are naturally wet-season activities, commencing in the first rains in April and ending with the last showers in November, though the main grain crop, the eleusine, is reaped early in the dry season.

(10) Azande have no domesticated animals other than dogs and chicken. Cattle, sheep, and goats, are not to be found anywhere in their country. This is presumably because these animals cannot survive where trypanosomiasis is prevalent. One might conjecture whether or not they would take to animal husbandry were their country cleared of tsetse, for stock, especially cattle, have none of the cultural, as distinct from food, value they have for their Nilotic neighbours to the north, who are interested in little else. Zande dogs are most delightful creatures—efforts, so far as I know unavailing, have been made to establish the breed

in England—and they are excellent hunters and highly prized on that account. In the past they were sometimes fattened up and their flesh cooked and served to an important guest. Chicken and eggs are regarded as great delicacies, but females are only killed for food on special occasions, when cocks are not available, because a plentiful supply of chicks is required for frequent consultation of the poison oracle. There can be no doubt that in the past some Azande were cannibals, and though it is now impossible to ascertain the facts with any certainty, it seems likely on the evidence obtainable that this was in the main a practice of some of the subjugated peoples and not of the Avongara-Ambomu, and that it was restricted to the eating of enemies killed in war, and executed criminals. It occurs in the tales.

(11) The produce yielded by cultivation is supplemented by hunting and collecting. Many Azande will eat almost anything they can lay their hands on—frogs, toads, snakes, caterpillars. Others are more fastidious, but even for them there is a wide choice of animal diet. The country is, or was, rich in many species of game, some of which figure as characters in the Trickster tales. Apart from casual hunting, mostly with the spear, and the use of snares and pits, there are two main ways of catching game. The first is used during the rains, when the grass is high. This is known as *gbaria* hunting, a *gbaria* being a stretch of bush in which animals are likely to rest, round which a path has been made by treading down the grass. By walking round this stretch of bush a man may observe from their tracks whether animals have entered it and are still in it. If there are tracks of entry and none of departure he summons his neighbours and they erect their nets as I have seen it, opposite the point of entry, station children on the two lateral sides to scare the animals should they try to break out, and then track them with the aid of dogs from the point of entry, to drive them towards the nets where men wait to spear them when they become entangled. The other method, referred to in some of the tales, called *tua*, is hunting by fire in the dry season. When the bush is burnt some stretches are not fired, and animals in what is otherwise open country seek cover in these unburnt stretches. Nets are then erected on one side and the grass is fired on the other sides. The animals, crazed

with fear of fire and blinded by smoke, dash towards the nets and are speared. In the case of elephant or buffalo nets are useless and the hunters hope that these beasts will be in such a state of confusion that they will fall to the spear. Fishing does not have so important a place, at any rate over most of Sudanese Zandeland, as hunting in the food supply, the streams which flow everywhere through the country being generally too swift for the Zande methods of fishing. The usual method, employed by women, is to double dam a stream and bale out the water till the fish are exposed and can be scooped out; though on some of the rivers men catch fish in traps, usually at waterfalls, and nets and baited hooks are also used, and also vegetable poisons.

(12) Many wild fruits are eaten, some of which figure in the tales, but the main harvest from the bush, apart from animals, is termites, which make excellent eating and are one of the most important constituents of Zande diet. The country is dotted all over with the mounds erected by these insects in the course of their excavations, and most families own at least one or two of them. Azande have ingenious ways of catching termites to which a whole paper might be (and will be) devoted. Here I mention only the commonest method, the one which figures in a high proportion of the tales. During the rainy season, if there is heavy rain early in the morning, called *sangu*, followed by strong sun, this brings about ground conditions which induce the winged termites to swarm at night. People in advance clear the grass and scrub round the mounds, dig holes where the runs indicate that the insects are likely to emerge, and collect reeds which they dry and bind to serve as torches. The habits of different sorts of termites are known, including the time of night they prefer to take flight. So the people, men and women, go to await the swarming, taking a firebrand with them to kindle a fire for warmth, protection against beasts of prey, and to light their torches. Every now and again they inspect the mound to see what the termites are doing. First some of the wingless insects, what Azande call their sentinels, begin to bore their way through the clay crust of the mound and peer out. If they like whatever it is they experience they continue this operation till the winged ones are ready to take flight. If they do not like conditions—if, for instance, it starts to rain—they retire to the interior

of the mound and there will be no swarming that night. Termites are very sensitive creatures and not only demand suitable
conditions but are also easily alarmed, so the watchers must
watch in silence. All being well, out the winged insects come
and take flight. Torches are then lit and held above the holes
earlier dug. The insects fly towards the flames, get their wings
singed, and drop to the ground, where they mill around till they
fall into the holes. It helps a lot if there is a crescent moon, for
if it is full moon the insects may fly towards the greater light and
ignore the torches. If left to themselves they fly away, dropping
their wings as they do so. When the swarming is over the insects
are scooped out of the holes, stuffed into bags, and taken home.
Those which are not dead by morning die when exposed to the
sun to dry. They are eaten as a relish, very often being pounded
into a paste which can be stored. Termites also provide Azande
with a secondary crop, mushroom beds cultivated by these
insects, each sort of termite having its own kind of mushroom.
These are also excellent eating. Another harvest from the bush
mentioned in the tales is honey. The hives of wild bees, ferocious
little creatures which attack on the slightest provocation, are
usually in tree-hollows, though in some parts of the country logs
are hollowed out and placed in the forks of trees to entice bees
to colonize them. Azande stupify the bees with fire and smoke
and scoop out the honey, bees and all. Also mentioned in the
tales is the making of salt. It is made by women, who burn
saltmarsh plants and make an infusion from the ashes.

(13) Frequent reference is made in the tales to food and eating,
as we might expect. I do not go into details, but a few explanatory comments are needed. Maize, ground-nuts, manioc, sweet
potatoes, gourds, and yams may be eaten roasted and by themselves. The main meal of the day, however, is *bakinde*, a mash,
usually of pounded and ground eleusine, which resembles solid
porridge and is stodgy and unpalatable by itself, and so is
served with a flavouring of cooked meat, chicken, fish, termite
paste, or oil (sesame or other vegetable oil). If these delicacies
are not at hand the housewife has to make do with vegetable
leaves, principally leaves of manioc, though this is regarded as
poor man's flavouring. The flavouring, whatever it is, is called
pasio, the more restricted meaning of which is 'flesh', and the

meal as a whole is generally referred to as *bakinde*, the accompanying relish being understood. A good deal of grain, mainly eleusine grain, is brewed into a thick but palatable beer which is almost as much food as drink.

(14) Products of craftsmanship figure in the tales, so passing reference should be made to the fact that Azande are acknowledged to be skilled builders of huts and granaries (on stilts), constructing them out of clay, wood, and grass; they are also potters, making many types of pots for drawing and storing water and for cooking and brewing; carvers in wood (gongs, drums, stools, bowls); smelters (smelting was seldom practised after the introduction of trade iron); smiths (spears, knives of many shapes, axes, billhooks, bells); and weavers (shields, baskets, and mats). Speaking generally it might be claimed that for a so-called primitive people they have a rich material culture.

(15) The labour of cultivating is shared between men and women, the men doing most of the tasks requiring greater strength, such as clearing the bush, but also taking their share in sowing, weeding, and hoeing. Men alone hunt; women do most of the fishing. Both sexes catch termites; men collect honey and wild fruits and yams; women make salt. The crafts are a male occupation. On the other hand, domestic chores are the women's portion: cooking, pounding, grinding, drawing water, gathering firewood, making up the homestead fires, cleaning the huts and courtyards, looking after the small children, and the many other tasks which the running of a home entails.

(16) I suppose that the simplest way of assessing an African people's way of looking at life is to ask to what they attribute misfortune, and for the Azande the answer is witchcraft. It is true that there is a vague belief in a rather shadowy person called Mbori, the word missionaries use for God in want of a better, who is regarded as being ultimately, but in a passive and permissive manner, the cause of what happens; in the Zande representation of him he is more or less otiose, and he has no cult. Indeed Azande show little interest in him. He is mentioned in the stories. It is true also that homage is paid to ancestral ghosts, though what a Zande has chiefly in mind are his dead father and

mother, the *atoro buba* and *atoro nina* of his supplications at his homestead shrine on such occasions as harvesting of first fruits and the building of a new home; but the cult is a purely family one and the intervention of the dead is a sanction only between members of a family. Should such conduct not be in question and a breach of the obligations of blood-brotherhood not be an issue, Azande will attribute misfortunes to witchcraft, *mangu*. As misfortunes are frequent, especially sickness or fear of it, accusations of witchcraft are equally frequent, and witchcraft is invoked as a cause almost spontaneously in most circumstances of failure in health, in hunting, in cultivating, in craftsmanship, etc. Indeed scarcely a day passes without one's hearing of somebody being bewitched. Witchcraft, it must here be said to avoid misunderstanding, is not an explanation of events alternative to what we should call natural causation, but a supplementary explanation of why a happening affects a particular person adversely. A man sustains an injury: he is injured by a buffalo while hunting. Witchcraft explains why he and not another was hurt, why on that occasion and not on another, why, that is, a particular person suffered at a certain time and place.

When a misfortune occurs, when for instance a man falls sick, a Zande hastens to consult one of his many oracles. The names of suspects put to the oracle are of those whom the aggrieved person believes are hostile to him. Envy, jealousy, hatred are the drive behind witchcraft, and hence the cause of failure, misfortune, and above all sickness and death. Witchcraft beliefs may thus be said to provide Azande not only with a theory of causation for particular events but also with a moral philosophy.

Lesser oracles may eliminate some of the suspects. The final judge of who is responsible is the poison oracle, and it is only on its verdict that a man can take action. A poison with strychnic properties (as we should regard it) is administered to a chicken and questions are put to it, the answers being established affirmative or negative, according to the way the questions are put, by the chicken's dying or surviving. The witch, having by this procedure been identified—shall we say as the person responsible for causing sickness—is then approached and asked to withdraw his witchcraft, which he does by swilling water in his mouth, blowing it out, and expressing his good intention. A Zande will also consult the oracle before starting on any major undertaking: marriage, hunting, a long journey, etc., and even about his health (at the beginning of each month), to make sure that a witch (a malevolent person with supposed psychic powers) does not lie in wait for him, or maybe a sorcerer (a user of bad and lethal medicines). He has other aids. He may summon witch-doctors to dance to diagnose the cause of his troubles. He is further protected and aided in his occupations by a vast number of magical medicines and charms; and all deaths, being believed to be caused by witchcraft, are today avenged by magical means; in the past, at any rate sometimes, it was by killing or exaction of compensation. Magical practices are a frequent motif in the tales.

King Gbudwe, I should say, did not approve of magic, except for a few traditional types; but after his death in 1905 new sorts of magic were taken over from foreign peoples and flowed into the country, and the volume was increased by the introduction of secret societies for the practice of magic, also taken over from foreign peoples. During his lifetime he prohibited these societies, which appeared to him to be subversive and a challenge to the authority of the royal Vongara house. He also tried, as did other rulers, to stop circumcision, which was likewise being introduced from foreign sources, together with a ceremonial of initiation which accompanied it; but when the power of the Avongara was largely broken by European administrations, they were unable to prevent the spread of circumcision any more than the spread of the secret societies, although these societies were prohibited by the European rulers.

(17) This has been a very brief account of Zande institutions and way of life, but no more, I believe, is required for an appreciation of the stories. Any reader who might wish to have more detailed information about them may consult some of the main sources listed below.

CALONNE-BEAUFAICT, A. DE, 1921. *Azande*. Bruxelles.

CZEKANOWSKI, JAN, 1924. *Wissenschaftliche Ergebnisse der deutschen Zentral-Afrika-Expedition 1907–8 unter Führung Adolf Friedrichs Herzog zu Mecklenburg*. Bd 6, 2: *Forschungen im Nil-Kongo-Zwischengebiet*. Leipzig.

EVANS-PRITCHARD, E. E., 1937. *Witchcraft, Oracles and Magic among the Azande*. Oxford.

EVANS-PRITCHARD, E. E., 1962. *Essays in Social Anthropology*, Chs.5–9. London.

—— 1965. *The Position of Women in Primitive Societies and other Essays in Social Anthropology*, Chs. 4–8. London.

'GERO' (GIORGETTI, F.), 1966. *La Superstizione Zande*, Bologna.

HUTEREAU, A., 1922. *Histoire des peuplades de l'Uele et de l'Ubangi*. Bruxelles.

LAGAE, C. R., 1926. *Les Azande ou Niam-Niam*. Bruxelles.

LARKEN, P. M., 1926. 'An Account of the Zande,' *Sudan Notes and Records*, vol. ix, pp. 1–55.

—— 1927. 'Impressions of the Azande', ibid., vol. x, pp. 85–134.

REINING, CONRAD, C., 1966. *The Zande Scheme*. Illinois.

SCHLIPPE, P. DE, 1956. *Shifting Cultivation in Africa*. London.

CHAPTER II

INTRODUCTION TO THE TALES

(1) GENERALLY speaking, anthropologists during the last few decades have ignored the folk-lore of the peoples they have studied. There have been exceptions, and I would like to pay tribute to an essay stressing their importance and discussing the manner in which they should be recorded and treated (E. J. Lindgren, 'The Collection and Analysis of Folk-Lore', in *The Study of Society: Methods and Problems*, 1939).

I have myself erred in this respect and this volume is an act of penance. Neither of my teachers, Seligman and Malinowski, showed much interest in the subject, and I do not think it would be an exaggeration to say that folk-lore was regarded by many anthropologists at that time as a peripheral subject, and folk-lorists as harmless old fogies; and not without reason, as anyone may judge for himself who cares to run through the pages of the Folk-Lore Society's *Journal*. I suppose it was because of this background that in my study of the Azande I took less interest in their tales for their own sake than I should have done. I took down a number of them, but mainly in the process of learning their language, as an aid to that end. These efforts are scarcely recorded here, because in that sense they are juvenilia and also because I have since been able to make use of other, and in many ways better, material.

(2) The Ture tales, of which this volume is a selection, have been compiled by several hands. In 1921 Mgr. Lagae published nine of them, with a French translation, in *La Langue des Azande*, vol. i. In 1926 the late Canon Gore published four in his *A Zande Grammar*, with an English translation. The Lagae collection was recorded in the Congo, the Gore collection in the Sudan. The late Mrs. Gore published a volume of fifty of the stories in the vernacular in 1931 (2nd edn. 1951 or 1954—the title-page bears both years): *Sangba Ture*. This collection, also recorded in the Sudan, has recently been translated by me and published in journals and privately printed papers (see Appendix II).

Fr. Giorgetti tells me that the first twenty-nine tales in the Gore collection were written by Antonio Kusakpio, a Catholic of Mupoi in Tembura District, who served as clerk to Major Larken round about 1920, when Major Larken was Commissioner for that district. When he was transferred to Yambio District he passed his copy of the original typescript to Mrs. Gore of the C.M.S. there, and she completed the collection and published it. We do not know who were the redactors of the last twenty-one tales, but it could have been Enoka Mangbondo, who wrote an introductory note to the collection. The provenance of the first twenty-nine therefore seems to have been the old kingdom of Tembura, and that of the last twenty-one the old kingdom of Gbudwe, and the dates for both were in the early 1920s. Between 1926 and 1930 I took down, as I have said, a number of the tales, and my at-that-time Zande clerk, Mr. Reuben Rikita, also recorded a number, in the Yambio District of the Sudan. I had begun to translate both when war broke out in 1939 and the task of translating these and many other Zande texts was abandoned till 1956. One text (N of Ch. IV) was written by a Zande schoolboy of Yambio District. Between 1961 and 1963 a Zande student at the University of Khartoum, Mr. Richard Mambia, made for me a new collection of the tales in the Yambio region; and in 1964 another student at the same University, Mr. Angelo Beda, added a few from the Tembura region. Most of these have now been published in vernacular and translation (see Appendix II). Fr. Giorgetti has recently got together a new collection and is preparing them for publication, with an Italian translation. He has kindly allowed me to include one of them in this volume. It was written by Mr. Raimondo Bitiringara of Tembura District. Except in the case of tales recorded by myself the redaction is almost certainly not a word-for-word rendering of the narrator's narrative but what the redactor wrote of what he remembered soon afterwards.[1]

[1] After this volume was completed Fr. J. J. Dijkmans kindly sent me his *Zande-Woordkunst*, a brochure published in 1965 by the Royal Museum of Tervuren. It contains a few short Ture tales written by Zande schoolboys in Lingala (with a Flemish translation), the lingua franca, and apparently at that time the language of instruction, in the Uele region of the then Belgian Congo. In the Zande section of the brochure, Ture is mentioned in three texts, but these are only fragments and seem to me to show missionary influence, though the author thinks the influence may be Semitic, through a different channel.

(3) For the first fifty tales I have retained the order they have in Mrs. Gore's collection, and to avoid confusion I have kept her titles also. However, where there is an alternative version I have often chosen it for inclusion in this volume in preference to the one in her collection. The versions I have used appear to me to have more of the flavour of the way a Zande tells the tales. Also, the Gore collection, being intended for use in mission schools, has sometimes been bowdlerized, either by the writer or by Mrs. Gore, and these expurgations of Rabelaisian humour lessen the dramatic effect. I may be wrong, but I further sense that here and there explanatory sentences have been inserted which would not be required in telling a tale to a purely Zande audience. The Gore versions are older, and it may be that in the later versions there is sometimes a slightly modern and literary touch, but these considerations are outweighed by those I have mentioned, and the further one that the literate Azande of a younger generation can write with greater ease than those, a very few, of the time the tales were written for Mrs. Gore; and their style is not so cramped and schoolboyish. The tales are consequently not all of the same period, not of the same quality. The tales recorded by Mr. Reuben Rikita have been translated by me; those recorded by Mr. Richard Mambia and Mr. Angelo Beda were translated by these two gentlemen, with some emendations of mine; those in the Mrs. Gore collection were translated by myself, with Mr. Angelo Beda's help; those in the Lagae and Gore (1926) collections have been retranslated by me. It must be added that there has been no attempt at collation; that would destroy the artistry of the stories.

(4) It is possible that the two Zande students who recently wrote some of these stories for me have been influenced by the Gore collection, either directly or through the tellers of them, but there is no internal evidence that this is so and I am assured by both that they were taken down from quite independent sources. In the case of Mr. Beda, he comes from an area where the Gore collection is not used for teaching purposes. Nor could the Lagae collection have influenced the tellers, as it was compiled in the Congo and did not circulate in the Sudan. With regard to Mr. Rikita and myself, I know that the tales were recorded from illiterate Azande who had never been to a mission school

or anywhere near one. It might be considered unfortunate that, except for the tales recorded by myself, the names of the tellers were not noted, but, even if noted, they would have been nothing but names, since in most instances the persons would have been unknown to me. Nor, I think, does it particularly matter who was the teller, for we are primarily interested in the theme of a story rather than its manner of presentation. The redactor's or compiler's initials or names are given after each title: R. R. (Reuben Rikita), R. M. (Richard Mambia), A. B. (Angelo Beda), L. (Lagae), G. (Gore, 1951 understood), G. 1926, T. (Tito), F. G. (Giorgetti), E-P. (myself). I say redactor or compiler, as almost certainly neither the Gores' nor Lagae's collections were recorded by themselves. They must, I think, have been written by mission boys.

(5) It cannot be said with any assurance whether the collection of plots in this volume is fairly complete. It is certainly not entirely complete, for I have heard others, not recorded. I say 'plots' rather than 'tales' because each time a tale is told it is in some degree a new tale, a point to be discussed later. It is not improbable, when we consider the vast area occupied by the Avongara-Ambomu, the different historical circumstances obtaining in the course of their expansion into different regions, and the different ethnic compositions met in them, that while some of the plots may be known throughout Zandeland others may have only a regional distribution. It is impossible to say whether this is so or not, because the Ture stories have been recorded in only a fraction of Zande territory.

(6) Ture tales are told after sunset, when the man of the home sits with his children, and perhaps also children from neighbouring homes, round the family fire in their courtyard. I must confess that I have not often heard them in this setting, it being a matter of chance whether one happens to stumble on a group while so engaged. As so often in Africa, it is regarded as improper, and also liable to bring about misfortune, should the tales be told in daylight. They are told by adults to children and mainly by men, though women also tell them. As far as I am aware adults do not tell them unless there are children present, for they are essentially stories for children, though this does not

mean that adults who happen to be present do not listen to them and enjoy them. The fact that the tales are familiar to them from their childhood, the plots and the development of them, incident by incident, being known to them as well as to the teller, does not seem to blunt their delight at hearing them again and again. Every Zande I knew, and I suppose every Zande, knew some of the tales and could tell them, though naturally some knew more of them than others, knew them better, and could tell them more expertly. The audience show their appreciation by their attentiveness, their laughter, their glee, their gestures, their chanting of the chants, and their responses to the teller's address to them: 'Children, here is a Ture story', to which they reply eagerly, 'Yes, yes, yes'; or again, 'Now it is time you were asleep', to which they reply, 'No, please tell us one more story.' 'No,' says the father, 'not tonight, I will tell you another one tomorrow.'

(7) This participation is lost in the tales as here set forth. Indeed they lose much of the vividness they have when recited. They are further dulled by translation for those unfamiliar with the setting in which action takes place and with those nuances of the Zande language that defy translation and are merely rendered ponderous if the attempt is made at a word-by-word translation; and they have also been impoverished in the process of recording them. In the absence of tape recorders they had to be taken down laboriously by long hand, and this in itself affects the narrative, leading sometimes to curtailed or garbled versions. The illiterate teller speaks too fast, and if persuaded to speak slower is checked in his habitual delivery. Then, either he or his redactor is inclined to omit repetitions and digressions and to shorten rather than spin out a tale; and I believe that there is a tendency to put direct speech into *oratio obliqua*, with a loss of vividness this entails. Further, the vivacity is lost: the tone of voice, the singsong of the chants, and the gestures and mimicry which give emphasis to what is being said and are sometimes a good part of its meaning. But perhaps most serious in the bare setting down of a tale in writing is the loss of the audience.

(8) The order in which the tales are presented is quite arbitrary. They cannot correctly be called a cycle of tales because there is

no conventional order in their recitation, and it is seldom that one story is connected with another. Each tale is complete in itself.

(9) We have no means of knowing when these tales originated or whether they all belong to the same period. One looks in vain for clues. They contain no identifiable archaism. Azande reckon historical time in the succession of their kings; but when, as is rare, the name of a king is mentioned, as in the case of Wando, this is an obvious adaptation to present circumstances.[1] None of our earliest authorities recorded any of the tales. All we can say definitely, therefore, is that the tales are at least fifty years old and that in essentials they are much the same today as they were then. Nevertheless, we may surmise that they are of considerable antiquity. In the first place Ture, the hero of the tales, means 'spider', so the Azande belong in this respect to a West African culture area (Ghana in particular). The tales could have spread to them by diffusion, but there are other indications of a western homeland. The matter is made more complicated by the poverty of ethnographical information in what used to be the French equatorial territories, and by the complex ethnic composition of the Azande, for we cannot be certain that they are all of Mbomu origin. Again, though in the absence of records one cannot be certain, the stories appear to be much the same over the whole of Zandeland, including, according to such information as I have received, the Azande and Nzakara under Bandiya rule. This would also suggest that they are of some antiquity and there are other indications that this may be so. Our own fairy tales are largely about kings and princes because they were part of our social order. Kings and princes with great authority have also long been prominent among the Azande, though their traditions relate that there was once a time when they had no such rulers, as I explained in Chapter I. It may therefore be significant that they do not play a considerable role in the tales, one commensurate with that which they have played in Zande history;[2] and it is worthy of note also that reference to them in

[1] Likewise, such expressions as 'as far as from here to Wau' or 'as far as from here to Mongala' also could not have been in the original tales, because the Azande had never heard of these places till very recently.

[2] It is true that the word for prince, *gbia*, occurs in the tales, but this word is used also in addressing any person of importance.

Zande proverbs, of which there are a vast number, is totally lacking. Then, Zande culture of today, and as far back as historical records go, is inconceivable without their poison oracle, so again it may be significant that it is scarcely mentioned in the tales. It may very well be that the Azande have taken over this oracle from some foreign people in the course of their migrations. Likewise, it seems curious that in the tales of a people so impregnated with witchcraft beliefs, witchcraft is scarcely mentioned (as also not once in their proverbs); and here again, on such slender evidence as we have, it is possible that witchcraft beliefs of the kind prevalent today were also taken over from a foreign people. Finally, as already remarked, it is highly probable that the Azande, today predominantly an agricultural people, were once primarily a hunting and collecting people, as the tales also suggest, their plots being mainly concerned with hunting animals and collecting termites, mushrooms, and honey. It is true that there could be other explanations; for instance, that kings and princes, poison oracle and witchcraft, are for Azande rather too close to the bone of harsh reality to figure in imaginative stories which take them into a world of fancy, but the suggestion I have tentatively put forward is also plausible.

While Zande culture and social life have undergone very considerable change during the last sixty years, this also is scarcely at all reflected in the tales. Modern changes have left almost no imprint on them. There is, for example, no reference to a hundred years of Arab and European occupation and no trace of missionary teachings, and there is no mention of what have become indigenous institutions, such as initiation rites and secret societies. Could this be because, as with our fairy tales (some may prefer the term 'Märchen', used by students of folklore), the world of make-believe, being largely beyond reality, is little affected by changes in it? Since this is the case for sixty years, we may have support for supposing that the tales, in much their original form, have survived the impact of cultural and social changes over a much longer period of time.

All this at least goes to show that the tales are not a sensitive celluloid plate which passively reproduces the pattern of social structure: the relations of princes and commoners, and those expressed in oracular consultations and accusations of witchcraft; and also such changes as occurred during the fifty years of British administration. This does not mean that sociological analysis is not required, only that it has explanatory limits. Clearly, to make any sense the tales must be in terms of the world around the teller and his hearers, imaginative constructions, like all conceptual thought, being derived from experience, including social relations.[1] They take place in a setting familiar to Azande, hunting, fishing, termite-collecting, eating porridge with sauces; and when in the stories the characters have animal forms, much of the sense depends on a knowledge of the habits and characteristics of the animals. Likewise, social relationships in them must evoke in Zande minds the idealized patterns to which they tend to conform. The behaviour in social relationships that Azande consider correct, and which on the whole they have learnt to expect, is figured in the stories: those of husband–wife, brothers (sons of the same mother), orphans, sister's son–mother's brother. Ture persuades people to help him by pretending that he is their sister's son because a Zande in trouble will hope for help from that quarter; the paternal uncle is regarded not so much as a friend in need as a disciplinarian. Another character is the orphan who speaks in a pleading voice. Azande regard a boy whose parents, especially the father, are dead as being a miserable person, for he has nobody to protect him or further his interests, especially by providing him with spears to marry. But we must not forget that though anchored to social reality, or the conventional image of it, the tales are fiction and present a caricature of it, almost an ironical parody, laughing at it, holding it up to ridicule.

(10) The teller takes his pick from his repertoire in what order suits his fancy. The structure of incidents which constitute the plot in each story is such that the stories could almost run into each other and cease to relate separate and distinct episodes. Tellers have, however, a device, not uncommon in fairy tales (e.g. in Greek fairy tales), for decisively concluding one tale before beginning another. This consists of a bit of nonsense in which the narrator says that when he was nearby he found people quarrelling; when he tried to pacify them one of them

---

[1] See F. C. Bartlett, 'Psychology in Relation to the Popular Story', *Folk-Lore*, vol. xxx (1920), pp. 264–73; also, e.g. Tom Beidelman: 'Further Adventures of Hyaena and Rabbit: the Folktale as a Sociological Model', *Africa*, vol. xxxiii (1963).

rushed at him and hit him over the head; and when he cried out the man gave him some meat, chicken, or eggs, some of which he ate and the rest he put on the lintel of the door over there: 'Boy, go and fetch it.' I was told that before a child gets to know that this is a joke he may go to look for it, but he soon learns that this is simply the way the narrator breaks off his story, and may also be a signal that it is bedtime. This tailpiece is omitted for the stories in the collection, except here and there where the recorder has bothered to add it. It is always more or less the same.

(11) Since Ture means 'spider' in Zande, we have to ask ourselves whether the Zande thinks of the character as a person or as an insect. There is no doubt that they think of him as a person. All our sources are agreed on this. Colonel Bertrand, the editor of de Calonne's book, equates him with Mbori, the word missionaries use for God, as a sort of culture hero.[1] Mgr. Lagae objects to this, for he says that Ture is not regarded with any respect, no more than is Uylenspieghel in our tales. No Zande takes him seriously, he is just 'un monsieur qui fait de sa poire'.[2] Major Larken[3] and Captain Philipps[4] agree on this point with Mgr. Lagae. All Azande with whom I have discussed the matter have told me that the character has the name Ture because he was so clever, like the spider which can make a web out of itself. Also, in the stories he is invariably given the human personal pronoun *ko* and never the animal pronoun *u*. A text I took down from Mekana Ongosi puts the matter in a way which I think would meet with general acceptance:

Azande tell the Ture stories to their children all the time. However, no one has ever seen him, though plenty of people think that Ture indeed once lived because everybody relates stories about Ture everywhere. That is why Azande say that they are true though no one has ever seen him. People think that Ture lived in the past on this earth with those people who were there then, although no one

[1] A. de Calonne-Beaufaict, *Azande*, 1921, p. 172.

[2] Mgr. Lagae, *Les Azande*, 1926, p. 73.

[3] Major P. M. Larken, 'An Account of the Zande', *Sudan Notes and Records*, vol. ix (1926), p. 28.

[4] Captain J. E. T. Philipps, 'Observations on some Aspects of Religion among the Azande ("Niam-Niam") of Equatorial Africa', *Journal of the Royal Anthropological Institute* (1926), p. 174. He was, I believe, much in debt to Mgr. Lagae and might not therefore be regarded as an entirely independent authority.

knows where Ture went to. Some people say that he went to the
Europeans and that he makes all those things Europeans possess.
That is why they hide him. They do not want to reveal where he is
to people in any circumstances. Azande say that if you go to the
Europeans and mention the name of Ture they will seize you and
will say to you, 'you reveal where Ture is, where you saw him'. So
Azande are frightened to speak about Ture to Europeans. However,
one thing is that people think that Ture is still alive today among the
Europeans. They say that the Europeans have hidden him lest many
people get to know about him. It is also he who has taught the
Europeans their skills. Azande begin to tell about Ture to their
little children while they are still little when they sit around the fire
with their father. Then their father begins to tell them stories about
Ture and also old affairs in which he himself took part in the old
days when he was at (King) Gbudwe's court. When these children
become men they in their turn tell them to their own children.

If it is thought that Ture may still be alive he must be thought
to be as immortal as the Scholar Gypsy or the Wandering Jew,
for in Sudan Zandeland, and possibly elsewhere, holes in rock
outcrops, presumably made by earlier occupants of the soil, are
sometimes said to be where Ture ground his grain and sesame
in ancient times.

The text I have cited above shows that Ture is thought of as a
person who at one time lived and may still be living, but there
is clearly some hesitation and doubt, and we might still ask
whether he is for Azande a real person or a fictional one. May
I first quote what I wrote thirty years ago:

It is very difficult to answer this question and perhaps the correct
reply would be that they half-believe in Ture. If you ask them they
reply, 'we Azande think that he must have lived because our fathers
have told us so . . .'. One can only say that Ture lives in the stories
told about him. It is no use asking who he was or is because Azande
only know him as the hero of a cycle of stories. Impossible things
happen in these stories—animals talk and so forth—but this does
not make Ture incredible to Azande. To them he is a real figure in
the situation of story-telling. But since he lives in the stories nothing
much is known about him outside them.[1]

Words like 'believe' and 'real' can have different senses.
Do we believe that Hamlet and Othello and Richard III were
real persons? Certainly there was a Richard III, but he was not

---

[1] 'Zande Theology', *Sudan Notes and Records*, vol. xix (1936), pp. 37–38.

the Richard of Shakespeare's play, who in a sense is more real
to us than what we may regard as the more shadowy historical
king, unless we are historians, and perhaps even then. In the
same sense Sherlock Holmes and Dr. Watson, although we
know them to be characters of fiction, are more rounded or
better defined figures for us than many of our flesh-and-blood
acquaintances. The question is perhaps irrelevant. We are
moving in a world of imagination, of the fairy tale and pantomime, in which the characters are real to us when we hear and
see them, especially when we are children, as are the Ture tales
to Zande children when they hear them told. Fiction imposes
itself on experience. Does one not experience Dublin through
the eyes of James Joyce?

A curious and ironical situation seems to have come about
when these tales were printed to be used as school-books by
C.M.S. missionaries. The only other reading for schoolboys was
religious texts, and since the missionaries vouched for the
authenticity of Bible stories they appear to have feared lest the
Ture stories, by being printed, should also be regarded as having
the same authenticity. So the Zande catechist(?) who wrote a
foreword to the Gore collection of the Ture stories was at pains
to warn the reader not to take them seriously, and above all not
to liken them to those of the Holy Book. Ture is a cheat, a
tempter who leads men astray, a liar, a thief, a murderer, etc.
But these are not true stories. They are children's tales. Ture
was the very opposite of Jesus Christ.[1]

(12) Another, and a similar sort of, question arises about the
animal characters in the stories, which act and speak like people,
but are at the same time animals with the characteristics of their
species. One can scarcely ask whether they are thought of as
animals or persons, though if the question be put directly to a
Zande he will say they are animals. But in the telling of the
tales, in the situation of the drama, they are both. They are
animals acting as persons and persons in animal forms. The
animal forms might be compared to the masks in Greek or

---

[1] One cannot, in the absence of Zande literature, set the tales against other
redactions and evaluate their representation of a literary tradition, as we can do,
for instance, in the case of *The Arabian Nights* (see *The Art of Story-Telling*, by Mia I.
Gerhardt, 1963, pp. 3–4).

medieval drama. These masks serve to depersonalize the other characters and to concentrate the drama on Ture, in whose person the plots are enacted.

Here again grammar helps us. The Zande language has five pronominal genders, masculine (*ko*), feminine (*ri*), animal (*u*), impersonal (*ni*), and neuter (*si*). Outside the stories a Zande would invariably, in my experience, use the animal pronoun when speaking of an animal, but in the Ture stories he will often use the pronoun for a person, *ko*, 'he'. Furthermore, he may in the same story switch from the human gender to the animal gender and vice versa. I do not think that this is due to inadvertence on the part of the teller or redactor. I think that a careful examination of the tales in the vernacular shows that the narrator used the one or the other gender according to whether the animal nature of the creature or the human qualities with which it is endowed in the story was present in his mind. Sometimes one is uncertain how to deal with the matter: when for instance we have such openings as 'There was a man called Leopard (*Mama*)' or 'There was a man called Vulture (*Nguali*)'. To avoid confusion I have sometimes used 'it' rather than 'he' for an animal character where the teller has used the animal gender we do not possess.

The dual nature of the animal characters in African stories has always confronted the translator with a problem in his presentation of them. Sometimes the difficulty has been got over by such titles as 'Mr. Leopard' and 'Mr. Duiker', but this does not look quite right. It clothes them too much in the garb of our own culture, makes them too Brer Rabbity, and deprives them of their distinctive animal traits, with which Azande are familiar. On the other hand, 'leopard' and 'duiker' do not look quite right either, when they are acting and talking like humans. In this quandary I have compromised, at the risk of seeming to be inconsistent, and have written the creatures' names with a capital letter where they act more or less like humans and with a small letter when they are presented more or less simply as creatures; but having embarked on one or the other course I have stuck to it in any given tale, in spite of the temptation to vary usage sometimes where the context suggests it might be appropriate to do so.

It should here be pointed out that the merging of human

personality with thunder is not so bizarre as it might appear to us, because for Azande thunder (*gumba*) has an animal nature, is some kind of creature. Consequently it is not out of place among the dramatis personae, as it is likewise not out of place among the Zande animal totems. As Gumba is also a personal name there might be some doubt when the character appears in the stories whether the word should be translated 'Thunder' or left as a personal name, were it not that the celestial, and, for Azande, animal, nature is sometimes clearly expressed in its exploding (*su*).

Although no examples are given, it should be mentioned that the Azande have other stories in which animals figure besides the Ture stories. They are on such topics as why frogs cry only in the evening; how hatred started between bushbuck and leopard; and how leopard was defeated by iguana. They are largely based on observation of wild life and they are to some extent aetiological. Although in them animals may sometimes talk and behave like humans, and one cannot make a hard-and-fast distinction between them and the Ture stories, one may assert that they are of a different genre. In most of the Ture stories the plot is focused on Ture—they are about a person—and the animals play only a supporting role. In the animal stories they are the main characters, and though they may be personified they are essentially animals. One might say that in the animal stories the animals are given such human attributes as are required for dramatic effect, whereas in the Ture stories persons are given animal forms. In the one animals act as persons, in the other persons act as animals.

(13) Although there is some substitution of one character for another in the tales, where substitution makes sense (e.g. in the Lagae version of Ture and Thunder's eggs, Crocodile takes the place of Thunder), animals cannot in many cases be interchanged without damage to the situations in which they figure. A fruit-eating bat steals fruit; it would not do to substitute a vulture. When one of the characters has to feign death, what more appropriate than the insect *kpikoro*, which does so in real life when disturbed? In the story of how Cicada fooled Ture who could play the part better than this insect with its six legs? Wagtails eat termites, and the story about Wagtail's sons would

be weakened if a bird which does not eat them were sub-
stituted for it. In the story of how Ture drove Weaver-birds into
the bush no other birds could take their place without making a
travesty of it, for the point of it is that these birds feed if they can
on grain and can play havoc with whole crops. Azande have
great knowledge of the wild creatures of their environment and
have selected to play parts in the tales those most appropriate
for them. It is possible that the characteristics of a creature may
have suggested the plot of a tale, as, for instance, in the story
about Cicada.

(14) It has been remarked that the depersonalization of the
characters by giving them animal forms tends to throw Ture into
relief. So also does the lack of characterization of the human
actors. Only Nanzagbe, Ture's senior wife, and Nangbafudo,
his second wife, are provided with anything like a personality,
just enough to act as foils to Ture. When other persons appear
on the stage they are nameless—a man, an old woman, an
orphan, a youth, a child, an ogre—or if they are named they lack
personal traits. It is not Hamlet without the Prince of Denmark
but Hamlet with only the Prince.

(15) Ture is best described as a trickster, to use the excellent
term employed by American ethnologists for the hero of
Amerindian tales (e.g. Paul Radin, *The Trickster*, 1956). This is
how he describes himself: 'I am Ture, the son of Ture's father,
who tricks people all the time.' The tales are almost all about
his tricks.

Ture is a monster of depravity: liar, cheat, lecher, murderer;
vain, greedy, treacherous, ungrateful, a poltroon, a braggart.
This utterly selfish person is everything against which Azande
warn their children most strongly. Yet he is the hero of their
stories, and it is to their children that his exploits are related and
he is presented, with very little moralizing—if as a rogue, as an
engaging one. For there is another side to his character, which
even to us is appealing: his whimsical fooling, recklessness,
impetuosity, puckish irresponsibility, his childish desire to show
how clever he is, his total absorption in song and dance, his
feathered hat, and his flouting of every convention. In spite
of his nefarious conduct he is never really malicious. Indeed he
has an endearing innocence. One is sorry for him when his

cocksureness gets him into trouble, when he overreaches himself and sheds frustrated tears. Then he is pathetic. We are ourselves acquainted with a similar figure in the folk-tales of our own and other peoples, and he appears in shadow-plays and Punch and Judy. And there is in him a touch of Don Quixote too, of Falstaff, of Charlie Chaplin of the screen, of Mr. Toad of Toad Hall. He is indomitable. In spite of every failure, misfortune, and humiliation he perseveres.

I do not suppose that any Zande would put the matter in this way but I think the character does appeal to them on the same grounds. I must confess here that I have often had the feeling that there is a good bit of Ture in the Zande character, or at any rate in the character of some of those I knew—a sense of humour, a tendency to show off, an admiration for slimness, and a preference for circumlocution. It is as though Ture had imposed his image on his creators. This is not a wildly fanciful suggestion. Whose personality among ourselves has not been in some degree shaped by characters of fiction with whom he has identified himself in imagination?

Perhaps Ture also appeals to Azande because he does what he pleases, what in their hearts they would like to do themselves. Indeed, the tales are rich in material for the psychoanalyst. What he would make of them I am not competent to judge,[1] but though a cobbler should stick to his last I cannot refrain from drawing passing attention to the many unedifying incidents, greeted with relish, in which Ture acts in a manner that would evoke horror and the strongest condemnation in any self-respecting Zande. He kills his father, he tries to kill his son, he attempts to murder his wife, he has sexual congress with his mother-in-law, and by implication with his sister also; and in the telling of the tales these monstrously uninhibited acts are accepted without demur. We may ask whether they are not pointers to dark desires. Perhaps an analytical psychologist could also offer interpretations of such monsters as the man with half a body (One-leg)[2] and the men with many ears (Big-ears), and also of how often in the tales it is an old woman against whom Ture matches his wits.

---

[1] They might be a problem for him, since there is nothing buried. All is on the surface and there are no repressed symbols to interpret.

[2] A half-man is a character in the tales of other African peoples.

Here I am out of my depth, but it may not be going too far to suggest that in the tales the opposite to the ordinary appears in the characters, as in pantomime. It is as if we were looking into a distorting mirror, except that they are not distortions. We really are like that. What we see is the obverse of the appearance we like to present. The animals act and talk like persons because people are animals behind the masks social convention makes them wear. What Ture does is the opposite of all that is moral; and it is all of us who are Ture. He is really ourselves. Behind the image convention bids us present, in desire, in feeling, in imagination, and beneath the layer of consciousness we act as Ture does.

(16) The tales are, of course, fantasy, they transport their hearers into an imaginative world, and in this respect they play in Zande life the role art plays in ours, and correspond to drama and fiction in our own society. But just as our drama and fiction mirror reality, so do the Ture tales. Here we must be on our guard, for much that appears utterly fantastic to us does not appear in the same light to Azande. There is nothing strange to them in magic. They practise it and see it practised every day. A story about oracles and magic that would be fantasy to us is common experience to them. So when we are told in the tales that a paste of vegetable ashes and oil (*mbiro*) is used to attain ends we would deem quite impossible of attainment, it is not the same for them, for they use these pastes to attain ends in ways which from our point of view are quite as irrational. Indeed, the point of a number of the stories is that the reason for Ture's failure is not that he uses magical means to attain his ends but that he uses the wrong kind of magic (medicines), or loses the medicines, or in his greed eats them because he cannot resist the taste of the oily paste. Nor were Azande unacquainted with cannibalism, for some of them practised it. Likewise, when in the stories people eat toads and caterpillars and grasshoppers this may for us add an element of fantasy to them, but it is not the same for Azande, many of whom would not hesitate to eat them if hungry, or even if not. Nor is the idea of incest, which was regularly indulged in by the class of nobles, unfamiliar to them, or even parricide, for it was taken for granted that sons of kings might kill them with sorcery.

Therefore incidents which may appear to us as going beyond the dramatic limits of fantasy, to be so preposterous as to lack excitement, humour, or even interest, intrigue and amuse Azande, because in them a sardonic twist is given to what could conceivably happen in a situation not wholly unfamiliar to them as it would be for us.

So, as they do not reject the possibility of Ture's being a real person, they do not reject the possibility of his exploits, however improbable they may seem to us. In the realm of magic nothing is theoretically (if we may so put it) impossible, provided you possess the right magic. In my experience Azande accept as true the exploits of two legendary witch-doctors which are just as improbable as those of Ture. This is one reason why it is so difficult to distinguish between myth and folk-tale. Both are imaginative constructions in which what we would regard as experience and make-believe are inseparable. We would say that when Ture eats a meal, what he is doing conforms to experience, and that when he goes to the sky, that is make-believe. But as parts of a story they are inseparable, and in the telling of the story if one is accepted the other is accepted too. You cannot move from acceptance to rejection without losing absorption in the story. In this matter I find myself, at least to some extent, in a comparable position, as I suppose many others do. Whatever the historians may tell us about King Arthur or Dick Whittington, one accepts them in a poem or on the stage as they are presented to us and the mind never entirely relinquishes that image. It must be remembered too that the Ture stories are implanted at an early age in the minds of children, who do not keep fact and fancy apart. Both are accepted in the tales as what happened, and though among ourselves, and among Azande also, the adult may have doubts about the validity of a tale, he continues to be emotionally tied to it. He cannot totally reject something out of which his imaginative life has been formed.

(17) It has just been remarked that no very clear distinction can be made between myth and folk-tale. This has been pointed out by others in reference to other peoples (e.g. Franz Boas, *Tsimshian Mythology, 31st Annual Report of the Bureau of American Ethnology* (1916), p. 880); and I would say that it is certainly

the case with the Azande.[1] It is true that Ture, like the Amerindian trickster, helps mankind. In the first three tales he gives
them successively food, plants, water, and fire, and these stories
might not only be given pride of place but also on that account
be labelled 'myths' and placed in a different category from that
of the rest of the stories; but they are told and received, so far as
I could observe, in exactly the same way and with the same
amusement as the others, the interest being in the tricks by which
Ture obtained these benefits rather than in the benefits themselves. Indeed it is clear from the sense of these three tales that
Ture was not motivated by charity, a desire to help mankind,
but by love of mischief, an irrepressible temptation to trick
people, to get the better of them and boast of his cleverness.

Only two widely known stories of the kind that would generally
be regarded as myths have been recorded for the Azande, one
relating how the royal clan originated and the other, earlier
referred to, how remarkable feats were performed long ago by
two witch-doctors. Azande speak about the events in them in
the same way as they speak about the incidents in the Ture
tales: 'People say this is what happened', 'We don't know
whether they are true or not but our fathers have told us that
these happenings really took place, so maybe they did', and
'Different people give different accounts, no one knows for
certain what took place'. I do not therefore think that Zande
myths can be demarcated from their Ture tales on the criterion
of credibility; it would have to be on other grounds, such as the
fact that the two myths give backing to the claims of a class and
a corporation, whereas the Ture tales have no institutional
significance.

(18) Two final topics remain to be discussed, albeit briefly:
the structure of the tales and some problems of translation. In
Propp's sense—he is concerned only with the morphology of
fairy tales (V. Propp, *Morphology of the Folktale* (1963), first published in Russian, 1928)—it might be said that there is only one
theme in the Ture tales, that of the trick. To use a simple termi-
nology we may, if we accept this, say that the theme is distributed throughout the tales in a variety of plots composed of a

---

[1] Miss Ruth Finnegan (Mrs. Murray) says much the same for the Limba of
Sierra Leone (*Limba Stories and Story-Telling* (1967), pp. 34–36).

number of incidents (the relations between which Propp calls functions). These incidents have an order required for artistic and also logical reasons: like the assumptions that you have to catch your hare before you can cook it, or that a detective cannot find clues before a crime has been committed. The mind will not endure fantasy if it is incoherent, and this imposes a certain degree of uniformity in the telling of a tale. However, so long as the story makes sense, incidents can be added or left out. One might say that they can be transposed from one story to another, were it not that there is no certainty that any particular incident belongs to one tale rather than to another. They are like beads on a string, you can take one off and put another on. Thus we find the same motifs in different tales, e.g. Ture puts custard-apple fruits over his eyes to deceive his pursuers; he uses the juices of a creeper to make those slip from whom he wants to steal; and he jams a boy's head into a bee's nest in the hole of a tree because he is piqued. Sometimes there is no ob-vious connexion between one incident and that which follows it, though there is absence of conflict, as in the tale of Ture, mush-rooms, and Death. One may even be in doubt whether to regard a story as a different version or a different tale. Thus in the story of Ture and the old hoe, incidents which form the plots of separate stories are strung together: how Ture swept around the grave of ghosts, and how Ture struck the ground-fruits for salt in vain. And are we to regard the two stories about the man with one leg as different versions of the same story or as different stories?

So we cannot correctly speak of variants of the tales, because there is no original to vary from; there are only different versions. The stories are never told in exactly the same way by different tellers, or even by the same teller on different occa-sions. They are not learnt by heart and merely recited.

Hence, since each individual creates, in the telling of it, a tale anew (see Albert B. Lord, *The Singer of Tales* (1960)), not only telling it in his own way but also, to some extent, in re-counting the sequence of incidents, dropping or introducing them or substituting one for another, improvising as he develops the tale, we may say that while there are a limited number of plots, there are as many versions of them as there are tellers, or even as many as the times a tale is told.[1] Nor is the audience

---

[1] Cf. the Revd. John S. Mbiti, *Akamba Stories* (1966), p. 26.

passive; by their response they also shape the tale. It follows that the plots, in the course of being shaped and reshaped by the innumerable re-creations of hearers and tellers, cannot be attributed to an author, but must be regarded as a product of a whole people, like language itself.

It follows also that as a tale goes from tongue to ear and from ear to tongue a story can in course of time be remodelled and undergo changes of emphasis and meaning. We know that this has happened, the story of Deirdre being a good example (Elenor Hull, 'The Story of Deirdre, in its Bearing on the Social Development of the Folk-Tale', *Folk-Lore*, vol. xv (1904)); but, as I have said, we cannot adduce evidence that this has happened to the Ture tales, the evidence being sparse and of little historical depth.[1]

(19) Passing reference may be made to style in the telling of the tales, as distinct from other Zande styles of speech, such as the historical narrative, court speech, and the conversational. It seems to me that these are definable forms on grammatical and other criteria, but clearly this is not the place to discuss the matter any further. What may be further remarked is that every teller of a tale has his own particular style, his modes of emphasis, intonation, chanting, gesturing, sentence construction, and choice of words and expressions, so that he makes the story his own not only by omissions, additions, selections, and sequence of incidents, etc., but also by his style, which is never quite the same as, and may be very different from, that of others; so much so that even after the lapse of forty years I can still tell by stylistic traits alone from whom I took down a story or other text.

(20) On the whole, translation of the texts was a fairly straightforward matter, though tenses, which are very complicated in Zande, were sometimes troublesome, especially as—Zande being a highly tonal language—one had to rely in translating from the Gore collection on the eye alone, without guidance from the

---

[1] Some experiments have been carried out to discover how a story can change from what is told to what is taken in and remembered and passed on, one of the first being F. C. Bartlett's 'Some Experiments on the Reproduction of Folk-Stories', *Folk-Lore*, vol. xxxi (1920), pp. 30–47.

ear. Here and there are sprinklings of idiomatic phrases which
require either a great knowledge of the language or help from
a Zande. Whether one may properly speak of a phrase as
'idiomatic' in a language that has no literary form might indeed
be questioned. Here the word is used in a special sense, to denote
such expressions as would not, if translated literally, convey the
meaning, or where a metaphor is employed which, for us, requires elucidation if the meaning is to be brought out. I say for
us, because for the Azande themselves the metaphor is familiar
and therefore the meaning plain. The chants are the most
serious translation problem. Sometimes they are onomatopoeia
or ideophones; sometimes they are incantations or spells; sometimes they seem to be quite meaningless, meaning being entirely
subordinate to sound, a sort of jingle. Even though an etymo-
logical derivation can be suggested, this must not be taken to
imply that that is what the sounds signify to Azande when they
hear the chants. When sounds in the chants appear to be meaningless they are left in Zande. These chanted pauses in the
narrative are very effective dramatically; they give the audience
the opportunity to participate, and they are also points from
which the teller can take his bearings and decide how he should
further develop an incident, or on which new one to start.

(21) Some of the proper names are suitably rendered into English:
e.g. *Baimiaboro*, Man-killer, *Bandurusa*, One-leg, and *Gumba*,
Thunder. Others would look incongruous if translated literally,
e.g. *Depago*, Cut into—side of—termite mound, *Nawongowongo*,
Mother (of)-the sound of grinding on a grindstone. These I
have left in Zande. Yet others appear to be just sounds, without
meaning but pleasing to the ear, e.g. *Nzanginzanginzi* and
Nzangirinza. Yet others appear to be simply proper names without any meaning connected with the story, e.g. *Nzuangba*,
Gburenze, and *Duwainga*, though all Zande names mean something. When they have no meaning relating to the story they
may get transposed, a character figuring under different names
in the same tale. I have not been entirely consistent in this matter,
even with animal names. Sometimes when the sense might suffer
were a name to be translated I have left it in Zande, and have
given the meaning of the word in a footnote, e.g. in the case of
Nguali, Vulture, in one of the stories.

(22) In some of the tales Ture or some other character consults an oracle called *Atari* which occurs only in the tales, not in real life. I have either left this word in the vernacular or just translated it 'oracle', because I have never been able to get a Zande to describe it other than as it describes itself in the texts.[1] Unlike oracles Azande consult, which take the neuter gender, *Atari* takes the animal gender, suggesting an animal nature, and it also speaks. The animal pronoun referring to it is in the plural form, *ami*, 'they', but for the sake of clarity I have used the singular, 'it'. The animal pronoun cannot be rendered by an English equivalent.

(23) A translator's task is not an enviable one. Translation from one European language into another is difficult enough; from a rich and complex African language into English is a yet more formidable undertaking. As one steers between the Scylla of too literal, and the Charybdis of too free, a translation, one is never quite satisfied with what has been achieved. It is some satisfaction, however, to be able to say that all the tales recorded in this volume have been, or are about to be printed in the vernacular in one place or another (see Appendix II), and are, or will be, therefore available to Azande themselves and to anyone else who can read their language or might learn to do so.

---

[1] Fr. Giorgetti discusses this oracle in *La Superstizione Zande* (1958), p. 96.

CHAPTER III

THE TALES

1. *How Ture got food from the sky* (R. M.)

ONCE there was no food on the earth. There was only one man who had food, and he had come down from the sky. When people began to die of hunger they went to that man so that he might give them food, but he chased them away. So, many people died of hunger. They told this affair to Ture, saying 'There is a man here with food, beside which he gets very angry.' Ture said 'You be silent, I am certainly going after that man.'

Ture went to that man's home and deceived him, saying 'Let us make blood-brotherhood, master.' It pleased this man very much. He and Ture made blood-brotherhood. Shortly afterwards Ture went to this man and said 'O my blood-brother, please give me some food, my children are dying of hunger.' Ture's blood-brother bent and said 'My blood-brother Ture, put your head between my legs.' Then this man flew with Ture to the sky. When they arrived there this man spoke to Ture thus: 'My blood-brother, collect some eleusine and some manioc and dig up twelve rats,[1] and then come and we will leave.' Ture did this completely. So once again this man bent and Ture put his head between his legs and he descended with Ture to this world here.

Ture returned to his home and gave the food to his wives. As they were eating this food Ture began to abuse this man, saying 'The man to whose home I went is bad. He told me to put my head between his legs before he would fly with me to get food.' This man heard what Ture said about him and he was very annoyed by it.

Afterwards, when the food Ture had brought was finished, hunger tightened on Ture and his wives. So he went to his blood-brother again and he flew with Ture to the sky. Ture

[1] *Akandu* are rats noted for their fat and are considered a great delicacy.

collected every kind of food there is in the world and put them into his big bag. But Ture's blood-brother went away from him and descended to earth here. Rain caught Ture in the sky and rained upon him till he was soaked. Ture then began to look for the way by which they had come. Ture found a very narrow path descending to the earth here. So he descended by this path to the earth. Ture walked for some distance and when he arrived at a bare stone-flat he tapped on a drum, and people came from all over the world. Ture distributed every kind of food to them and he returned home with his also. Because of Ture people eat today.

2. *How Ture released the water* (R. M.)

THERE was an old woman who planted many yams. They yielded (swelled) abundantly. People used to come and work for her and she used to cook them for them. But she never gave water to the people. She alone possessed water, which she dammed from other people. So whenever a man ate the yams they stuck in his throat, and when he writhed with them this old woman attacked him with her big knife and cut his throat with it. This woman killed many people in this way. However, Ture heard about this woman and arose and went to her home to work for her for yams. Ture already knew that she was hiding water from people. So Ture went and searched all around until he found the water she had been keeping from people. Ture drew some of this water in his bottle-gourd and put it in his bag. Then he went also and cut a hollow grass[1] and put it (one end of it) into his water. After Ture had worked for this woman she took a very large pot and filled it with yams and boiled them. She put them before Ture and went and sat down with her big knife and watched Ture closely, so that when he choked with the yams she might cut his throat. Ture then ate the yams and when they stuck in his throat he sucked up his water with that hollow grass he had put into his bottle-gourd in the bag. So Ture ate up all the yams without their sticking in his throat. This old woman went

---

[1] The Zande name is *mbepe*. It is *Beckeropsis uniseta* or *Pennisetum unisetum*.

again and cooked more yams for Ture, nice mealy[1] ones, and sat down again to watch Ture closely for the yams to choke him. Ture ate up all these yams of hers, for whenever they stuck in his throat he drank some of his water. The old woman went again and cooked yams even more mealy than the previous ones. Ture ate only a little and put all the rest in his bag. Ture then took one yam to eat it. After that he began to open wide his mouth and eyes as when something chokes a person. So this old woman jumped up from her place with her big knife and attacked Ture to cut his throat. When she was close to Ture he sprang up and landed a distance from her, and he started off at full speed and fled by the path to her water. She cried out, saying 'Ture, there is no way there. Ture, that is the way to excrement. Ture, there is no way there. Ture, that is the way to excrement.' Ture continued to run straight ahead and she shouted after him in vain. Ture then broke her dam and the water flowed everywhere. Ture stood on the far side (of the water) and said 'It is I here, I am Ture, it is I who have dealt with you.' That is why water is found all over the world.

3. *How Ture spread fire over the earth* (G.)

TURE arose to go to his maternal uncles, who were the Abare peoples,[2] and he met them under their forge, beating out their iron. They greeted him. Ture began to work their bellows for them. With deceit he came and took fire for everybody, for once upon a time people did not have fire. Ture went on blowing the fire, then he left, telling them 'I will return on the morrow to dance for you.' When the morrow came Ture gathered worn-out barkcloth around him at his home, a big stretch of it, and came and blew fire for a long time, and he arose and put his foot over the fire on one side, and his barkcloth glowed (caught fire), and the people put it out; and he jumped over the fire to drop on the other side, and the fire caught his old barkcloth, and they put it out again, but it was not

---

[1] *Upeupe* is a word applied to boiled or roasted tubers to indicate that a tuber is so thoroughly cooked that there remains no water in it.

[2] Two foreign peoples who form part of the Zande ethnic amalgam but have retained their languages.

extinguished, they tried in vain to put it out. Oh no! It glowed on Ture's barkcloth. The Abare gathered together to put out the fire on Ture; they tried in vain to put it out.[1] Oh no! Ture ran away with this fire and went with it into dry grass, and the fire spread everywhere in the dry grass in Ture's tracks. Ture went on running and stopped to speak his speech to the fire in a song, saying

'Fire you, I go on my way oo oo
Until you stay that wood of fire-sticks
And everybody has it oo oo.'

It was Ture who wanted to set light to his barkcloth to run away with it to that dry grass. Once upon a time people did not have fire, only those men, they blew fire. Ture went and showed people its place, and they knew about fire by this.

'I went here and saw men quarrelling, and as I tried to calm them one of them broke away suddenly and hit me hard, and when I cried out he took a small piece of meat and put it in my hand. And I brought it and put it on top of the doorway there, child, you go and fetch it.'

4. *Ture and Nanzagbe's termites* (R. M.)

RAIN fell. Ture and his wives set off to wait for termites (to rise). Ture went by himself and crossed a small stream. After collecting termites Ture began to return home. As Ture was crossing the brook a termite rushed out of his bag and fell into the water. A certain little fish called *pedi* suddenly appeared and snatched this termite, swallowed it, and sang a little song for Ture,

'Ture when you treat me thus
Ture it pleases me
Tiriri riri tiriri riri riri.'[2]

This song delighted Ture so much that he took some more termites in his hand and poured them into the water. The *apedi* burst out singing melodiously. Ture put the bag of termites down and began to dance with his feathered hat on his head. Ture was really doing something. The *apedi* ate up all these

---

[1] Barkcloth smoulders slowly.　　　　[2] This line is meaningless.

termites and ceased singing. Ture then rushed to his bag and gathered up termites in both hands and sprinkled them into the water. While the *apedi* ate them they sang their song and Ture was hovering in dance. When he was absorbed (in the dance) he lifted the whole bag of termites and emptied it for the *apedi* into the water. The song rang out in the stream jabberingly. Ture was totally absorbed in his dancing. The *apedi* ate up the termites, and Ture also grew tired of dancing. Ture took his bag and hung it on his shoulder. He said 'What shall I say to my wives presently, since I have poured all the termites into the stream for the *apedi*?' So Ture stumbled on purpose and fell into the water together with his bag. Ture was thoroughly soaked and his bag was half-full of water. Ture poured the water out of the bag, leaving just a little there. After that he dashed off home to his wives and said 'Something happened, it rained over there heavily. The termites did not swarm on account of this rain. That is why you see me here soaked through by it.' He poured out the water which was in the bag in their presence. His wives said 'Ture, with that foolishness of yours, whose termites will you eat?'

After that Ture's wives carried their termites to a stone outcrop to dry them on the surface of the bare rock. Ture said to himself 'What shall I do to eat the termites of these women?' While they went to a stream to draw water Ture scraped the bark from an *ndiri* tree[1] and twisted it over his wives' termites and they reddened (from the sap) like blood. When they returned Ture said 'Something has happened. Your brothers came and fought here and were speared. What you see on the termites is their blood. What will you do?' Nanzagbe cried out and said that while she looked the other way Ture should carry those termites to the bush. Nangbafudo on the other hand refused to listen and winnowed all her termites and carried them home. Ture then began to carry all those of Nanzagbe into a disused termite mound.[2] After that he returned home to Nanzagbe and said to her 'My sister, since you lack termites, grind some flour and give me salt that I may go with them to hunt meat for you in the bush.' Nanzagbe did accordingly. Ture went off with the flour after Nanzagbe's termites to the disused termite

[1] One of the *Euphorbiaceae*, probably *Bridelia feruginea*.
[2] A mound deserted by termites.

mound, where he pounded them and then cooked the flour (made porridge) to go with them. After a short time Ture had eaten up all the flour. So he returned again to Nanzagbe and said to her 'My sister, I have hunted in vain. I speared a beast but it got away. You grind me some more flour and maybe this time I shall kill a beast.' She did accordingly. Ture returned with this flour to the disused termite mound and ate it all with Nanzagbe's termites. So Ture went again to her for more flour. She said to herself 'Since Ture is full of trickery, what is he really doing in the bush? Whenever I grind flour (for him) I do not see anything which he brings for me from the bush.' So she ground some flour for Ture into a basket and then she made a hole in the bottom of this basket. Ture hung it on his shoulder and as he went on his way it fell speck by speck behind him. Nanzagbe began right away to follow Ture by the trail of flour and arrived at his disused termite mound. When she listened into the mound she heard the noise of Ture pounding termites and singing a song:

> '*Turu turu*,[1] if it had not been for Nanzagbe
> Where could I have eaten these (termites)?'

Nanzagbe took a little earth and threw it at Ture. Ture said 'You ugly lizard, if you throw earth into my termites you will get something (you won't like) right soon.' She threw some more earth, and Ture said 'You lizard, if I rush out at you right now, *he*?' When she threw earth the third time Ture then came out and saw that it was Nanzagbe. She said 'O Ture, what things you do! Have you not deceived me to carry my termites to eat them in the disused termite mound? Presently you will get something (which you won't forget).' Ture said 'O my sister, let me first eat my porridge. When I have had enough, stand well astride so that should I try to rush out you can cut down into me with your big knife on account of your termites.' So Ture ate up all his porridge, and he took his bag and hung it on his shoulder and gathered up his spears. Ture then said 'Nanzagbe, you stand astride at the entrance, and as I am about to dash out you can cut me with your knife.' Nanzagbe stood astride the entrance and raised high her knife. Ture deceived her by merely showing his head (outside all of a

---

[1] *Turu turu* is the sound of the pounding of the termites in a small mortar.

sudden) and withdrawing it. She tried to cut his head but she cut her own leg instead and fell down and fainted. Ture jumped over her springingly and alighted on the other side, and said to her 'I have got the better of you, it is I, I the son of Ture's father.' Ture then ran away. Nanzagbe limped home.

5. *First account of Ture and Depago* (R. M.)

THERE was once a man called Depago[1] who speared his father to death and burnt his father and ground his ashes into a horn.[2] This man was not in the habit of building huts. Ture wandered and met this man near a termite mound. Very heavy rain was about to fall. Depago said to Ture 'Friend, come, let us shelter from the rain.' Ture said 'But where is a hut?' He said 'Just come.' When the rain began to fall Depago took some of his father's ashes and wiped them on the mound, singing his song, which is

> 'Depago, Depago, quagmire,[3]
> Depago has cut a pool in the earth,
> Quagmire.'

The mound opened up, and they entered it. Ture then saw Depago's wives and his children and his home, and he was astonished. Depago brought food for Ture, and he ate it. When the rain stopped Ture said 'My friend, how did you acquire this skill?' He replied 'I killed my father and burnt him and ground his ashes into a horn.' Ture jumped to his feet and ran and rushed at his father and speared him, and he burnt him and ground his ashes into a horn. After that, Ture dashed to his wives and said 'You burn down all the huts, I have already found my hut.' As they delayed, Ture took fire and burnt down all their huts, but Nangbafudo alone prevented Ture from burning her hut. Ture said to her 'If I see you in my new home I will spear you with my spears.' After a little while the sky was cloudy and heavy rain approached. Ture told his wives and his sons 'You come and we will go to our new home.' They went until they found a big termite mound, and Ture said 'Here is our

[1] Depago means cut into (*de*) the side of (*pa*) a termite mound (*go*).
[2] He made a paste of oil and the ashes. This mixture into a paste of oil and ash of medicines is a common form of Zande magic.
[3] This could mean an underground hollow or pit.

new home.' When the rain began to fall Ture took his father's
ashes and wiped them on the mound, singing this song:

> 'Deture, Deture, quagmire,
> Deture has cut a pool in the earth,
> Quagmire.'

But the mound did not open. So the rain beat on Ture and his
wives and his children. Then Ture's wives set on Ture and he
fled from them. So they returned and begged that wife of Ture
who had not burnt her hut, and she opened her door for them
and they entered to shelter from the rain. Ture returned and
started to rebuild his wives' huts. It taught Ture that it is not
wise to jump at (imitate) what other people do (without
having their skill).

6. *The honouring of Ture's son in the place of Ture* (R. M.)

AFTER spending many days (without seeing his in-laws) Ture
decided to visit them. So he said to one of his sons 'Wana,[1] get up,
let us go to my in-laws. I haven't seen them recently. My good
thing (delicious food) may have gone bad at my mother-in-law's.'

When they were near the home Ture took out his fine black-
dyed barkcloth from his big elephant-hide bag and, hiding
behind a bush, he dressed himself in it, and he then admired
himself in it. It was most attractive. He came out to his son and
said 'Wana, walk behind me as we go.' When they had gone a
short distance Ture's son's barkcloth, flapping beautifully
about him, sang

> '*Hue hue* son of Ture,[2]
> *Hue hue* son of Ture,
> *Hue hue* son of Ture.'

But Ture's barkcloth sang thus:

> '*Gagariga* Ture, *gagariga* Ture,[3]
> *Gagariga* Ture, you will be put to shame today.'

---

[1] *Wana* is 'you there' or 'somebody', no name being mentioned.

[2] *Hue hue* is a pleasant sound made by something soft. The garment was beautiful
and in harmony with the wearer.

[3] *Gagariga* is the opposite of *hue hue*. It denotes something dry and unyielding
and out of harmony.

When Ture heard this he turned round and said to the boy
'*Wana*, take off your barkcloth and give it to me.' They exchanged their barkcloths. When Ture's son put on his father's
barkcloth it sang beautifully, just as his own, but Ture's son's
did not sound well on his father's loins. So Ture said 'As things
are thus, son, when we get near the home you had better first
stay on the path here; when I arrive you may then come yourself. Give back my fine barkcloth and take back this (ugly) one
of yours.' When Ture got near the courtyard his relatives-in-
law heard the sound (music) of his barkcloth and rushed to
meet him and carried him on their heads to the homestead.
Some of them spread mats for him to walk on. They treated
Ture with great respect and prepared him superb food. Ture
felt like a king. Ture washed his feet and raised them on to a
stool where his wife's younger sisters anointed them with oil
and red stain. While they were engaged in all this they heard
coming from the path the sound of Ture's son's barkcloth
singing

> '*Hue* son of Ture, *hue hue* son of Ture,
> *Gburunze, gburunze*[1] son of Ture,
> *Hue hue* son of Ture.'

Everybody started to praise the sound of the barkcloth of Ture's
son, saying 'Ture, the music of your barkcloth was not so sweet
as this. So you have not left off your fooling!' They kicked Ture
off the stool and rubbed him in dust, and he was very white
(with dust).[2] They said 'Only Ture's son is a proper person.'
They placed his son on a stool and put down a mat for his feet.
They relegated Ture to an inferior position, and he was just a
miserable person. While roasting chickens for Ture's son they
cooked just manioc leaves for Ture. While Ture's son was
getting fat with good food Ture was wasting away with
poor food.

    They spent many days in this manner and then decided to
return home. On the way they saw the bird called honey-bird,
which shows people the way to honey when it is singing melodiously. Ture said 'O my son, I have become very thin because

---

[1] *Gburunze, gburunze.* Mr. Richard Mambia's comment: 'If I wear a well-cut
suit that fits me well, it may be described as *gburunze*.'

[2] *Kpou* expresses the degree of whiteness.

of hunger; follow that honey-bird for honey so that I may eat
the honey and grow fat.' Ture's son followed the honey-bird
on and on until it stopped in a tree. The boy found honey in
this tree. So he made fire with fire-sticks. He lit then a bundle
of grass stalks and climbed the tree to fetch honey for his
father. Before he had pulled out two handfuls of the honeycomb
his hand was stuck in the hollow of the tree. The boy cried out
to his father on the path in a song:

> '*Nzingi nzingi* Ture oo,
> *Nzingi nzingi* Ture o,
> Your son's hand is caught in the hollow of a tree,
> Ture o, your son is stuck in the opening of a hollow!'

This song so pleased Ture that he forgot all about his hunger
and he put his feathered hat on his head and began dancing
with the utmost vigour[1] as if his head were on fire. Though the
boy was crying out in supplication Ture just went on dancing.
Ture was having his revenge for what had happened in the
home of his in-laws.

Leaving the boy at the opening of the hollow, Ture ran and
dashed up to the boy's mother and said 'O my wife, I left your
son at my in-laws. He said you were to cook a chicken in oil
and keep it ready for him; his mouth is sour from manioc leaves
in the home of the kin of Nanzagbe (his first wife).' Nanzagbe
was on the way to draw water when Ture said this about her
people's home. While Ture's wife was cooking the chicken he
went round and hid just behind a bush. When he calculated
that the food was ready he came to the path and hurried home
like somebody who has important news. When near the home he
ran with all speed and dashed up to the boy's mother breathing
in gasps like a woman making salt (by evaporation). 'O my
wife, fighting has broken out on the path to my in-laws. I have
just met my blood-brother on the way running to his home. He
told me that no child is safe on the path. Give me quickly the
food you were preparing so that I may run with it to the home
of my in-laws for your son. I don't know what is happening
there. Woman, wrap up the food quickly so that I may run for

---

[1] *Yera gbere ni kina boro ome*: lit., 'to cut the dance with great force': he danced
with great enthusiasm.

my son.' So Ture took this porridge and chicken and walked until he arrived under the tree up which his son was, and he sat down to eat it. Ture would eat for a short time and then climb up the tree to his son and wipe a chicken bone on his mouth. Meanwhile the boy was almost dying from hunger.

When Ture had finished the food he started dancing again. The boy sat up in the tree by the mouth of the hollow entreating his father in song:

> 'Father o, it was not my fault,
> Father o, hunger is going to kill me,
> Mother o, father is going to kill me,
> Mother o, it was not my fault.'

The mother of the child, as she waited at home her heart was pounding (with anxiety). So she got up and went to the path to go and see what was happening at the home of Ture's in-laws, not caring about war or death. She heard her son's cry on the tree supplicating for mercy. She tiptoed towards him and there she saw Ture dancing under this tree. She was seized with great pity for her son and her breast was burning against Ture. She dashed at him with her knife. But Ture had already picked up his bag, and leaving her there, fled with all speed. She climbed the tree after her son and then pulled out his hand from the hollow and took him home. Ture disappeared to his maternal uncles' homes and spent many months there. When he thought his wife's anger had abated he came and appeared humbly in his home in the evening, whimpering, saying 'O my wives, a deadly snake has bitten me on the path there, I am going to die soon.' The mother of the boy to whom Ture had done ill and his other wives gathered round their husband, and the affair of the boy and the chicken and the hollow in the tree was forgotten by the boy's mother. Ture pretended for a month that he was dying from a snake-bite and then he tried walking little by little. A full year passed before Ture mocked his wives, saying 'I have been fooling you all this time. Who told you that a snake had bitten me o?'

'I went walking and found Baru beating his wife almost to death. When I said to him "Baru, such fierce fighting is not good, you will kill the woman", he hit me on the head with his spear-shaft. When I cried much from it, he told his wife to boil some eggs for me. I brought the remainder and left them on the lintel of the door. Tore go and bring them to us so that we may finish them.'

7. *Ture's wife and the great bird Nzanginzanginzi* (G.)

Now there was once a great bird called Nzanginzanginzi, and it resided near a granitic outcrop to swallow people. It was not possible for a man to pass by there, it swallowed him. Ture's wife began to come and go by this path. She ground flour to go with it to her mother, and she took a millipede and put it on top of it, on account of this great bird. She went on her way and arrived at this large outcrop, and when this great bird looked and saw her it at once came forth and settled and said to her

'That's fine! Where are you going to?
Deboropepekua I am going to swallow you right now.'

While she remained silent this millipede began to sing a song to this great bird, saying

'*Zaza ngo* you let her go, she will arrive there,
Zaza ngo she loves her mother, love of mother,
Zaza ngo, zaza ngo.'

It flew and arrived and settled in its place. She continued on her way until she reached the top of the outcrop, when it came forth and came and settled beside her, saying

'That's fine! Where are you going to?
Deboropepekua I am going to swallow you right now.'

The millipede sang the same song and it went to its place. She passed by and arrived at her mother's home, and took this millipede and put it in a pot, and sat down. She stayed there a short time, and when her mother poured hot water into this pot she poured it on to the millipede. It was all scorched, near to death. When its mistress saw it, O sir! She came and saw that it was badly scorched. She said to her mother that, alas, she would not survive this great bird, she must go home. She started off and

took this millipede, scorched as it was, and put it on top of
her flour.

She arrived again at the outcrop. This great bird came forth
again and waited, and said

> 'That's fine! Where are you going to?
> *Deboropepekua* I will swallow you right now.'

The millipede cried with the (pleading) voice of an orphan,
saying

> '*Zaza ngo* you let her go, she will arrive there,
> *Zaza ngo* she loves her father, love of father,
> *Zaza ngo, zaza ngo.*'

The great bird then waited again in its place. She went on a
little way and it came forth again and waited and said

'That's fine! *Deboropepekua* I am going to swallow you right now,
   sisi!
That's fine! *Deboropepekua* I am going to swallow you right now,
   sisi!'

But the millipede was dead. The great bird dashed forward at
once and swallowed her.

So, when Ture heard about it he went to the *Atari* oracle. He
struck the top of the *Atari*. *Atari* rushed off and fell into the fire.
That astonished Ture, who therefore began to depart, and
when he was on his way he met *Atari* coming. *Atari* said to him
'You go and forge many little knives and let it swallow you and
then you can kill it and your wife will be saved.' Ture began to
quarrel with the oracle, saying that if it spoke about his affair
thus someone might hear it, as he himself already knew its
advice. The like of it knew nothing. Ture then went home and
forged many little knives and went to this large granitic outcrop.
When he had arrived there the great bird saw him and came
forth slowly and said

> 'That's fine! Where are you going to?
> *Deboropepekua* I am going to swallow you right now.'

Ture said to it 'Please come and swallow me.' It then swallowed
him. When he arrived inside it and saw those people it had
swallowed still alive, and his wife also, he distributed his little

knives among them all, telling them to cut the guts with them. When it was in great distress it cried out in song, saying

'*Deboropepekua* I have swallowed a strong man, Ture, into my inside,
Ture eats my entrails closely like stomach-ache so!
It began o o o, it began o o so!'

It kept on singing this song. When Ture heard this its cry with which it cried thus, he urged on those people in its inside, telling them to cut into it with force. They set upon it to cut it up, and as they cut it up it sang just this song. They went on cutting it up, and then it died. So Ture and his companions cut into its stomach to get out with those people it had swallowed.

'I went here and saw a man beating his wife, and I thought I would calm him, but he hit me on the head. When I cried out he took a little piece of meat and gave it to me. I came and put it there, child go and fetch it.'

8. *Ture and Depago again* (G.)

TURE began to go again to the home of a man called Depago, which man did not sleep in a hut. He (Depago) ground a paste and filled a horn with it, and then he used to smear some of it on to a termite mound, and it opened, and he entered into it with his wives to live there. Ture came and arrived, and when it was going to rain Ture said to him 'Let us shelter, rain is about to fall.' Depago said to Ture 'You get up, let us run from the rain.' They ran and ran and arrived at this mound, and he scraped out some of the paste and smeared it on the mound and said in song

'Depago, Degago, Depago, quicksand,
Depago cuts a pit, quicksand.'

The mound opened and he and Ture entered. Ture saw a fine homestead there which was that of this man, and he gave Ture a meal. When rain ceased they started to go out, and he did what he had done before and it yielded passage. Ture said to himself 'O, what shall I do to get hold of this paste?' He stalked it and stole it and took it away with him and went and appeared in his home, and said to his wives 'You burn down the huts.' They said to him 'If we burn down the huts, where shall we sleep?' He told them to burn them, they would find others for sure. The other wives all burnt theirs down, only Nanzagbe, she alone left hers unburnt, for she knew only too well his foolishness to burn her hut. Ture told them to come and he would show them huts. They went until they found a mound, and he smeared some paste on it while he sang a song as that man had done, saying

'Deture, Deture, Deture, quicksand,
Deture cuts a pit, quicksand.'

The mound opened and he entered with his wives. He said to them 'Here are your huts, I go to look for mine.' He said to them 'Don't in any circumstances eat caterpillars, for such is the rule of this paste.' He then went and found another mound and smeared the remains of his paste on it and sang the same song as he had sung before, and it yielded passage and he entered it. But it happened that there was no food in his mound as there was in Depago's. He slept and when day broke Ture saw caterpillars in this mound and they looked good to him. He began to eat them and the mound closed behind him, and although he smeared on it the last bit of the paste he had stolen from Depago he was unable to open it again.

That wife who remained outside, she looked for him in vain. He slept another night there. So, it alarmed his wife, and she started to go after this man whose paste Ture had stolen. She came and said to him 'That paste Ture brought here, he came and burnt the huts, the whole lot of them, saying that he was going to just live in a mound, and after he went off to do so we have not seen him again. It is for you to come and search for him in a mound.' She and he came and appeared, and he asked them 'Where is he?' They said thus, 'He went off among these many mounds.' He went and smeared paste on one of them and looked into it in vain, and he went and smeared it on another and saw Ture in it. Ture came out with those of his wives who were in that other mound. This man took his paste to return with it to his home.

'I went and saw men quarrelling, and when I tried to pacify them one of them made for me and hit me on the head, and when I cried out *ii* he took a chicken's leg and gave it to me. I brought it home with me and put it on the lintel of the door-way here. Child, go and fetch it.'

9. *How Ture cheated the Prince Man-killer* (R. M.)

TURE was just living quietly, and then he heard about a notorious man called Man-killer. Human skulls surrounded his court. Ture visited the court of this prince and sat down and played the hole-game[1] with the prince's son. This prince called his son and inquired 'Who are in the court?' The boy replied 'There is only one man there.' The prince said 'Take this food and take it to him and eat it with him.' The boy brought this food and placed it before Ture and they ate it together and finished it. When the boy wanted to return the pot and bowl Ture said 'O child, you are as black as charcoal, is your mother that black?' The boy went and reported it to his father, saying 'Father, there is a man here who says "Boy, you are very black, is your mother also so black?" ' The prince was very annoyed and told the boy 'Go and ask that man his name.' The boy went and asked Ture 'What is your name?' Ture just laughed and said 'Did you say "What is your name?" ' Ture got angry with the boy and said 'My name is all over this world, who is asking for it?' The boy said 'Tell what your name is right now, otherwise you will die. Don't you see the skulls of others?' The boy asked Ture in vain, so he went to his father and said 'When I ask this man for his name he just jokes.'

Man-killer dashed out to Ture in the court. Ture cried out, saying 'O prince, let me first go to my home and prepare food for you, after that you can come and kill me in my court.' Ture deceived the prince with this talk. When he got home Ture ran to his wives and his children and said 'Come, let us dig a tunnel which will go very far under the ground.' They dug the tunnel throughout the night until dawn.

Very early in the morning Man-killer appeared in Ture's home. Ture said to him 'My wives are preparing food for you to eat first, and then you can kill me.' Ture went after his wives and said to them 'That man who wants to kill me has come.

[1] A widespread African game, in which pieces are moved from hole to hole on a wooden board or in the ground.

Collect everything and run into the tunnel we dug last night.'
Ture remained himself to deceive Man-killer. Ture caught a
chicken and tied it up, and when he pulled the cord it cried.
Man-killer thought from that that Ture's wives were still in the
home, whereas they had already disappeared into the tunnel.
Ture would sit for a short time and then go and shake the
chicken. He told Man-killer 'That chicken which cries out, it is
the one they are making porridge to go with it for you.' Man-
killer was very happy. Ture got up and went to his homestead
(leaving Man-killer in the court) and pretended to urge on his
wives, saying 'This food you have been preparing for a long
time, is it not ready yet, as my friend is dying of hunger?' After
he had said this he went into the tunnel after his wives and
children.

Man-killer sat in vain for a long time and then decided to go
and look for Ture, but in vain. He searched for Ture in every
one of the huts and in the granaries; but oh no! Man-killer then
lifted up the eleusine-grindstone and saw a hole under it and
Ture's footmarks at its mouth. So he entered it and began
pursuing Ture and his wives, together with his children.

Man-killer went and overtook Ture's wives and he said to them
'It has nothing to do with you, it is only between me and Ture.'
He chased Ture till the tunnel came to an end, and Ture rushed
out. When Ture was exhausted he ran to knock the *Atari* oracle
on the head, and *Atari* said to him 'You go and take just an old
tattered net and set it up and stand by it with a little worn-down
spear.' Ture went and made blood-brotherhood with a man who
gave him a net. Ture set it up and stood beside it with a worn-
down spear. Man-killer came running and came and found
Ture standing beside the net, looking fixedly towards the
bush (expecting an animal to come out from there). But Man-
killer did not know it was Ture. When he asked, saying 'Man,
have you seen Ture here?' Ture brandished his spear, and said
'Man, you stop your talk beside my net; don't you realize that
my animals are in that piece of bush?'[1] Man-killer was scared
and took to his heels. Then Ture said 'It is I, I brother of
Nangbafudo,[2] I have tricked you, as I have often done to

[1] Talk would scare them away.

[2] Nangbafudo is elsewhere presented as one of Ture's wives. 'Brother' here may
be intentional and sinister, for though a man might address his wife as 'my sister' he
would never speak of himself as the brother of his wife.

others.' Man-killer said to Ture 'I have abandoned the idea of killing you, Ture. You are very clever. It is better that we make blood-brotherhood, so that you may teach me some of your tricks.'

'As I was returning from my uncle's home I met Depe dragging his son on the ground because the boy had been out the whole day. When I tried to plead with him for the boy he hit me on the head with his spear-shaft. When I started to cry he consoled me with some boiled fish. I put it near the door. Will one of the children fetch it for us?'

10. *How Ture fought with Nzangirinza* (G.)

THERE was a man called Nzangirinza who had many animal snares at the foot of a hill. He constantly inspected his traps and found only the heads of animals in them, without their bodies, just their heads. He was very tired of this and so one day he went to keep watch over his traps to see who was removing the animals, leaving only their heads. He hid himself and stayed still. Then he saw just Ture coming with his big knife with which he used to sever the heads of animals caught in Nzangirinza's snares. Ture came and stood without knowing that the owner of the snares was nearby in hiding. Suddenly the owner of the snares, Nzangirinza, dashed out at him and said 'O Ture! So you are the one who is stealing and eating my animals.' He got really angry with Ture and gave him a hard blow. Ture also gave him a hard blow and they fought together. They fought for a long time and the man knocked Ture down and beat him very much on the ground. He told his page Katikati to strip bast to bind Ture with it. Nzangirinza called the boy to bring cord quickly so that he might beat Ture properly. The boy sang

'I cut that fine cord *kpakpa*,[1]
I cut that fine cord *tutu*.'[2]

The struggle went on and on and on. Ture turned under the man and he ran out from under the man with all speed and escaped from the man. Ture went after the boy who went to

---

[1] The sound of breaking bast. [2] The sound of bast breaking easily.

fetch cord to bind him, just because of what the boy sang in his song. He put on his feathered hat and began to dance to the boy's song. He put down his elephant-hide bag and asked the boy 'Why did you go to strip bast for me?' He gave the boy a hard blow, and the boy gave him also a hard blow. They fought together for a time and after a time the boy knocked Ture down and beat him very much on the ground. He then got up from over him and went after Nzangirinza, and they went home.

'I was just taking a walk here. I came across men who were quarrelling. When I tried to calm them one of them hit me, and when I cried out he took a piece of meat and put it in my hand. I brought it and put it over the door over there. Boy, go and fetch it.'

13. *First account of Ture and One-leg* (R. M.)

THERE was once a one-legged man whose home was close to Ture's, though there was bush between them. This man did not like that people should see him. Therefore he only went out of his hut at night. Nobody ever saw him at all.

There was a termite mound in the middle of the bush between Ture and One-leg. Whenever it was getting dark One-leg would appear, come and climb that mound, and call to Ture in his home, saying 'O Ture, have you ever seen me?' Ture would reply 'Oh no, I have never seen you! What do you look like, eh? What do you look like?' One-leg would say 'A very handsome man, more handsome than anyone else.' One-leg would then descend from the mound and return home dancing. He was very happy because no one ever saw him at all. Every night One-leg used to trouble Ture.

One night Ture said to his wife 'If One-leg summons me tonight again, speak the same words that I speak to him every night.' Ture said 'What will you say to him?' She spoke the very words Ture used to say. So Ture went and hid in the bush near One-leg's mound. When it was dark One-leg came and climbed up the mound and called Ture: 'Ture oo have you ever seen me?' Ture's wife said 'Oh no, I have never seen you! What do you look like, eh? What do you look like?' One-leg said 'A very handsome man, more handsome than anyone else.' He then came down from the mound and returned home rejoicing. However, Ture had completely seen him. Ture then ran to his wife at home and said to her 'My sister,[1] that man who has been troubling me here, he is simply an ugly thing with one leg, one arm, one eye, one nostril, one ear, only a portion of his head on one side, and only one enormous tooth.' Ture's wife burst out laughing and laughed. When it was dark the next day One-leg came and jumped on to the top of the mound and called Ture and said 'Ture oo have you ever seen me?' Ture said 'ooo I have seen you.' One-leg hastily asked, saying 'What do I look like? What do I look like?' Ture said 'You are simply an ugly thing, with your one leg, your one arm, your one ear, your one eye, your one nostril, only a portion of your head on one side, and your one big tooth.' One-leg was pained with anger, and he saw red that someone had allowed Ture to see him. So he rushed after Ture to his home. Ture took to his heels from this dangerous man. As One-leg chased Ture he sang this song:

> 'My sisters have seen me if Ture has seen me,
> Where has Ture seen me?
> My mothers have seen me if Ture has seen me,
> Where has Ture seen me?
> My fathers have seen me if Ture has seen me,
> Where has Ture seen me?'

One-leg sang this song as he bounded (hopped) after Ture. Ture for his part cried, saying

> '*Roo roo* Ture o I die like a dog,
> *Roo roo* Ture o beasts eat me,
> *Roo roo* Ture o I die like a dog.'

One-leg chased Ture all over the world and they spent many years in running. After five years Ture's children said 'Let us follow our father.' They forged their spears and knives and throwing-knives and began to pursue Ture and One-leg.

Ture's children ran and ran till they stopped to ask, and they were told that the two men had passed there a long time ago, five years since. They sped on their way and when they asked,

---

[1] See footnote 2 on p. 53.

they were told that the two men had passed that way a long time ago, four years since. They sped greatly for many months and asked, and they were told that it was three years since the two men had passed that way. When they stopped to ask again, they were told that the two had passed there last year. When they asked further on they were told that the two had passed there last month. They ran and ran and when they asked, they were told that the two had passed there the previous day. Further on they were told that the two had passed there that morning. They went on running and when they asked, they were told that the two had just passed there. Then Ture's sons increased their speed and when they looked ahead they saw One-leg chasing Ture while singing his song:

'My sisters have seen me if Ture has seen me,
Where has Ture seen me?
My mothers have seen me if Ture has seen me,
Where has Ture seen me?'

For his part Ture cried, saying

'*Roo roo* Ture o I die like a dog,
Roo roo Ture o beasts eat me,
Roo roo Ture o I die like a dog.'

Ture's sons pitied him and they overtook One-leg and speared him with their spears. Ture then fell down, being emaciated, and said 'O my sons! You have saved me from that terrible man. How good it is to have children. You cut him up like an animal and give me his head to carry, and let us return.' They did this as he asked. Ture started with his sons to return home. On their way they saw a rubber-vine above, which bore rich red fruit. Ture put down One-leg's head and climbed up to cut the fruit. While Ture was up, One-leg's head was restored to life and sat looking up at Ture. He said to Ture 'Hey Ture! Throw me down some rubber-vine fruits.' As Ture looked down he saw the same One-leg. Ture trembled all over, and said 'What shall I do now to escape from this man?' One-leg said 'Ture, how will you now get down?' Ture said to him 'The true rubber-vine fruit will fall slowly but that which will fall fast is not rubber-vine fruit.' Ture threw down to One-leg a fruit. While he was eating it, Ture squeezed himself into the shell of a rubber-vine fruit and fell to the ground. As One-leg lifted up his eyes he saw Ture and at once started to rush at him. Ture then appealed to his sons, saying 'O my sons, I am dead from One-leg!' Ture's sons rushed to their father and slew One-leg and said to Ture 'Don't take this man's head from its place again.' Ture and his sons then set off for their home.

12. *How Ture lacked termites because of dancing* (G.)

LITTLE Dog went with his mother after termites. When they reached the termites little Dog lay in the middle of the path. Ture was going after his termites also, with his elephant-hide bag and his torches. He came suddenly and stumbled over little Dog, not at first seeing him. As he was falling to the ground little Dog began to sing his song:

> '*Tao tao oo tatarito, tao tao oo tatarito,*
> Ture has stumbled over my foot, he is dancing,
> *Tatarito, naringinza oo* Ture dances *tatarito.*'

Ture turned back and said 'Ture, what is that I have stumbled over which sings a song? Let me stumble over it again.' He came and stumbled again. Little Dog sang the same song. Ture inclined his ear to listen to it and it pleased him very much. He took his elephant-hide bag and threw it aside and threw away his torches also into the bush. He turned back again and stumbled over little Dog. When little Dog sang the song he began to dance wildly, leaping widely around. He turned and stumbled over little Dog again and when he sang he departed, dancing far away, and when he returned to stumble over little Dog he did not find him. He and his mother had collected their termites and gone away.

When this happened Ture had put on his big feathered hat to dance with. He said 'Confound little Dog who deceived me with a song, and I just danced and missed my termites.' As Ture had not thought of the termites but only of dancing he thought of the termites too late. As he had thrown away his elephant-hide bag into the bush he lit a fire to look for it in the bush, and he fell into water and was soaked through. He gathered to his chest some dry twigs (for firewood) and went home with them, shivering with cold. He did this to deceive his wife Nanzagbe, so that she might think he was overcome by rain and therefore it spoilt the termites for him. He arrived home when people were going to sleep and he found Nanzagbe and Nangbafudo had collected a good harvest of termites. They asked Ture, saying 'Where are the termites?' He replied 'Just look at my body! It rained there really hard.'

On his arrival he first stood outside, and they asked 'Who is moving outside?' 'I am the one' he answered. They opened the door for him and he entered, and they then asked him about the termites. 'We know all your tricks,' they said, 'you just danced and left the termites, and you soaked yourself in a stream to deceive us that we might think it was rain. As you let the termites fly away, you will not eat our termites.'

'I was just going home and saw men quarrelling, and when I tried to pacify them one of them attacked me and knocked me hard over the head. When I cried out he took a piece of meat and gave it to me. I have just put it over there. Child, go and fetch it.'

13. *Eye-bees and Big-ears* (R. M.)

ONE day Ture and a boy went to visit Ture's father-in-law. There they spent some time and then Ture was given his wife to take home. Ture then said to this boy 'As you accompanied me to my in-laws what do you want me to give you?' The boy replied 'I don't want anything.' Ture said 'Shall I give you a spear?' The boy refused. Ture said 'What about a hoe?' The boy just shook his head. This boy refused everything. Then Ture said 'What then do you want, boy?' The boy replied 'I want that we halve the woman with you.' Ture said 'oo! Boy, you are talking too big.[1] Whose wife do you say you want, to cut her in two?'

So they went on their way until they met some men called Big-ears. These men had many ears at the sides of their heads. This boy made a case against Ture before the Big-ears, saying

---

[1] *Na kii ba apai ti ro* means that the boy was attaching too much importance to himself.

'I went with Ture to his in-laws and now I want to halve the
woman with him but he was angry with me.' The one who had
three ears said 'If this is so it will be good because I shall taste
blood.' Another one with five ears said the same thing. The
one with ten ears appreciated the idea. While they were thus
talking the chief of the Big-ears appeared. Ture reported the
case to him. He said 'It is a very good thing, we are going to
taste blood.' So this their chief sent Ture to fetch leaves on
which his wife would be cut. Ture was very sorry for his wife
and he felt very sad at heart for her. Ture went to the Big-ears'
enemies, the Eye-bees,[1] and pleaded with them, saying 'O my
blood-brothers, my wife is going to be cut in two by the Big-ears,
come and help me please.'

Now, there was much hatred between the Big-ears and the
Eye-bees, so that it greatly pleased the Eye-bees to go and cut
off the Big-ears' ears. After that the Eye-bees entered Ture's
bundle of leaves and filled it. Ture tied them in the bundle
very tightly and brought them and put them down in the midst
of the Big-ears. Their chief urged them on to cut the cords binding the leaves quickly for cutting Ture's wife on them, so that
they might taste blood. The one with five ears got up, took a
machet, and when he cut the cords on the leaves the Eye-bees
rushed out to chop off the Big-ears' ears, saying

'*Waa*,[2] for my harp,
Waa, for my drum,
Waa, for my harp,
Waa, for my drum.'

So the Big-ears fled as fast as they could, leaving Ture's wife,
and Ture took his wife and went with her to his home.

'I went there and arrived and found a man beating his wife.
When I tried to stop him he hit me over the head with his
spear-shaft. When I cried out he gave me little cooked eggs.[3]
I put them on the lintel of the doorway; you child, there, go
and fetch them and we will eat them.'

---

[1] *Abanvunvuranvu* are a species of insect, said to be big, swift, and with extremely
short mouth-parts.

[2] *Waa* represents the sound of cutting something off at once.

[3] Eggs are first boiled, then shelled, and the egg is mixed with paste, such as
ground-nut or sesame, and wrapped in leaves, such as banana leaves, and boiled
in water.

14. *The running of Ture and One-leg* (G.)

A TRACT of bush was reserved to be burnt in hunting, and it was burnt. Next morning Ture took his spear-shaft and went into the burnt bush. When he saw a hole he would put the shaft into it and poke it there. He went on doing this from hole to hole until he poked it into a hole in a tree where there was a one-legged man. He began to chase Ture, singing thus:

'*Vugu vugu*, even the smallest hole, Ture will look there.'

Ture sang also, thus:

> '*Ro ro oo* Ture o, I shall die like a dog,
> *Ro ro oo* Ture o, animals will eat me,
> *Ro ro oo* Ture o, *ro ro oo* Ture o.'

The man chased Ture year by year. He chased him in all parts of the world for years. His children whom he had left at home as babies grew up to manhood, and Ture was still being chased. They heard of One-leg, that there was a man who was chasing their father continuously. They forged spears for themselves and, when they were ready, collected food for the journey, and they followed Ture with it. They then set off. They came to a homestead and asked 'Have you seen Ture here?' They were answered 'Ture passed by here years ago.' They went on and arrived at another homestead, where they asked 'Have you seen Ture and another man here?' The people said 'Yes, but they passed by here five years ago.' They went on ahead and asked ahead and they were told that four years had gone by since Ture and the man had passed. When they asked again they were told that Ture and the man had passed three years ago. They continued going on and on and on until they came to where they were told that Ture and the man had passed just this year. They went on and inquired and were told this time that they had passed only last month. They went on and asked in another homestead, where they were told that they had passed there that month. They went on further, and when they asked people they were told that they had passed there twenty days before. They went on and on, and inquired again and they were told that Ture had passed there three days ago. They asked again and were told that Ture had passed two days ago.

On their next inquiry they were told that Ture had passed there the day before. When they went further and asked in another homestead they were told that Ture had passed by there that morning. They began running, and when they asked in a further homestead they were told that Ture passed by there at midday. Ture's sons were glad, and they ran further on, and when they asked in another homestead they were told that the men had just passed by there. On their next inquiry they were told that the men were going over there. The sons of Ture saw their father and they saw the man also. The man was saying

'*Vugu vugu*, even the smallest hole, Ture will look there.'

Ture was saying

'*Ro ro oo* Ture o, I shall be eaten by vultures,
Ro ro oo Ture o, I shall die like a dog,
Ro ro oo Ture o, I shall be eaten by animals,
Ro ro oo Ture o, *ro ro oo* Ture o.'

As the sons of Ture heard the speech of their father thus, they took pity on him. They ran ahead and lay in ambush. Ture and the man were approaching. His sons extended in a line.[1] Ture came and passed and they knew him. When One-leg came and tried to pass, the first of Ture's sons hurled his spear at him and missed him. The second son also missed him. The third son also missed him, and so did the fourth son. Only the last son speared him and he fell. They came and stabbed him and killed him. The sons of Ture sat with their father at last for the first time since he went away leaving them as small children. They said to him 'O Father, since you departed from us this is the first time that we have seen you.'[2] They gave him what was left of their food and he ate and revived. Ture then skinned and cut up the man as though he were an animal. They cut off his head and other members. Ture's sons told him they were going to carry the head, but he said 'No, it is I who am going to carry it, as he has much wearied me.' They argued with him for a

[1] The Zande is *tenge da soro*. It denotes that there was a passage between two hills through which the men would have to pass. Ture's sons stood across the passage, but they also lined the sides of the hills in an extension or overlap up the sides of the hills. The phrase can also be used for standing in a courtyard.

[2] The Zande text has *yangara bi ro ani abi ro re*. Literally this would mean 'this is the last time for us to see you', but here it has the sense of 'this is the first time we have seen you'.

time, but in vain, so they let Ture carry it. They went home, and on their way home they came across the fruits of a rubber-vine, fully ripe. They put down the man and climbed up to eat the fruits. The head of the dead man recovered and began looking up at Ture, saying 'You fellow, Ture! Pluck one for me and throw it down to me here.' Ture became terrified and said 'alas! This man has revived to trouble me.' Ture said to him 'The one which I throw and it falls slowly is the rubber-vine fruit, but the one which will fall quickly is not the rubber-vine fruit.'

Ture threw one and it came down and fell lightly. When One-leg got it he found nothing in it. He threatened Ture, saying 'Confound you! Where will you get down today?' Ture squeezed himself inside the rind of a rubber-vine fruit and fell to the ground. The man began to chase Ture again. Ture cried out to his sons, saying 'Oh! One-leg is killing me.' His sons ran to his aid and killed One-leg again. Then they said to Ture 'Do not again carry his head. We told you before not to carry the head of this man. Now you have seen it!'

'I was just going here and found a man beating his wife and when I stopped him he knocked me hard over the head; when I cried out he took a piece of meat and gave it to me. I brought it and put it on the shrine over there. Go boy, and look for it.'

15. *Ture and the woman's dogs* (R. M.)

THERE was once a very rich woman called Nawongowongo. She had many granaries of eleusine and ground-nuts, sesame and dried meat. She established her home very far across a mighty river. She lived entirely by herself. However, she kept her five huge dogs. She used to go hunting with them in the bush, and they would catch her all sorts of animals. This woman used to eat meat all the time when other people were suffering from lack of meat. Ture heard of this woman and went as far as the shore of the mighty water across which her home was. Ture looked over the sheet of water and he said to himself 'O Ture! What shall I do to go and eat this woman's meats?' Ture then made a big rope and set a snare with it (at the edge of the river) and by putting one of his legs in the snare it snatched him and landed him across.[1] Ture then set another snare on that side, and it snatched him again and landed him on the first side. Ture said 'So I shall eat the things of that woman.' Ture put one of his legs again in the snare, and it threw him across. He stalked the home of that woman. Ture looked in vain for this woman, she had gone into the wilderness to hunt animals with her dogs. Ture dived into that woman's granary of meat and came down with dried flesh, broke it into a pot and stood it on the fire. While it was stewing Ture climbed into the granary of sesame and came down with much oil-paste to season his meat with it. After the meat had been cooked, Ture put the porridge-pot on the fire and went and collected some of the woman's eleusine and pounded it and ground it and cooked porridge. Ture ate this porridge with the meat and when he was satisfied he put what was left over into his elephant-hide bag. After that Ture appeared beside Nawongowongo's grindstone, which used to sound like a bell. Ture sounded her stone, and it sounded '*Wongo wongo* Ture *wongo*.'[2] This woman heard the sound of her stone right away in the wilderness. She stood right where she was and shouted, saying 'Who is sounding Nawongowongo's stone, eh?' Ture replied

> 'It is I, I am Ture,
> Whenever I sound Nawongowongo's stone
> It sounds *wongo* Ture *wongo* Ture.'

This woman started off with her dogs to chase Ture at her home. When they arrived at the edge of the courtyard she saw Ture and cried to her dogs, calling them by name, saying 'You seize Ture.' Ture started off to rush to his snare. The dogs pursued him at full pace. The woman cried to her dogs to catch Ture. When they were almost up to Ture he put one of his legs in his snare and it lifted him and landed him across the river. Nawongowongo an' her dogs just stood gazing at Ture on the other side of the river. Ture then said (mockingly) 'It is I, I Ture, who have eaten your meats. What will you do to me on this side of the river?' Then Ture went away.

Ture went to his friend, who was little Bushbuck, and said

---

[1] This conveys to Azande the picture of one of their snares: a stake is fixed in the ground and is then bent over in such a way that the bent end flies upwards with the noose if a creature releases it by treading on the noose.

[2] '*Wongo*' is the sound of the stone.

to him 'My friend, I have been and eaten Nawongowongo's
meat, as much as I could, you try some of it.' Ture offered
little Bushbuck (some of) the left-overs he had put in his bag.
It tasted good to little Bushbuck, and he said 'O my friend, let
us go there tomorrow so that I may eat some of this nice meat.'
Ture said to him 'You come early tomorrow morning, so we
go.' Very early next morning little Bushbuck arrived at Ture's
home and they went and reached the shore of the great river.
They then set two snares and put their feet in them, and they
snatched them and landed them across. Then they set two more
snares on that side and left them and went stealthily to Nawongowongo's home, and when they arrived there they looked for
her in vain, for she was out hunting with her dogs. Ture sent
little Bushbuck to the eleusine granary to get some and grind
it for his part. After that Ture climbed into the granary of
(dried) meat and came down with a very big lump of meat and
broke it up into a pot, poured water over it, and placed it on
the fire to boil. After that he climbed into the granary of ground-
nuts and came down with ground-nut paste to go with his
meat. After the meat had been cooked they put the porridge-pot
on the fire. While it was cooking Ture spoke to Little Bushbuck thus, 'My friend, I am going to the bush.'[1] Ture then
went to the bank of the river and tied up the snare of little
Bushbuck, and then returned to him at the homestead. Ture
and little Bushbuck cooked porridge and ate it until they were
satisfied. Then Ture put what was left over of it into his bag and
went to Nawongowongo's grindstone, which used to sound like
a bell. He sounded on it, and it sounded

> '*Wongo* Ture
> *Wongo* Ture *wongo*.'

The woman heard the sound of her stone in the wilderness and
asked 'Who is sounding Nawongowongo's stone o o?' Ture
said

> 'It is I, I am Ture,
> I sound on Nawongowongo's stone,
> It sounds *wongo wongo*,
> *Wongo* Ture.'

---

[1] A euphemism for going to empty one's bowels.

Nawongowongo appealed to her dogs, saying 'Not again today. You catch Ture right now.' Then the dogs took heed and ran after Ture and his friend to the homestead. When they were near to the courtyard Ture and little Bushbuck took to their heels to get to their snares. Just as the dogs arrived Ture stepped on his snare and it threw him to the other side. But when little Bushbuck tried to step on his it could not lift him. The dogs reached little Bushbuck and seized him and killed him. Ture stood on the other side congratulating himself. Nawongowongo said 'Ture, you yourself, I will catch just you.'

After that Ture went and deceived little Digdig and treated him as he had treated little Bushbuck, and the dogs killed him. So Ture went to Grey Duiker and said 'My friend, let us go and eat meat from that ugly woman over there, who is Nawongo-wongo.' Grey Duiker came to Ture very early in the morning and they went and set their snares at the edge of the great river to lift them to the other side. They also set other snares (on the other side) and went stealthily to this woman's home. They looked for her there in vain. So they began to cook porridge as before. While the pot of porridge was on the fire Ture said 'My friend Grey Duiker, I am going to the bush.' Ture went and reached and tied up altogether Grey Duiker's snare. Then Ture returned. Grey Duiker then said also in his turn 'Ture, I am going to the bush.' Grey Duiker went to the side of the river and found his snare completely tied up by Ture. Grey Duiker kept quiet and returned to Ture without setting his trap in order. After they had eaten the porridge Ture sounded Nawon-gowongo's stone as before. When her dogs arrived Ture and Grey Duiker took to their heels to get to their snares. Grey Duiker left Ture well behind and sped ahead towards Ture's snare. Ture yelled, saying 'Grey Duiker, your snare is not there, Grey Duiker, yours is not there.' But Grey Duiker did not listen to what Ture was saying. Grey Duiker ran on and stepped on Ture's snare and it snatched him up and landed him across. Everything was against Ture. Ture was very angry with Grey Duiker on the other side. The dogs then began to pursue Ture and chase him hotly at the side of the river, to chase him hard. And Nawongowongo ran after them and urged them on to seize Ture. Ture continued in flight and turned round a termite mound and plucked red fruits of the Kaffir apple and hung them on his eyes and climbed up a tree and sat up there, and brought out his harp and played it, singing

'I am he who looks up,
I look down, all men die.'

The dogs came and passed Ture. Nawongowongo asked Ture, saying 'O man, have you seen Ture here?' Ture did not answer her but went on singing his song while playing the harp. She asked him again and he said to her 'Woman, I only look upwards. If I look downwards men will all die.' She could not even recognize Ture. Ture then said to her 'You tie up your dogs right now to a tree, for otherwise I am going to look down and you will die.' The woman was afraid and tied up all her dogs to a tree. Ture then dropped down, for it was only of the dogs that he was afraid. He turned behind a termite mound and set up another snare and it threw him across. He stood there and said to her 'It is I, I the son of Ture's father; I have eaten all your meats and again deceived you. What will you do to me then, eh?' Ture returned to his home with the debt of Nawongowongo's things.

16. *Ture and Thunder's eggs* (R. M.)

ONCE upon a time there was a man called Thunder. Thunder used to put many eggs in his hut; some were white and some were red and some were black. There was a big river near Thunder's home with plenty of fish in it. Therefore Thunder closed this river with his fish-trap.[1] Every morning Thunder used to empty fish from this his fish-trap, so there was no lack of 'meat' in his home. One day Ture got up and went, as his habit was, and wandered along the river bank setting on fire the bush to chase out reed-rats. Ture went on wandering until he found a piece of bush with lots of spoor of reed-rats leading into it. Ture spread his net quickly and ran to the other side of the bush and set it on fire, and when it was burning he hurried to stand by his net. No sooner had Ture reached the net than he saw a reed-rat caught in his net. Ture threw down his spears and

---

[1] A stream is dammed to stop fish from swimming downstream. There are apertures in the dam in which are placed conical traps which allow water to pass through but hold up fish.

when he tried to pounce on it,[1] it slipped out of the net and ran into the (burning) bush. Ture thought 'If I spear it I shall spill my fat (in the rat's belly) on to the ground.' That is why he threw down his spears in order to pounce on it (and strangle it).

When it jumped back into the bush Ture cried 'O the son of Ture's father, such a big animal should not escape! I will see where it will go today.' He jumped into the dry bush after it and chased it noisily. Ture was so occupied with the animal that he forgot about the fire.[2] So he ran into the middle of the bush and was trapped by the fire there. When Ture looked about him he saw fire roaring and spreading towards him on every side. Ture would look this way and that way and his eyes met only fire. Ture was at the end of his wits. Thinking of nothing but his life he dashed through the fire.[3] When he emerged on the previously burnt bush his barkcloth and his hair were burning fiercely. His body was just one big sore from the fire. Ture then thought of nothing but water. He dashed to the river and plunged headlong into the water. The current snatched him and tossed him about with first his head downstream and then his legs downstream, and took him downstream with tremendous force. The current carried him and dumped him in Thunder's fish-trap as if he were a huge fish. As Ture always was lucky, at about the same time Thunder came to empty and reset his fish-trap. He heard Ture struggling in the trap and thought that it was a big fish. He pulled the trap out on to the bank, only to discover Ture in it. When he was pulling Ture out, Ture burst out, saying 'O my maternal uncle, so you are still alive! My mother told me that if during my wanderings a current of water should carry me into a fish-trap, then I would know that it is the trap of my maternal uncles. O my friend, are my uncle's wives in good health?' This was pleasing to Thunder's ear. He therefore took Ture home with him. Thunder's family all gathered to admire his nephew and

---

[1] Reed-rats and other small animals are not usually speared but are either beaten to death or strangled. This saves the net from injury.

[2] '*Bangiri ture ki su kina kuti nya . . .*': literally, this means 'Ture's eyes burst at the animal . . .'. When a person has seen a thing and his desire for it blinds him to everything else, this is the phrase to express it.

[3] '*Ture ki ta e ti ko a he boro ki gu a gu ki ti ku bangiri we yo*': literally, this means 'Ture left himself and leapt and fell into the fire'. When a person plunges into water, fire, thick bush, or whatever it may be, on a sudden impulse, this phrase may be used.

to hear how he fell into the fish-trap. When Ture opened his mouth to give them his story,[1] their mouths hung gaping (with wonder). When it was dusk they showed Ture to a hut. For many a day they nursed Ture and bathed his burns.

Whenever people dispersed into the cultivations Ture would stretch himself walking about the courtyard. When he reached the edge of Thunder's courtyard he saw big egg-shells, black ones, red ones, and white ones. Ture exclaimed '*Wo wo!* What wonderful eggs are these whose shells look like this? How shall I see them o?'

When Ture's wounds were completely healed he went to Thunder and said to him 'O uncle, that hut in which I sleep, I constantly have bad dreams in it. There is not a single night that I can get any repose in it.' Thunder's wives and children occupied all the huts except Thunder's hut of eggs. Ture understood this perfectly well. Ture had not done anything bad at all while in Thunder's home. Therefore Thunder prepared a bed for Ture in his hut of eggs and said to Ture in the evening 'My sister's son, this hut here, people do not sleep in it, but just you alone are going to sleep there. Do not touch anything there at all except your bed.' Ture accepted this arrangement, rejoicing in his heart.

Ture spent ten nights in this hut. Every night he used to light a big fire and sit in its light to look over and admire Thunder's eggs. Desire for them itched him like *abakpa*.[2] One morning Ture said 'O my maternal uncle, tomorrow I am returning to my mother to relate to her the good things you have done for me.' Thunder said 'Very good Ture.' That evening Ture went and stripped some bark of the kind that sparks when set light to, and he placed it near the fireplace where everybody could see it. That evening Ture went to bed as soon as he had had supper, saying 'Uncle, I shall leave very early tomorrow, so I will turn in early tonight.'

Ture made a big fire in the hut in Thunder's home like that

---

[1] '*Ture ki zoro ngba ko yo fu yo . . .*': literally, this means 'Ture came down in his mouth to them'. Ture was telling some lies but, being a good talker, they were convinced. This expression has usually a slightly derogatory sense, being used when the speaker is thought not to be telling the whole truth.

[2] *Abakpa* is a creeper which has fruits resembling soya beans in shape. On these fruits are fine brown hairs which, if they have been in contact with a person's skin, cause most unpleasant itching; probably one of the *Papilionaceae* genus.

by the light of which witch-doctors dance at night. As soon as people were quiet Ture crawled to Thunder's eggs, and he took one red one and put it aside, took one black one and put it aside, and took one white one and put it aside. Ture then sat down to eat up the rest of Thunder's eggs, broiling them one by one at the side of the fire. When one was cooked it burst, '*bu*',[1] and Ture started to eat it. When Thunder heard the bursting eggs he asked Ture 'Ture, what bursts like that?' Ture answered quickly 'It is just the bark you saw today which is popping!' When another one burst and they asked Ture, he gave the same answer. In this manner he went after Thunder's eggs and ate most of them up, leaving by this trick only those he had put aside before. When he was satisfied he put the remaining (broiled) eggs into a bag he had borrowed earlier from Thunder.

Early in the morning Thunder was at Ture's door and said to him 'Show me my eggs which are in that hut, show them to me one at a time by their kind.' Ture took out the white one and showed it to Thunder. Thunder said 'Put it back; another one again.' Ture showed him the black one and he said 'Put it back; another one again.' Ture showed him the red one and he said 'Put it back. Now show me a white one again and a red one and a black one.' Ture showed him the same ones as he had shown before. Thunder's anxiety was relieved and he commended Ture and urged on his wives to prepare food for Ture to eat, as he was about to depart.

Ture finished his meal. However, Thunder did not enter the hut of eggs. So Ture started on his return home. Thunder and all his family got up to accompany Ture, except for a little girl who remained at home. When this child entered the hut (Ture had left) the shells of Thunder's eggs met her eyes,[2] and she saw only those three Ture had been fooling Thunder with. She rushed out of the hut and ran after Ture and Thunder and his wives, calling out, saying 'As you are accompanying Ture thus, he has eaten all our eggs ooo.' But they did not hear it at first; only Ture heard it. Thunder asked 'What are they shouting behind?' Ture answered quickly 'They say "See me off

---

[1] '*bu*': the sound of the bursting egg.

[2] '*zo bangirise ti e*': 'to burn the eyes on something', a strong expression for a discovery of something dreadful or unexpected.

quickly." ' The child was running hard,[1] shouting after them.
They asked again, saying 'What is that child talking about o?'
Ture was beginning to be very much afraid in his heart. He
said 'She says thus, "You go on accompanying me till you cross
the stream over there." '

When they got to the bank of the river the child was getting
very near. Ture hastened till he was on the bridge. When
Thunder said farewell to Ture and was returning, the child
arrived and said 'Oh! There are no more eggs at home. Ture
has eaten them all.' While she was saying this[2] Ture destroyed
the bridge by throwing its supports into the river with all his
strength. He was destroying it after him while he was running
ahead. Ture dashed to the other side and stood there and
displayed Thunder's eggs to him on the other side: 'Look at
your eggs; are not these they in my bag? I am Ture who
always fools people. I have got the better of you.' He took to his
heels, leaving Thunder on the bank in great anger and sorrow
for his eggs.

17. *The shooting of guinea-fowl by Ture and the Orphan* (R. M.)

NANZAGBE's brother, Orphan, went to Ture's home to visit
his sister. He was just a young boy. When guinea-fowl were
eating up Ture's durra in the cultivations Ture and his brother-
in-law carved wooden arrows to go and shoot the guinea-fowl
with them. Ture carved arrows till his quiver was bursting with
them, and Orphan carved only one, being a child.

They then took themselves to the cultivations to wait for the
guinea-fowl. The guinea-fowl settled in the cultivations till it
was dark with them. When Ture saw so many of them he
prevented his brother-in-law from shooting at them, saying
he himself would shoot them. The boy said 'So be it sir, you
shoot them.' Ture shot one arrow but only into the ground; all
his many arrows went into the ground and all his arrows[3] were

---

[1] '*Kpe oto*': an 'idiomatic' expression for running either in flight or for some other
purpose.
[2] '*Si kina ku ngba ri . . .*': lit., 'while it was still in her mouth', i.e. 'while she was
still speaking'.   [3] *Kumu* indicates a great number.

exhausted in the ground, and he had not shot a single guinea-
fowl. So he called upon Orphan to come and shoot his single
arrow. When the boy shot his single arrow the guinea-fowl died
like locusts. They gathered these guinea-fowl and returned
home with them to Ture's wife. No sooner had Ture arrived
than he called his wife. 'Nanzagbe, that brother of yours is a
very poor shot! It was I who shot all these guinea-fowl. Take
them and cook them for me, madam.'[1] Ture's wife cooked
these guinea-fowl, and took just their entrails and cooked them
for her brother because he was such a poor shot, so Ture had
related. The boy sought for a good bit of guinea-fowl meat
among the entrails, ate it, and left the entrails untouched in the
pot. This boy began to get thin because he was not eating well.

When Ture and his wife had eaten up these birds, Ture and
the boy carved more arrows to go after guinea-fowl. The boy
carved just one arrow, Ture's quiver was full as before. The
guinea-fowl flew down as before. Ture's wife said to herself that
as Ture had always been fond of wantonness she would follow
them to the cultivations to see what really happened there. She
went and stood still. Ture was shooting his arrows into the
ground as before and they were finished. Orphan came with his
single arrow and when he shot it the guinea-fowl died till their
blood flowed into the river. Ture's wife ran to the cultivations,
saying 'Hey Ture, didn't you tell me that it was you who shot
these guinea-fowl? Whereas it is indeed my brother who shoots
these guinea-fowl!'

When they got home she cooked the guinea-fowl for her
brother, and she cooked only their entrails for Ture. Ture
refused to eat them. When Nanzagbe gave her brother a stool
to sit on he said he would not sit on Ture's stool. She entered
her hut and brought out a spear and compensated him[2] and
he sat on the stool. She gave him water but he rejected it, but
when she had compensated him he washed his hands and
began to eat his food. When greed overcame Ture he came and
sat near the boy, begging for a leg of guinea-fowl from him.
The boy said 'When you were eating your fowls which I had
shot for you, did you see me begging for them?'

---

[1] *Na*, 'madam', and *ba*, 'sir', when used thus at the end of a sentence have a touch
of asperity suggestive of reproach or impatience.

[2] A Zande who has been insulted will not relent until he is made a gift.

Next morning Ture said 'Friend, let us go and collect honey today.' When they reached a hollow tree in which there was a nest Ture said 'Let us gather up the honey with our heads as there is no fire.[1] Each one will put his head into the hollow, and when the bees are tired of stinging it he can thrust his hand in to pull out the honeycomb.' Ture employed this method first and drew out his honeycomb. He then called Orphan to the mouth of the hollow also. When the boy put his head into the hollow tree Ture pushed his head down and put a stone in by his head so that his head was stuck in the hollow of the nest. When the boy was weeping and begging for mercy Ture was dancing. When Nanzagbe heard her brother's cries she left her home and ran with her pestle in her hand. Before she arrived Ture fled as fast as he could. She came and rescued her brother and took him home with her.

That is why when somebody has done something bad or something foolish we say 'Even Ture who did many foolish things, did he do that?'

18. *How Ture swept around the grave of ghosts* (G.)

THE termites rain fell and Ture and his page Katikati went to look for their termites. They went and found a big mound. As Ture scraped it the eyes of people appeared and he thought they were the tunnels of termites. But it was the place where the ghosts buried their dead under a tall mimosa tree.

Ture cleared around the mound and as the sun was setting he was happy at the thought of these termites. When it became dark he went with his boy to beside them. Before, when Ture was sweeping around the mound, he found a staff with an old blunt hoe on it lying beside it, and he took it and dropped the hoe into his bag, not knowing its owner, and he threw the handle (staff) away. Ture waited and then he lit a torch to inspect these termites and he found people's eyes on the mound, and he thought that they were the termites making their runs, whereas the mound was a grave, a grave of the ghosts. They seated themselves and soon afterwards they heard the owners of the grave come singing, saying

[1] Bees are dispersed with fire and smoke.

'Let me be taken under the mimosa tree.
Which mimosa tree?
The one which Ture is on its mound.'

Only the boy heard it, Ture did not hear it. This boy Katikati said to Ture 'What is sounding like this? Let us listen for a while.' As they listened they heard them coming again, saying

'You take me under the mimosa tree.
Which mimosa tree?
The one which Ture is on its mound.'

Those ghosts were coming out to bury their dead in that mound where they usually buried them. When Ture heard it he said to his page 'Let us run away.' Ture told him 'I am going to run in that direction' and said that Katikati should run the other way by himself and then they would join up ahead.

As they listened they heard a thud, '*kpu*',[1] near that grave. The ghosts had dropped their corpse near the mound Ture had cleared around. These ghosts asked 'Who swept this place?' They looked in vain for their old blunt hoe and found only the handle lying down. They asked the handle, saying 'Where is the old blunt hoe?' The handle replied 'A man called Ture came here and took me and threw me away into the bush and went away with the hoe.' These people then called aloud to the hoe, saying, 'Old blunt hoe o!' The old blunt hoe answered, and they asked 'Where are you?' The old blunt hoe said 'I am here in Ture's bag.' These many ghosts started to chase Ture in the darkness. They called out to the old blunt hoe again, saying 'Where are you?' It said 'I am here in Ture's bag.' When Ture heard it he took the old blunt hoe out of the bag and threw it into the bush, but it came back and entered into Ture's bag. He took it and threw it very far away, and it came back and entered Ture's bag. So, as it troubled Ture much, he took it out of the bag and threw it away and ran away from it.

[1] The sound of the dropped corpse.

19. *How Ture chased the Weaver-birds into the bush* (G.)

TURE went with Orphan to the home of the red Weaver-birds. They found them cultivating eleusine for a beer-feast. Ture tied a cord round his leg and went stealthily and tied the other end of it to the legs of the Weaver-birds. He tied another cord to Orphan's leg and tied the other end to the legs of the Weaver-birds. The Weaver-birds were not yet aware; they were just chatting away in their usual speech, and when they saw Ture and Orphan they flew away in flocks, going here and there. They watched them and they settled in their nests, flying high and then low to the ground. But they did not know that Ture had tied their legs to that of Orphan.

Ture ground a red gravel like blood and gave it to Kpikoro[1] to deceive the Weaver-birds with it. He sent Kpikoro deceitfully to the Weaver-birds to bring him fire to light his pipe. He told Kpikoro to go and scatter the fire of the Weaver-birds. He went and scattered the fire. A young Weaver-bird was angered about their fire and he sprang and hit Kpikoro hard with his wing. Kpikoro fell down as though dead. Kpikoro lay there and rubbed his mouth with the flour of the red gravel. It appeared to the Weaver-birds to be blood and they feared that they had killed Kpikoro. Ture did that to deceive the Weaver-birds. Ture called out to Kpikoro 'Kpikoro, where are you?' The young Weaver-bird said 'Is it not Kpikoro whom you call? He is just lying down. I just slapped him and he fell down as though dead.' Ture continued to call and when he came and saw Kpikoro the Weaver-birds flew in flocks and went to the bush, thinking that Kpikoro was dead. In the past the Weaver-birds lived in the homes of people. It was on account of what Ture did that they went to live in the bush, thinking that Kpikoro was dead. That is why they eat all kinds of human food—eleusine, durra, maize—it is because at one time these were their food (when they lived with people).

[1] An insect which when disturbed feigns death. It is wingless, has a hard body, and is black in colour.

20. *How Ture lacked termites because of fear* (G.)

THE rain of termites fell and Ture went with his page to collect the termites. Little Bushbuck was by himself in the forest and was saying

'I have swallowed Ture *gororo*,
I have swallowed Ture *gororo*.'

As he was saying this Ture's page heard it, and he asked Ture 'What is sounding like that?' They went and lit a light, and they saw the termites making their runs. When they came to wait for them to swarm they heard little Bushbuck walking on dry leaves together with the same chant, saying

'Little Bushbuck is strolling in the forest.
I have swallowed Ture *gororo*,
I have swallowed Ture *gororo*.'

When Ture heard it he said to his page 'Let us run away, let us go and meet ahead.' They ran with all speed from this animal and went home. They went and saw Nanzagbe, who had collected an abundance of termites, and they told her that it had rained and the termites had not swarmed. She asked Ture's page, saying 'Is what Ture is saying true?' Katikati told her that it was a lie, they had run away from little Bushbuck.

The rain of termites fell again, and she said 'Ture, as you ran away leaving those termites, I am going myself.' She went after the termites with Katikati. The animal made the sound near them but they did not fear and they collected their termites.

Ture had remained near the (other) termites near the homestead. Ture waited and then he heard something saying

'*Dingi dingi ti bu Ture.*'

When it sounded like that and Ture heard it he was very much afraid, and as his fear increased he got up, saying 'Let me go inside from fear.' They were still making the noise and coming near the hut. Ture left the termites and ran inside for fear of the birds which were deceiving him. Ture said 'Let me close the door, provided nobody is ordering me to close it.' He closed it. Then these birds came and stood just outside the hut. One stood behind the hut and the other stood at the door, and they were making the same noise which Ture had fled from. Ture said 'Let me lie down, provided nobody is ordering me to lie down.' He put out the fire in fear so that the birds might not see him in its light and kill him. Ture covered himself with a broken pot and said 'As I cover myself with a bottomless pot, will it be said that somebody ordered me to cover myself?' It dawned and then the sun rose and other people all came out-doors, and still Ture was inside, while those birds had already gone. Ture still went on hiding in the hut from fear.

Nanzagbe and Katikati came back from the place of their termites. They arrived at the place of those termites they had stationed Ture near them, and they did not see any trace of Ture near them at all. They saw the fallen wings of the termites as they had flown off by themselves when Ture fled from them in fear. They looked for Ture in the homestead in vain and saw no sign of him, and they said 'Where has Ture gone?' They called out to him in vain, and then they looked in the hut and looked under the bed in vain. They searched all over the hut and then they looked under the broken pot and found Ture there. She asked him, saying 'Ture, where are the termites you have collected?' He said to her 'Something was making a noise here last night and I did not know what kind of animals were making the noise.' She said to him 'Was it not the birds? They have been making that noise here before, but I did not fear them. I continue collecting my termites when those birds are there.' She went on, saying to Ture 'As you were afraid by your termites, you won't eat mine.'

21. *How little Monkey consumed Ture's porridge* (R. M.)

TURE got up and when he was going to his in-laws he met little Monkey on the way and he said to him 'Friend, come and accompany me to my in-laws.' When they arrived at Ture's in-laws, 'Whatever is done for Ture', little Monkey said, 'since we came together, you do the same for me also.'

When they prepared porridge for Ture he demanded that they should prepare the same for him; when they kindled fire for Ture little Monkey demanded that they kindle his also; when they showed a hut for Ture and his wife he said he wanted to sleep there too. Ture slept for a long time and when he awoke he found little Monkey sleeping between him and his wife. So Ture got up and beat little Monkey and threw him out. Little Monkey said 'If people travel together why should they sleep apart?'

In the morning they made a porridge-and-honey mash for Ture, and little Monkey said the same should be done for him. The hosts refused. After that Ture poured his porridge into his bag, thinking that he would eat it at home when little Monkey would have gone to his home. So Ture and little Monkey set off to return to their homes.

When they were on their way Ture got angry and chased little Monkey from following him, but desire for Ture's porridge was itching little Monkey. So he started searching for a trick whereby he might eat Ture's porridge.

Little Monkey ran ahead of Ture and turned himself into a beautiful knife and lay on the path so that if Ture threw him into his bag he could then eat up his porridge.

Ture came and saw the knife and said '*Hu!* Is it not little Monkey pretending?' He passed it by. Little Monkey then changed himself into a fine spear and lay on the path ahead of Ture. Ture came and saw this fine spear and just remarked 'Little Monkey, you trouble yourself to no purpose! You will never eat this porridge of mine today.'

So little Monkey turned himself into a beautiful small woman's toilet knife, resembling that of Ture's wife Nanzagbe. He then lay beside the spring near Ture's home. As Ture was returning home he decided to pass by the spring to drink some water. When he looked he saw the toilet knife. He exclaimed 'Oh, look at Nanzagbe's toilet knife, she must have dropped it while drawing water.' Ture picked up this knife and put it in his bag. Little Monkey changed back again to his usual self and ate up Ture's porridge, leaving only a small bit.

When Ture arrived home he called to his children to bring a bowl for him to pour the porridge into it for them. When Ture began to open the mouth of the bag little Monkey jumped out and took to his heels. When Ture looked into the bag he saw only a small remnant of the porridge. When Ture put in his finger and tasted it it tasted very delicious, and then real tears ran down Ture's cheeks.

22. *How Ture lacked termites because of laziness* (R. M.)

IT had not rained at the favourable time for termites to swarm[1] for a long time, and then one day rain fell until everything was soaked. When the rain stopped everybody dispersed after termites[2] like animals in the dry season.[3] The bush was teeming with people.

Ture also took his bag and threw into it his hoe and matchet for cutting grass stalks.[4] Leaving his wives, Nanzagbe and Nangbafudo, near the termites close to the homestead, Ture declared that he was going right into the bush where he had termites which swarmed in great numbers.[5] When evening came, Ture took the path to the termites. Ture travelled on[6] until he was near his termites, when he met Elephant balancing his great bulk near his termites.[7] Ture put down his bag, wishing to see how this big lump of a heavy fellow[8] swept around his termite mound.[9] Elephant blew away leaves from near his termite mound with his great trunk and pulled out small bushes and grass nearby with his great trunk. Ture said he would see how he would make the hole.[10] Elephant backed a bit and came and planted his heavy foot in the courtyard[11] of his termites

[1] *Sangu age*: rain that starts at dawn and stops before midday. It causes the termites to swarm.

[2] That is to say, they all went to prepare their termite mounds in preparation for the swarming of the termites.

[3] When the bush is fired in the dry season the animals run away to seek shelter. They are dispersed as are the people who have all left home to prepare for the harvest of termites.

[4] To make torches to inspect the termite-runs.

[5] *Wiso*: a word used in connexion with termites. It indicates that a mound has many termites which will swarm.

[6] *Paka*: a verb which gives particular force to the idea of travelling or walking.

[7] *Tundurundu* indicates a great block or bulk of something.

[8] *Kakputukakputu*: with rough ridges on the body.

[9] Clearing around the mound, sweeping a clean space, and digging a hole into which the termites will fall.

[10] For the termites to fall into.

[11] The cleared and swept place before the mound.

once, and when he lifted his heel, lo! there was a large hole for the termites. Ture then appeared before Elephant and said 'O friend, so this is how you dig your termites-hole; mother told me that if I went in search of termites and found an elephant treading his termites-hole I should know that he is my friend.[1] So you there, my friend, when you have finished treading out your termites-hole, please come and tread out mine.' Elephant replied 'You go and clean their courtyard first, and when the termites are about to swarm I shall at once come to tread your hole for you.' When Ture heard this he rejoiced in his heart, saying 'I have saved myself digging a termites-hole, son of Ture's father. Who would see me messing myself with earth of the hole today? That ugly fellow Elephant will come to tread the hole for me with that big heel of his.' Ture went and cleaned around his termite mound and then took and threw away his hoe[2] and wandered away to eat wild fruits. When it was time for the termites to swarm he came and made a fire before the termite mound and sat waiting for Elephant. Ture waited and waited, but Elephant did not come. When he was tired of waiting[3] and the termites were showing themselves[4] he was crying, calling Elephant ceaselessly, and Elephant was hearing this as if he had no ears in his head. When the termites were already in flight Elephant just shouted to him 'I am not coming. So you did not dig your termites-hole thinking that I was going to tread it for you! I am collecting my termites, man.' Ture jumped up and dashed off to look for the hoe he had flung into the bush. While he was there all the termites flew away. Ture went without termites as a dog goes without its sister's bridewealth. He returned home and simply told his wives that his termites had not come out. Nangbafudo made faces[5] at him, saying 'Just say that you left the termites and went after your dance. What a man you are! Why did we ever marry you?'

So people say if you go in search of something, such as

[1] Lit., 'blood-brother', but used also for 'friend'.
[2] Which he had brought for digging the hole.
[3] When it was too much for him.
[4] The termites perforate the mound with their runs, through which they come out. First wingless termites come out to make sure that conditions are suitable for the edible winged ones to swarm: this is *kparia*.
[5] A woman or child who is displeased may turn her or his face away, closing the eyes for a few moments.

termites, with somebody, don't expect him to do your work for you. How do you know whether he will refuse? You can never tell what is in the heart of the other man.

23. *Tortoise and the termites of Wagtail's[1] sons* (R. M.)

THERE had been a heavy rain for termites, so Ture and that wife of his, Nanzagbe, went to clear around their termite mounds. They would arrive at one termite mound, but Ture would say that those termites did not usually swarm in great numbers. Ture and his wife wandered until they had visited almost all the mounds and they found a mound which Ture said had plenty of termites. They cleaned around it. When it was dark these termites did not perforate (the mound).[2] It was an empty mound Ture had cleaned around. Ture said he would be the one to inspect the termites by torch-light. He went and looked in vain for their runs. He returned and told Nanzagbe that they were about to come out. Termites started flying everywhere. Ture's wife said to him 'When will ours swarm, man?' He replied 'They will start swarming right now.' Ture and his wife waited and waited, and when his wife went to inspect the mound by torch-light she saw not a single termite-run. She nagged at Ture all the way home.

That night Wagtail and his children collected termites till their baskets and pots were all full. In the morning they went to dry them on a granitic outcrop[3] over a large area.[4] Wagtail's sons hid themselves on the edge of the outcrop to guard the termites. Ture went round to see who had collected lots of termites. He reached Wagtail's termites and he looked around to see if there was anybody present, and there was nobody. Ture gathered up some of them and poured them into his mouth and as they were delicious in his mouth he decided to sit down and eat them. While he was doing so Wagtail's sons sprang up and began lashing vigorously at him with switches.

---

[1] *Ngbia* is the wagtail.
[2] They did not make runs along which to emerge and swarm because the mound was a deserted one.
[3] A *munga* is a granite outcrop and suitable for drying things.
[4] *Kpai* seems here to indicate the area over which the termites were spread.

Ture fled with all speed. Ture continued running until he was near home, when he stopped running. Ture's body was smarting from the switches. Ture called Nanzagbe loudly,[1] 'Bring my bag, woman, and take that big basket of ours. My friend Wagtail has given me termites. You were quarrelling with me yesterday, now aren't you going to be spoilt with termites?'

Ture led the way with his elephant-hide bag slung across his shoulder, and his wife followed him carrying her big basket on her head. Soon they arrived at the stone flat where Wagtail's termites were. Ture told her that those were his termites, given by Wagtail. The man was sick of termites. Ture turned up his bag and pressed termites into it. As for his wife, she was crying out for another big basket. When they lifted their loads to go home the sons of Wagtail rushed out and attacked them with switches and began lashing them like a feast.[2] Ture's wife tried to throw away the termites to run away, but her desire for them was too much for her. Wagtail's sons stopped whipping her and gave her some termites to take home. On her way home she was threatening Ture. She arrived home, and looked in vain for Ture, he had disappeared. Wagtail pounded his termites and they filled every pot and gourd.[3] Wagtail invited people to come and eat termites in his home as was expected of an elder. But the main part of the termites, that which a person stores to eat when the termite season is over, was in the granary. When people were feasting on the termites Wagtail's young grandson arrived and told Wagtail that his father (Wagtail's) was dead. People were comforting Wagtail while Ture was tapping his big toe on the ground.[4]

Wagtail and his children all went to the funeral of his father. Wagtail asked 'Who will guard my termites which are in the granary?' Ture cried out that he would do so. They asked Ture to climb into the granary. Ture quickly climbed into the granary and came down. They asked Tortoise to climb, but when he tried to climb he fell down. He said 'I never climb granaries myself, sir.' Wagtail said that Tortoise was to guard his termites. Ture was very sad and blamed himself for having run up the ladder and dropped into the granary so easily: 'O

---

[1] *Boro ari yo*: lit., 'very high'.
[2] They beat them like millet being threshed for a feast.
[3] *Kpete* indicates a great quantity.　　　[4] A sign of delightful expectation.

son of Ture's father, so I was being tricked by Wagtail!' The people dispersed leaving Tortoise under the granary. No sooner had Wagtail and his children set forth than Tortoise dragged out the prop of the granary roof and lifted it up. He did not repeat the trick he had played before. He easily climbed up and dropped into the granary[1] after Wagtail's pounded termites and settled down cosily to eat them. Tortoise didn't come down from the granary till he had eaten up all the termites. Tortoise was eating the termites day and night. He emptied each container and set it aside for his excretions. When he had eaten all Wagtail's termites he came down and went to a stream where he hid in the water.

Wagtail buried his father and built a hut over the grave. He then left with his children to return home to prepare a feast for raising a memorial on his father's grave.[2] When Wagtail was near his home he saw his granary open[3] as Tortoise had left it. When he stepped to the mouth of the granary only Tortoise's dung was smelling nastily[4] in the granary. Wagtail jumped down and he and his children went around asking about Tortoise. Ture said to them 'You have got it. You said only Tortoise was your friend. Let nobody bother me for my part! I don't know Tortoise's whereabouts.' It was Ture's wife who said 'Is it not Tortoise whom I often see on the river bank basking? Whenever a person shows his head he plunges into the water.' Wagtail went and made blood-brotherhood with Kite and said 'My friend Kite, that ugly little savage[5] called Tortoise has done me a great injury by eating all my termites while I was at my father's funeral, and on top of that he excreted into my granary and my pots and gourds and has now fled to the river. You go and wait for him for me and if he attempts to come out snatch him and fly away with him, and when you find a rock let him go and smash himself on it. If he is not shattered, then you are not Kite!'

[1] *Karakara* indicates that he climbed both fast and skilfully.

[2] A feast is given and today a mound of stones is erected on the grave—in the past it was a hut.

[3] The movable roof of the granary was partly raised, leaving a space between the roof and the wall of the granary. This gap is referred to as its *ngba*, 'mouth'.

[4] *Gbada*: an adverb which indicates that the smell was horrible. It is used with *fu*, 'to smell'.

[5] *Uro* means 'foreigner', but as Azande look down on foreigners with scorn the word 'savage' is perhaps permissible here.

Kite waited for Tortoise and when he next came out to bask
Kite attempted to snatch him but Tortoise withdrew into his
shell. Kite dropped down beside him to deceive him, saying that
he was his friend. 'Friend, I am coming to you for conversation
but you are withdrawing into your shell. Is that how you treat
your friends?' Tortoise already knew his plot, and that is why he
said to him 'I talk only when I open my bottom, and the person
who puts his foot into it, he is the one with whom I converse
well.' Kite could not see why he should be afraid of Tortoise's
bottom. So when Tortoise opened his anus he put his foot into
it. They conversed. They talked for a while and then Tortoise
closed his anus tightly on Kite's foot in his shell and ran into
the water. Although Kite was fluttering and crying, Tortoise
dived with him into the water. So Kite was drowned, and
Tortoise remained living near the water.

So people say if you interfere with somebody who has
committed some offence you will suffer at his hand,[1] for an
offender never forgets. He is always insecure and continually
schemes against his enemies.

24. *Ture and Bat and Duiker and bread-fruit* (R. M.)

THERE was a man who had many children. This man built
an extensive[2] homestead on a river bank. On the river bank was
his bread-fruit tree which he and his children guarded jealously.
Nobody could pick his bread-fruit. The man was about his
bread-fruit as hot as a potsherd for (roasting) tobacco (leaves).
Whenever one fell he instantly arrived to see who had shaken
it down or whether the wind had blown it down. If it was the
wind which blew it down he took it home, where his wife
roasted it (the seeds) for his children and himself also. Desire
for this bread-fruit was one day making Ture itch as though he
had been rubbed with *abakpa* beans.[3] So he went to the bird
called Bat in his home and proposed that they should go and
pick the bread-fruit that ugly man was so jealous about. 'Who

---

[1] *Dia we a dia fuo ni*: lit., 'take fire after a person', i.e. to suffer some calamity.
[2] *Ti ki ni ga wa yo*: 'it extended far'. How far is left to the imagination.
[3] See footnote on p. 69.

does he think he is to insist on eating this good bread-fruit all by himself!'

On their way they met that small beast Duiker. Ture said 'Friend Duiker, we are going to pick that fellow's fruit who is so mean about it over there.[1] Aren't you coming as well?' Duiker, who had been coveting the fruit before, followed them. After they had arrived beneath that bread-fruit tree in the evening Ture climbed up it, and whenever he picked one of the fruits Bat would soar up and catch it in mid air and lay it down gently. They picked a lot of the fruit in this manner till they had a great heap of it before them. They took it to Ture's home, and his wives roasted it and it filled a bowl. Ture then said 'Friends, since I was the one who climbed the tree I shall start eating it first, as I might have fallen from the height. When I am satisfied I shall give what remains to you.' They agreed to this. Ture sat down and ate the fruit till he left only a small portion, which hardly covered the bottom of the bowl, for Bat and Duiker. When they had eaten it and were leaving, Ture then said 'Friends, as the bread-fruit has been delicious in our mouths, very early in the morning tomorrow, come, let us go and pick some more. It is very delicious.'

At cock-crow Bat and Duiker arrived. They at once went again in a body to the man's bread-fruit tree.[2] Ture said 'Since it was I who climbed yesterday, you, Bat, will yourself climb and I shall spread myself out on the ground here for the fruit to fall on me, so that people do not hear it fall.' Bat flew up and as he picked the fruit it fell on the belly of Ture. Bat thought that since Ture got the largest share of the fruit yesterday because he had climbed up the tree, it would be his turn to get the largest share this time. Therefore he was sending down the fruit in showers as if for a feast.[3] Ture's belly was smarting from the fruits. Suddenly Ture saw a very big one whirling down to him.[4] Ture was terrified by this and when he moved a little

[1] *Enda pati e*: this has the sense of meanness. *Ka enda na he* has the sense of boasting about something or being proud of it.

[2] *I ki gbedi ti yo berewe ku pati ga kumba pusa yo*: lit., 'they pulled themselves again to the man's bread-fruit'. The expression suggests being drawn irresistibly towards something.

[3] At a feast everything is in abundance. So anything in abundance may be compared to a feast.

[4] *Boro* is used for emphasis. *Wiriwiri* denotes the rotating of roundish fruit as it falls. *Fuo ko* suggests the fruit coming down with the intention of hurting him.

aside the fruit smashed on the ground with a deep noise, *nduu*! The owner of the tree cried out 'I have heard it oo, I have heard it!' He urged on his sons and they rushed to the bread-fruit tree with their big spears in hand. Before they arrived Bat had flown away. The men pursued Ture and Duiker, just behind them, running after them at a terrific speed.[1] Ture and Duiker ran until they found a cave and plunged headlong into it, and they hid there breathing heavily (*vavaa*). Duiker said to Ture 'I am going to put my horns in the way so that when they push a stake after us here they will poke my horns and think they are just pieces of wood.' Ture said '*Hii*, what do you know, being just a child? I will spread myself in the way and when they push in a stake they will poke my flesh and think that it is just earth.' They argued much about this. When the men approached and they could hear their heavy steps (*züzü*) Duiker said 'All right Ture, let us see you do it.' The men swarmed to the cave and cried, saying 'Look you, people are here. Cut a stake quickly so that we may probe with it into this hollow.' They took a long stake and pushed it into the cave and it struck Ture's thigh. The men poked Ture with the stake for a long time. He writhed with the pain but in vain, and he burst out crying: 'O Ture, Nangbafudo's brother,[2] my thigh ooo!' The men said 'Ah, there is somebody there, drag him outside, people!' They struggled with Ture and pulled him out of the cave and asked him, saying 'Who else is there?' Ture cried out that Duiker was still in there. When they pushed in the stake again Duiker put his horns in the way and the men's stake hit them. They thought that there was nobody else there, that it was just Ture trying to fool them, as was his habit. In vain Ture kept on telling them that it was Duiker's horns they were poking, the men would not listen to Ture. They beat Ture and bound him and stumbled over the ropes and fell down.[3] When they left Ture there and went home, Duiker came out slowly[4] from the cave and cut the rope with which Ture had been bound, saying 'See what I was telling you, the men have really punished you!' Ture could not answer a word.

[1] The word *wakawaka* indicates great speed.

[2] Nangbafudo in these stories was one of Ture's wives. See footnote on p. 53.

[3] *Ki vo ko koto ti giri ko ti*: the sense here is that the men tied Ture up without mercy.

[4] *Ki kakasa ti ko*: he came out cautiously.

So people say it is not good to do everything and give other people no chance; and no good comes from stubbornness. If Ture had listened to Duiker he would not have been beaten so much.

25. *Ture's fear at a fire-hunt* (R. M.)

AN old man lived for a long time, and then death took hold of him. When he knew that he had finished with this world he summoned his eldest son and blessed him with spittle.[1] He said 'O my son, as I am dying and as the Azande are very mean about meat I don't want you to suffer lack of meat. Before people arrive near my corpse cut off my big toe, the left one, and bury it on the path to your home. When you summon people to hunt let them all leave your home by that path while you chant the death of animals.' Bakoakpi[2] buried his old father and two months later he summoned a hunting party. It was a hunt where dogs are not used but only people enter the bush and chase out the animals to the nets. People came to Bakoakpi's hunting as they would attend a feast. When the sun was high in the heavens the men shouldered their nets and their big spears and left for the hunt. While they were leaving Bakoakpi's home they stumbled over his father's toe, while he chanted

> 'Let only animals die,
> Let no man die.'

The men went and ran with their nets round a big stretch of bush and spread them properly.[3] When they were ready Bakoakpi ran along the other side of the bush with the boys and women to scare the animals into the nets. The animals ran and fell into the nets and were speared till their blood (water) flowed into the river. There was an abundance of meat.[4] The people erected huge drying platforms and cut up the meat to

---

[1] A father blesses his son by spitting on him.

[2] *Bakoakpi* means *ba*, 'father'; *ko*, 'his'; *a kpi*, 'is dead'.

[3] *Mbegumbegu* indicates how well and completely the nets were spread and supported. Cf. *ri ki mbakadi ba mbegumbegu*, 'she made the bed faultlessly'.

[4] Heaps of meat. Any other vast quantities of anything may be referred to in the same way.

smoke it, and the platforms creaked under the weight of meat.[1]
It was not possible for anyone to go home. The people roasted
and ate meat. When it was dusk people prepared sleeping
places and fell into a deep sleep, the sleep of those glutted with
meat. There was a little boy with them who was an orphan.
People refused to give him any of their meat. He gathered up
just some left-over intestines of the animals and erected a little
clumsy platform for them at the edge of the camp and made a
fire under it and lay down, easing his misery by playing on his
harp. At midnight when everybody was asleep a big bird which
used to swallow people arrived.[2] First came a great wind and
passed. After that it flew heavily[3] and perched, singing

> '*Hiki*,[4] I swallow people,
> I will swallow you today, *hikii*.'

This boy heard it. He was the only one awake. All the others
were in the deep sleep of meat. He said 'My father told me that
if ever I spent the night in the forest I should not fall asleep
quickly.' He took his harp and while playing on it he sang
thus:

> 'Princes' talk, talk of *ripopo*,[5]
> Princes' talk, talk of *ripopo*,
> I am a land-dweller, I am a vigilant one,
> I am a land dweller, I am also a river-dweller,
> I see a big bird, I shoot it with my arrow!'

When the big bird heard the orphan's song it moved back and
sang its song again, and he sang his too. So it was afraid, for
it did not swallow people when they were awake. It therefore
flew back to its place and these many people were saved because
of this orphan. In the morning, when he said what had
happened, they were angry with him, saying 'Whom can a
poor thing like you save? You shut up, you!' They seized him
and beat him and rubbed him on the ground till he was white
with dust, and then they threw him down at the edge of the
camp.

---

[1] *Nyokonyoko*: an abundance of fresh meat spread to smoke dry. Rarely used for other things.

[2] 'It started from its place to come.' This has a sort of threatening sense; the coming of the bird spelt some trouble.

[3] The heavy way a big bird flies is thus expressed.

[4] The threatening noise the bird made in its throat.

[5] *Ripopo* does not seem to have any meaning.

That day their meat was not dry enough for them to carry it home. So they spent the following night in the same camp. At midnight a great storm came and passed, and after that the big bird arrived as before and found only the orphan awake. When it sang its usual song he played his harp of sorrow while singing the song he had sung before. When it backed a little he woke the people quickly, saying 'Get up and see the big bird I was talking about today, and you beat me!' When they got up and saw the big bird they were all shivering in great fear. They shouted and beat things to frighten away this big bird. It flew heavily away. In the morning they took the orphan and washed him clean and gave him so much dried meat that he did not know how to carry it! Everybody tied up their meat and went home, including the orphan.

The news of this big hunt and the great quantity of meat went round and came to the ears of Ture. Ture seized his spears and burst in upon his father, speared him to death, and cut off his big toe, which he took home and buried on the path to his home. Early the following day he summoned a big hunting party. Azande came for the hunt as numerous as grass. They shouldered the nets and went off to the hunt while each of them stumbled over the toe of Ture's father and he chanted

'Let animals not die,
Let only people die.'

During this hunt buffaloes rushed out of the bush and began to toss people and killed many of them. Only three buffaloes were killed. Some people made stretchers for this meat while others carried their dead relatives home. At dusk Ture took his harp and lay down with it at the edge of the camp to await the big bird that used to swallow people. A big storm blew as before. When it had passed the big bird arrived. Meanwhile Ture was falling into a deep slumber. When it sang its song and Ture sang the orphan's song it backed away. When it sang again sleep had overcome Ture. It sang again but there was no response. It sang again; oh no! Whenever Ture tried to open his mouth sleep seemed to say 'Will you open that mouth of yours today?' The big bird swallowed very many of the people. The rest of them awoke and fled in fear, leaving the meat. Ture too awoke and in haste made off to his home.

This is why when a person jumps at a new thing (or idea) people first stand aside to see how he gets on,[1] for they say 'That is how Ture put people's feet in fire.'

26. *How Ture struck the ground-fruit for salt in vain* (R. M.)

THERE was a man who had a block of salt at the back of his head. This man loved to eat ground-fruit[2] more than anything else. Every year when the bush was burnt he would go there and pull up a fruit and break it open and rub (the soft inside of) it on his salt at his nape. When it hissed, *waa*, from the salt[3] he would throw it into his mouth and swallow it and move on to the next one. This salt of his, he was born with it, so all the girls rejected him and he remained a bachelor.

When grass was burnt this fellow went as usual to eat his ground-fruit. Ture also for his part went in search of ground-fruits and met this man eating ground-fruits as he had been doing for years. When Ture saw it, he too wanted to do it. Ture broke up his ground-fruit but when he rubbed it at the back of his head he only saw lice eggs on it, and he threw it away. Ture therefore ran to the *Atari* (oracle) and hit it on the head, and when it jumped into the fire and fumed Ture fled. It called Ture back, saying 'Didn't you come so that I could foretell your future?' Ture said 'O *Atari*, how can I obtain the block of salt I have seen at the back of a man's head in the burnt bush?' *Atari* said to him 'Go and cut the slimy creeper, dip it in water, and make the door of his hut very slippery while he is eating his fruit. Then you go and attack him and chase him to his home, then you will get that salt.' Ture said 'You ugly thing you! Did you think I didn't already know of that trick?'

Ture ran and made this man's doorway very slippery with the creeper and went to the burnt bush to look for him. Ture found

---

[1] Lit., 'to see their legs with it': wait and see whether they will be successful or not.

[2] *Nonga* is a red acid ground-fruit.

[3] When the inside of the fruit is brought into contact with salt some kind of chemical reaction produces a hissing noise like '*waa*'. Salt makes the fruit lose some of its acidity.

him and dashed at him with big spears, and terror of Ture
seized him and he fled as fast as he could. Ture pursued him and
when he tried to take shelter in his hut he slipped on the juice
of Ture's creeper and fell heavily on his back[1] and the block of
salt fell from his nape. When he fled inside the hut, Ture took
this block of salt and ran to the burnt bush after ground-fruits.
Ture plucked up the ground-fruits till he had a great heap of
them before him. He sat down and tied the salt to the back of
his head. He broke open a ground-fruit, but when he rubbed it
on this salt it did not hiss *waa* as it did for the owner of the salt.
Ture tried everything but the ground-fruit never became
salty for him. Ture tied it to his leg; oh no! He tied the salt to
his belly, but no use! He tried to tie it on every part of his body
and then he lost his temper and flung it away and went to his
home. When the owner of the salt followed Ture, he came and
found him struggling to produce the right effect with his salt.[2]
So when Ture discarded it he took it, fixed it in its position, and
went on his way enjoying his ground-fruit as before.

That is why people say that if you are greedy after a man's
thing when only he knows how to work it, it will be too much
for you[3] as the man's block of salt was too much for Ture.

27. *How Mbiangu saved Ture from death by fire* (G.)

THERE was a man whose name was Mbiangu. He left all other
places and built his home amid dry grass. When people set the
dry grass on fire and it flared up, going towards his hut, he
danced and sang thus:

'Mbiangu o, Mbiangu sesame oil, Mbiangu o, Mbiangu
sesame oil,
As I dip my head into sesame oil the fire is completely
extinguished,
Mbiangu o, Mbiangu sesame oil.'

[1] *Yoro ti ko ku ari yo ki mere ti ko sende*: lit., 'he went up and fell heavily to the
ground'. The expression emphasizes the heaviness of the fall.

[2] *Ko ki ni saki ti ko na ga ko tikpo*: lit., 'he was turning himself with his salt', i.e.
he was trying very hard to make it work. He was very preoccupied with the salt.

[3] *Aura ti he*: to attempt to do something which you don't know how to do, or are
not sure of being able to do.

Then the man dipped his head into sesame oil with his hat on, and as he shook his head the fire went out.

Ture came and saw the man doing that. He went home and went among dry grass where he built his hut and waited for the dry grass where he had built his hut to be set on fire. The fire was approaching the home of Ture. In imitation of the man, Ture said

'Ture o, Ture sesame oil, Ture o, Ture sesame oil,
I dip my head into sesame oil and the fire is completely
    extinguished,
Ture o, Ture sesame oil.'

But when he dipped his head into a different oil and shook it, oh no! The fire increased. Ture, realizing that there was nothing he could do, called for Mbiangu. Mbiangu then hastened after Ture to save him from the fire. He dipped his head into sesame oil and shook it, and the fire went out completely. He said to Ture 'Do not do this again since you do not know how to do it, otherwise you will die alone from fire. Had I not been near at hand you would have died.' Ture told him that he would not do it again.

But Ture was just waiting for Mbiangu to depart. When he left, Ture went again and built his home in a large piece of dry grass, and he told people to come and set fire round the dry grass. They came and set fire to it, and as the fire was getting near to him he sang

'Ture o, Ture sesame oil,
I dip my head into sesame oil and the fire is completely
    extinguished,
Ture o, Ture sesame oil.'

He dipped his head into different oil and shook it, oh no! The fire at once reached Ture and seized Ture and killed him. This time Mbiangu was absent and Ture called for him in vain. When he heard of the death of Ture he came as quickly as he could and dashed to Ture and scraped out some of his (magic) ash and rubbed it on Ture's lips; and Ture was saved again from death.

28. *How Ture killed Big-tooth for bread-fruit*
(R. M.)

THERE was a man called Big-tooth who had a big African bread-fruit tree in his courtyard. This bread-fruit tree bore abundant fruit,[1] and Big-tooth kept angry watch over it. Whenever he caught anybody with his bread-fruits he would cut him in two with one blow from his single huge tooth. He also had many children.

Ture arose and went to Bat and said to him 'My friend, come let us go and pick Big-tooth's bread-fruit.' So Ture and Bat went together and climbed this bread-fruit tree, picked the fruits while Big-tooth was asleep, and then climbed down with them and went home with them to shell them (the seeds, after eating the fleshy part). After they had roasted them (the kernels), Ture said to Bat 'My friend, I am going to draw water so that we may drink after eating our bread-fruit.' Ture only pretended to go all the way and turned back and came and stalked Bat till he was near to him, and then, disguising his voice, he said 'Cut Ture right through, cut Bat very deep.' Bat was scared and ran away with all speed, and Ture came forward and ate up all the bread-fruit. Ture always tricked Bat in this way to consume the bread-fruit they used to steal.

One night while they were stealing the fruits one fell down and woke Big-tooth from sleep and he trapped Ture in the tree, whereas Bat had already flown away for his part. Big-tooth said to Ture 'Today you will die. Who told you to come and steal my fruits?' Ture pleaded with him, saying 'O master, as your tooth is very long just lean it against this tree on which I am so that when I climb down I may fall on to it.' Big-tooth did so. Big-tooth and his sons gathered spears and sat beneath Ture to watch him above. After a while Big-tooth's sons fell asleep; then Big-tooth also fell asleep. So Ture climbed down quietly, took a spear and speared Big-tooth with it and shouted, saying 'Gbudweee,[2] let us spear Ture.' Big-tooth's

---

[1] *Zoozoo*: their fruits were so many that the weight was almost breaking down the branches.

[2] The name of a Zande king. Azande were accustomed to shout the name of their ruler when hurling their spears. However, the story is probably much earlier than the reign of this particular king, in whose one-time kingdom it was recorded.

sons awoke from sleep and began to spear their father to death,[1] thinking it was Ture. Ture left them there, and having run away he stood far off and said 'It is I, I am the son of Ture's father, I have tricked you into spearing your father.' Ture then ran off as fast as his legs would carry him and escaped from Big-tooth's sons.

They began to mourn for their father and bury him. After that they made a big feast to lament their father with it. Ture heard about this feast, so he went and knocked on the oracle *Atari's* head, and when *Atari* staggered and fell into the fire and began to melt Ture took to his heels. *Atari* came out of the fire and called to Ture, saying 'Didn't you come so that I might consult the rubbing-board oracle for you?' Ture said to him 'What can I do to go and attend the feast of Big-tooth's sons without their recognizing me?' *Atari* said to him 'Cover your head with the flowers of the spear grass[2] and wear leaves like an old woman and take a very small animal with you as though it were a baby and go; they will think you are their old grandmother.' Ture said 'You ugly thing! Did I not know all that before?'

Ture did what he was told and went to the feast of Big-tooth's sons. When Ture appeared at the edge of the courtyard they went to meet him, saying 'Grandmother is coming, grandmother is coming, grandmother is coming, grandmother is coming.' Ture was comforting (sympathizing with) them, and after that they showed him a place to rest. Ture then took the little monkey he had wrapped up in barkcloth and pinched it, and when it cried Ture said it was crying for bread-fruit. So they roasted bread-fruits and gave them, but it was Ture who ate them all, pretending to feed the baby. In this manner Ture was eating up the fruits of the sons of Big-tooth which nearly filled a granary. After five days Ture said he was going to depart. The sons of Big-tooth accompanied him till they reached a river. Ture then threw down the little monkey and jumped into the river and swam to, and appeared on, the other side; and he then pulled off his woman's dress and dressed himself in man's dress, and then he started to boast to the sons of Big-tooth, saying 'It is I, I am Ture the doer of things. It was

---

[1] *Gbanguagbangua*: 'fast and thorough'.

[2] These are white.

I who killed your father, and I have deceived you again and have eaten your bread-fruits.' Ture then made off quickly, leaving them in great wrath.

29. *Ture and Cicada* (R. M.)

TURE and Cicada lived close together. When the season of yams came Ture went to Cicada and said 'My friend, let us go out today to look for yams. People dug them up yesterday, I was astounded at what they collected.' They found yams and dug out great quantities.[1] There were great lumps of excellent yam[2] about them in abundance.[3] When Ture saw these yams his greed overcame him. He didn't want to take them home to his wives; he said 'Friend Cicada, I am tired of digging yams for those women at home. I am going to eat these yams right here in the bush in return for the twigs and thorns which scratched and cut me searching for them. Are you taking yours home?' Cicada answered 'Let us boil our yams here in the bush and eat them all up. While I am gathering firewood, you go to your home and fetch a pot for us to boil them in.'

Ture dashed home and cried to Nanzagbe to bring out for him the pot[4] in which she cooked sweet potatoes: 'I have found honey in a hole in the ground and if it were not that I lacked something to put it in you would be eating honey by now.' She brought out the pot and gave it to Ture. Ture ran with it to Cicada and found that he had already got a fire going. So they carried the lumps of yam to a stream, washed them, and put them in Ture's wife's pot and returned and stood the pot on the fire Cicada had made. When the yam had boiled and was cooked, Cicada said to Ture 'Comrade, let us go and drink water before we eat our yam.'

When they reached the river again Cicada said that as there were many crocodiles in that river, and as also the current was strong, each should hold the other by his legs so that he might

[1] *Pumburupumburu* denotes great quantities.
[2] *Muro gbara*: the most 'fleshy' yams.
[3] *Gusoguso* has the same sense as *pumburupumburu*.
[4] *Bunga* is a medium-sized pot used for boiling things or carrying water by young people. It is larger than broth-pots and smaller than pots for cooking porridge and brewing beer.

put his head into the water to drink. He told Ture to come first and he would hold his legs while he was drinking water. Ture put his head down to the water and Cicada held him by the legs.[1] When Ture had drunk enough water he said 'Comrade, you pull me from the water, I have had enough water.' Cicada then said 'Hold my legs firmly, I am very thirsty. I shall spend some time drinking.' So Ture gripped[2] Cicada's thin legs while he, unlike Ture, plunged into the water, leaving only his legs outside. Shortly afterwards he came to the surface and told Ture to hold only one leg (of his six) lest his hands might tire. Cicada, under the water, broke off the leg Ture was holding and swam under water till he appeared far downstream. Cicada ran very fast on his remaining five legs and dashed off to the yam, and he put it off the fire and began to gobble it up. While he was eating it his children arrived. They had gone out in search of their father, since, when he had gone in search of yams, he had not stayed away so long as this time. What might Ture have done to him? Cicada wrapped up the well-cooked starchy[3] yam in leaves and made every one of his children carry some of it, and they went their way home.

Meanwhile Ture continued sitting with Cicada's leg in his hand, thinking he was waiting for his friend who was drinking water. Ture said 'Comrade, what water are you drinking like this, into what stomach will you eat the yam?' Ture went on waiting and when his patience was exhausted he became furious[4] with Cicada, saying 'You, fellow, come out of the water, somebody is going to eat up our yam in the burnt bush.' When he tried to pull Cicada out of the water he pulled out only the broken-off leg. Ture at once understood Cicada's trick, so he dashed with all speed towards the yam. When he looked around only his wife's pot told him that he was alone there. Ture was speechless. When he recalled those wonderful lumps of yam tears flowed down his cheeks.

Ture put his wife's pot into his (leather) bag and began to return home. When he was near home to took Nanzagbe's pot

---

[1] *Pi ti ndu boro*, 'to lie at a person's feet', is an idiomatic expression with the sense of 'to lay hold of'.

[2] *Ka ku ti* has the same sense as *pi ti ndu*.

[3] *Mutemute gbara*: 'very starchy when cooked'. It means almost the same as *muro gbara*.

[4] *Gbi ku ti boro*: lit., 'to burn against a person'.

PLATE III

a. Gong and Drum

b. This could be Ture

and smashed it on the ground, and he rubbed himself in dust, put grass in his hair, tore his barkcloth, and scratched himself with thorns until he looked like one who has been beaten on a (dead) elephant.[1] Ture then took a piece of the pot and ran with all speed and dashed up to his wives, and breathing heavily he said 'A dreadful thing has happened! I have escaped from a band of men[2] on the path here, for legs are excellent things. The men beat me hard and broke Nanzagbe's pot in my hand. Only this one piece here, I snatched it to come and show it to her.' When Ture's wives saw his torn barkcloth and dust and grass in his hair and his body all scratched, they could not dispute what he said.

30. *Ture and Red Duiker* (G.)

TURE was taking a walk in the burnt bush when he met Red Duiker and they continued their walk together until they became hungry. So Ture said to Duiker 'Since we are hungry allow me to tie you up and exchange you for termites, and when a person takes you in exchange, if he puts you in a hut, then dash out and come running to me so that we may eat the termites with you.' Duiker agreed to the proposal. Ture tied him up and went around with him until he came to the homestead of a woman. He said to her 'This is my meat which I want to exchange for termites.' Meanwhile he had already said to Duiker 'You see that big tree over there; I shall sit under it and await you with the termites for which I am going to exchange you. When you escape from them run there.' The woman exchanged the animal with him for as many termites as filled his elephant-hide bag. Then she took Duiker and put him inside the hut on the platform there, where she left him, and came out to wash the pot in which she was going to cook him. When she

---

[1] In cutting up the carcass of an elephant people are sometimes injured, either by accident or in a quarrel. So the simile of being beaten on an elephant suggests that a person has been really badly beaten.

[2] According to Mr. Mambia, *Abaigo* 'refers usually to some legendary lawless fellows who roamed the countryside in groups'. It may now have come to have this meaning, but when I was in Zandeland the word was the name of King Gbudwe's leading company of warriors.

had finished washing it she sent her daughter to go and fetch Duiker so that she might cook him.

When this woman had gone out Duiker began to release himself as Ture had told him to do. The girl came and saw Duiker untying himself and she said to her mother 'My mother, the animal you exchanged is getting away.' But her mother got angry, saying 'Since your father has been killing his animals has he given them to me?' The daughter said 'As you talk like that, you will see something today!' She tried to go and take it to cut it up into the pot but when she stepped across the threshold of the hut Duiker suddenly dashed out and ran towards the place Ture had pointed out. But he looked there in vain for Ture, he had gone off ahead. Duiker found and kept on following Ture's tracks.

Ture had gone off and met a man hoeing in his cultivation and he said to the man 'Let me hoe your cultivation and you go and pound my termites for me.' Ture hoed that man's cultivation while the man went to pound his termites. He pounded them and filled three pots with the paste and he put them in Ture's bag and took them in it to him in the cultivation, though Ture did not see his bag when the man brought it; so he continued hoeing.

Duiker followed after Ture till he came to the home of the man, where he asked that man 'Where is Ture?' The man said that Ture was hoeing in the cultivation. Duiker asked him again 'Where is Ture's bag?' The man replied 'It is in the cultivation with Ture.' So Duiker came running and went straight into Ture's bag and ate up the termite-paste without Ture's knowing. Ture continued hoeing and then, when he saw his bag, he asked the man 'Have you pounded my termites?' 'Yes' the man replied. Ture asked 'Where is my bag?' 'It is here' replied the man. As Ture looked, there he saw his bag shaking and he said 'What kind of creature is shaking it like that? Whatever creature you may be, if you eat my termite-paste I shall eat you all up with your dung!'

He went again and continued hoeing, and he hoed for a short while and then wanted to go and taste some of the paste. When he came near, Duiker dashed out of the bag with all speed and stood near to Ture and Ture saw him. When Ture looked in the bag he saw something else which Duiker had put in the pots and he thought that his paste was still in its place. But Duiker had put something else[1] into the pots, which filled them, and had spread a layer of paste on top to deceive Ture so that he might think that his paste was still intact. In fact, when Ture saw the thing he thought that his paste was intact; so he said to Duiker 'Look at my termite-paste.' Duiker said to Ture 'Taste some of that paste of yours.' When he scraped out some of the paste he saw something else. He swore 'By the brother of Nangbafudo!'[2] He threatened Duiker and clapped his hands to his head from the shock he received on account of his termites. When Duiker saw that Ture was seriously threatening him he ran away and escaped from him.

31. *How Ture's page got the better of him by trickery* (G.)

TURE and his page were going to the home of his in-laws. On their way they saw firewood and Ture told the boy 'When we reach the homestead I shall send you to come and gather this firewood.' The boy assented. He then let Ture go ahead and he remained behind and broke off the firewood and took it with him in the bag. He followed after Ture and as they continued on their way Ture saw nice leaves and he told the boy 'When we reach the homestead I shall send you to come and pluck these leaves.'[3] The boy assented. He let Ture go ahead and remained behind and plucked the leaves and put them in the bag and then joined Ture again. They continued on their way and Ture saw a very good dry piece of grass and he told the boy 'When we reach the homestead and they give us some ground-nuts I shall send you to collect this dry grass.'[4] The boy assented. When Ture went ahead he collected the dry grass and put it in

---

[1] Another version of this story says that Duiker had excreted into the pots. So when Ture earlier threatens 'I shall eat you all up with your dung' this gives an added touch of humour to the trick played on him. In the Gore Collection, being a missionary school textbook, the word for 'dung' is avoided. The word I have translated 'dung' is a euphemism: *negbo*, waste matter.

[2] See footnote on p. 53.

[3] Either for drying the hands or for placing food on.

[4] For roasting the ground-nuts.

the bag and then went and joined Ture. They continued on their way and came to nice clear water and Ture said to the boy 'When we reach the homestead and are given food I shall send you to draw that nice clear water so that we may wash our hands with it before eating the food they will give us.' As Ture was going ahead the boy drew the water and put it in the elephant-hide bag. In this way the boy gathered all these things that Ture spoke to him about without Ture's knowing he had gathered them. They arrived at the homestead and sat down, and the people of the home gave them food.

When Ture told his page 'Go and draw the water we saw earlier' the boy put his hand into the bag and took out the water and gave it to Ture to wash his hands with it. Ture rejected the food, blaming the boy because he had drawn the water beforehand. The boy ate the food alone. They stayed on and after a while they gave them ground-nuts and Ture told the boy 'Go and collect the dry grass we saw earlier.' When the boy put his hand in the bag and brought out this dry grass Ture rejected the ground-nuts, so the boy ate them alone. In the evening they gave them fire and Ture told the boy 'Go and bring the firewood we saw earlier.' When the boy put his hand into the bag and brought out the firewood for the fire Ture refused to take it, only the boy used it. Ture was trying to send the boy away by trickery to eat up all the food by himself while the boy was absent.

32. *Ture's war with Gburenze and his sister* (R. M.)

THERE was great lack of meat in the country and people's mouths were sour from eating leaves of manioc and of sweet potatoes. So two women went to catch fish so that they might collect at least small fish to bring and broil. One of them was pregnant, and she in particular, saliva was dripping from her mouth.[1] They went along the bank until they found a stretch of water in which fish were feeding.[2] They dammed it and were

---

[1] A person who has not eaten meat for a long time, or a pregnant woman, has a great desire for meat. This expression is then used.

[2] The fish were eating in it and thereby made a noise.

skimming it ardently with a wooden bowl[1] as hunger for meat drove them on. When the water was getting lower they could see the fish turning about in it. While they were intending[2] to jump into it with their fishing-nets to catch the fish, that little bird Bulbul flew and perched in a tree above this water and sang

'Women, as you are just catching fish, war has come,
Pregnant one, you are only fishing, but death has come,
Women, war has come, death has come.'

The pregnant one scraped up some marsh mud and threw it at him. He flew to another tree and continued singing there. The other woman broke off a piece of wood and flung it[3] at the bird. He escaped it, thanks to his ghosts (good luck). He therefore flew off, saying to them 'I was good enough to warn you of the war.'[4]

The women caught so many fish that their containers were all full. They got out of the water on to the bank and were cutting up the fish, laughing and rejoicing. Then they heard away, heard grass shaking and trees breaking and spears clanging against one another. They were unable to move because of the great fear that had seized them.[5] One of them cried that Bulbul might have been speaking the truth: 'O sister, we are dead.' When they tried to run away two men burst in upon them with fire in their eyes. The women prayed them to spare their lives and take them for their wives, but the men had been in war for a long time and had killed many people and did not heed their supplication. People's blood had turned their eyes into those of fierce savages.[6] One of them dashed at the pregnant woman, and when she tried to plunge into the water he cut open her belly at the edge of the water and

---

[1] Women dam a section of a stream. They then skim out the water with wooden bowls and catch the fish in conical fish-traps or nets.

[2] Lit., 'when they were in the sleep of that', i.e. when they were thinking only of that.

[3] *Vugumo* is to throw something longish in shape which then rotates in the air. The verb also implies that the object is thrown with considerable force and usually in anger.

[4] Lit., 'to scratch the news of war to you', i.e. to tell secretly and in advance.

[5] Lit., 'they became rotten from fear', i.e. fear paralysed them.

[6] *Akare* means 'strangers' or 'foreigners', but here it has the sense of wild and brutal people.

only her corpse dropped into the water. The twins who were in her womb spilled out alive into the water. The men had already speared the other woman and they gathered up their fish and went on their way.

These twins remained alive in the water and they ate just sand till they grew up. They were a boy and a girl. When they reached the age when children can be sent to fetch water and fire they came out on to dry land. Their skin was very light as they had grown up in water. The boy was very handsome; and as for his sister, her beauty defied description. Her brother used to collect wild fruits for them to eat. He carved wooden arrows with which he used to shoot birds and rats which they roasted and ate. The children grew up to be adults. This young man became a great hunter, his strength was that of two. They left the river bank and went wandering over the countryside. They went on till they arrived at the homesteads of the people killed during the war and found dilapidated huts and granaries and also hoes and other tools left by the dead. So this youth built a hut for him and his sister to sleep under, and then prepared cultivations and planted in them the seeds they had found in the old dilapidated granaries. Their home was very fine, but nobody would have much to do with them because they did not want to visit the homesteads[1] where people had been killed and their blood[2] had flowed into the streams. Only some men who had gone hunting came and appeared in their home. They were astonished at this splendid homestead. But when the head of the home appeared before them they were struck dumb by his grace and beauty, who had such wonderful soft hair. Whoever saw him was at once made aware of his great strength. When his sister came out to give them water, as they were very thirsty, they could not take their eyes off her. They even forgot about the water. In all their lives they had never seen a woman as beautiful as she. As the young man and his sister resembled each other as two termites, for they were twins, the hunters at once knew they were brother and sister. So

---

[1] *Gbaria* originally meant an area marked out for hunting. It was then applied to settlements in which the Government of the Anglo-Egyptian Sudan compelled the Azande to live. In the sense in which it is used here it is therefore an anachronism.

[2] 'Blood' is understood here.

when they returned to their home they spread the news about Gburenze—as they called him on account of his hair[1]—and his sister. People came from afar[2] to see them.

The renown of Gburenze's sister came to Ture's ears. Ture then bundled his wives, Nanzagbe and Nangbafudo, off to their brothers' homes. Ture then gathered fighting men whom he sent against Gburenze to go and kill him and bring his sister to him. That evening Gburenze's sister went to fetch water and she saw a fish on the surface of the water which said to her 'Men of war will burst upon your brother to kill him on your account.' She returned and told Gburenze. Very early in the morning Gburenze came out and sat on his stool with his curved knife in his hand and looked towards the path. After a short while men rushed at Gburenze. His sister sat on the verandah of their hut singing this war song:

'Gburenze, fight the war brother,
Gburenze, fight the war brother,
Ture has gathered all the people,
To come and kill Gburenze for me ooo,
Gburenze, brother of Nangume,
Gburenze, chop the men to pieces.'

When Gburenze threw his knife at the men they were all killed except a left-handed man who escaped. He fled with all speed to Ture and told him 'Alas, Ture; but oh no! Everybody is dead save me who have run to tell you about it.' Ture was enraged with the left-handed fellow.[3] Ture nearly speared him to death but he escaped because his father's ghost was with him. Desire for Gburenze's sister gripped Ture's heart and he set up and sent another war party against Gburenze, but only what happened before was repeated and the left-handed man escaped. He fled again to Ture. Ture dispatched yet another war party. When this party arrived Gburenze's sister did not sing her song. Gburenze flung his knife to no purpose; the

[1] *Gburenzegburenze* generally has the sense of something which is graceful, especially in motion. The name is descriptive of the boy's grace.

[2] This phrase in Zande suggests a vague sense of direction and distance. The people did not come from any particular place but from every direction and distance.

[3] Lit., 'his heart burnt like the potsherd in which tobacco is dried', i.e. he was in a great rage.

men did not die as before. The men-at-arms surrounded him and speared him. The men rushed to lay their hands on Nangume[1] to carry her off to Ture, but when she sang this song:

> '*Hii*,[2] who told you people to touch
> Gburenze's sister! Your hands will stay
> Now at your breasts!'

the hands of the men became stiff on their breasts. She sang again:

> 'Stand away from Gburenze's sister—
> Your hands will be loose as before.'

When they backed away from her their hands became as supple as before. They said among themselves 'Let us tie up her brother to carry him to Ture. She will follow after us.' They bound the body but when they tried to lift it it was as heavy as a rock. The men strove in vain to lift Gburenze's body, it would not move from the ground. The men were wet with sweat and their barkcloths were torn off their loins, but alas, no! Gburenze lay on the ground like a rock. Then Nangume said 'Gburenze, my brother, let us go please!' When they tried again to raise him he was as light as a dry leaf. Nangume strapped her door and followed them. They arrived at Ture's home with the body, but when they tried to put the body down, oh no! It was a rock! Ture rushed out of his hut where he had been preparing a bed, thinking that Gburenze's sister had arrived. He saw only Gburenze's corpse. When he started to insult his captains they said 'Ture, Gburenze's sister is already approaching the home. A princess does not walk like a slave.' Ture sat down without taking his eyes from the path. The carriers stood waiting with the corpse of Gburenze on their heads. Ture's eyes were fixed on the path, so he did not notice what was happening with the corpse of Gburenze. Suddenly Ture saw Gburenze's sister herself coming like a princess walking on the ground. Ture gazed at her with his mouth hanging open. Her beauty stunned Ture. He could not imagine himself being good enough for her at all. She came and told the men to put down the corpse. They

---

[1] Nangume, 'mother of sand', on account of her having been nurtured on sand.
[2] *Hii* is an exclamation used by women. It has the sense of a negative assertion. It can scarcely be rendered into English.

put it down. She cast her eyes about her and saw Ture looking at her as if she were god.[1] She then sang

'O Ture, Ture has killed Nangume's brother,
O Ture, you stay in your place please!'

When Ture tried to stand he was as if glued[2] to his stool and the stool as if glued to the ground. Whenever Ture looked at her, tears fell from his eyes. People said to him 'Well, Ture, you often claim to be a worker of wonders, is that not a beautiful woman you are facing?' She went and sat very close to Ture. Ture was imploring her to let him loose. She would only answer 'Ture, I shall let you loose. But rest first in that position.'

The men started cutting up Gburenze's body into a pot and they made a fire, and when they tried to lift the pot into which they had put the body for cooking it was too heavy for them. Nangume sang a song and they lifted the pot and put it on the fire. They replenished the fire beneath the pot in vain, Gburenze's body would not cook. His sister sang and the flesh was cooked. She sang a song and they put down the pot from the fire. When they tried to eat Gburenze their mouths seemed to have been tied in place with leather straps. Nangume sang and they ate up Gburenze. She said to them 'O sirs, gather his bones for me when you have eaten all your flesh.' They gathered up the bones for her and she wrapped them up (in leaves), and leaving Ture where he was, she left for her home with her brother's bones. When she was on her way Ture would have speared himself to death if there had been a spear at hand. Terror of her seized those people present and nobody wanted to approach her. After Nangume had gone Ture's wives heard that the woman for whose sake he had chased them away had pinned Ture to the ground beneath his granary and that all had deserted him and he was almost starved to death. So they returned to their husband and fed him in that place of his.

Nangume went home with the bones of her brother and covered them with a small pot and sat beside them, singing. She did not eat that day. At night she slept near the pot. When

---

[1] So Mr. Richard Mambia translates it, giving the word *toro* an appropriate modern sense. In old Zande the word *atoro* means 'ghosts of the dead', with no singular form, *toro*, which missionaries have given to refer to 'spirit'.

[2] The Zande word is *rungo*, 'sew', but 'glued' would be a suitable idiomatic word in translation.

she turned it over the following morning she saw a lizard under the pot. She put the pot back and sat singing more songs without eating. The following morning she opened it and saw a rat, and she covered it again. The third day she found a baby under it. She covered this baby under a large pot. The fourth day she found a young boy under it. She took him and put him on a bed, closed the door, and sat outside the door weeping. When she entered the hut the following day she saw a handsome young man inside. They thus lived in their home as husband and wife.

When they had become husband and wife they spent two days, at the end of which she said 'My husband, come let me show you today the man who sent a force against me because he wanted to marry me.' She concealed from him that he had come out of her brother's bones. Until their death he never knew this fact. He had found a beautiful woman and did not want to ask her questions lest she reject him. He believed that that was how people were born and that was how they found their wives. It was only when people resettled that district that their children found husbands and wives for themselves. As soon as they reached Ture's home Nangume said 'Ture, get up to salute my husband please.' Ture then sprang from that spot to which she had bound him. Fear of her seized Ture, for he was afraid she might do what she had done to him before. He therefore fled and hid himself in the bush until Nangume had left with her husband. When he came out of the bush his wives jeered at him on account of this woman he had wanted to marry.

33. *Ture and Nzuangba* (R. M.)

TURE started to walk and went on till he found a man called Nzuangba, who said to Ture 'Friend, I have a hunting area to be fired,[1] it will be fired tomorrow.' Ture replied 'That's fine my friend, I shall await the firing to spear animals in it.'

Early next morning Nzuangba took his wives and children and also Ture and they went to build a hut right in the centre of this dry grass. Then Nzuangba told the people to set the

[1] See pp. 8–9.

bush on fire all around. The bush burnt with roaring fire. All
sorts of animals began to flee to the middle of the bush because
it was burning on all sides. The animals were rushing on
Nzuangba in the middle of the bush and he was spearing them.
He killed many animals: elephants, buffaloes, and waterbuck.
Meanwhile the fire was approaching Nzuangba's hut and Ture
began to be terrified until the seams of his barkcloth were
shaking. He said 'My friend, as we are surrounded by fire, by
which way shall we escape?' Nzuangba said 'Ture, we shall be
saved.' The fire came fiercely and with great violence towards
Ture and Nzuangba. Wherever Ture looked there was nothing but fire. Meanwhile Nzuangba's wives and children were
preparing (skinning and cutting up) the animals. When Ture
was about to start wailing Nzuangba took sesame oil and
smeared it on the heads of his children and wives and of Ture
also. Nzuangba then started to dance, singing

'Nzuangba o Nzuangba sesame oil,
Nzuangba o Nzuangba sesame oil,
I put my head into sesame oil,
And the fire goes out completely.'

The fire, which was very near, was extinguished. This affair
pleased Ture. Ture said 'My friend, please give me a little of
that oil.' Nzuangba took some of the oil and gave it to Ture. So
Ture dashed off to his wives and ordered them 'Burn all the
ground-nuts and sesame, from now on we shall be eating only
meat.' Ture's wives burnt their sesame and ground-nuts, except
for his wife Nangbafudo, who showed temper about her sesame
and ground-nuts. Ture marked out a large area of dry bush
with plenty of animals in it, and went and built a hut in the
middle of it and went there with his wives and children. He
then went to invite his friend Nzuangba to come to spear
animals. Two days before the bush was to be burnt Ture brought
out the oil which Nzuangba had given him and tasted it at the
tip of his finger. It tasted delicious to Ture, so he ate all the
sesame oil and went and prepared ground-nut paste and
poured it into the place of the other.

The time for burning (the bush) came. Ture went to the
centre (of the bush) with his wives and his children and
Nzuangba also. The bush was set fire to all around them. The

fire drove the animals towards Ture in the middle of the bush and Ture and Nzuangba speared animals without ceasing. The fire began to get close and Ture's children began to wail, and Ture shouted 'Hey you, shut up and come here.' Ture took ground-nut paste and wiped it on their heads and those of his wives. Afterwards he started to dance, chanting

'Ture, Ture sesame oil,
Ture, Ture sesame oil,
I put my head into sesame oil,
And the fire goes out completely.'

But oh no! The fire was coming nearer Ture and was not put out. Ture began yelling out this song. Alas, no! Ture's children were all crying. As the fire was on top of Ture he thrust his hand into the ground-nut paste and began to sprinkle the grasses with it. Alas, no! The fire was getting nearer all the time. So Ture wailed and cried out to Nzuangba to help him. Nzuangba then smeared Ture's children with his sesame oil and sang his song, and the fire was extinguished. Nzuangba then mocked Ture, saying 'Who told you to eat up the oil I gave you?'

34. *Ture and Man-killer again* (R. M.)

THERE was a man called Man-killer. He hated people very much, and did not want anybody to go to his home. Whenever a person went to his home he killed him. He carved a very big gong inside which he used to kill people. When a man visited him he would ask him to sleep inside this big wooden gong, which was like a hut. When he got the man to sleep he would come and stab him to death.

Now Ture heard of this man and got up and went to his home. Ture sat for some time and then he said 'My friend, show me a hut so that I can enter to sleep now by day because I don't go inside to sleep at night.' He showed Ture his big wooden gong, which was like a hut, because he intended to kill Ture as he had been in the habit of killing other people. Ture entered it knowing that Man-killer used to kill people inside it. Now Ture entered and just sat inside it. This man said to Ture

'People don't sit inside it, they lie down.' Ture replied 'I don't feel sleepy, I entered just to sit down.' He said to Ture 'No, you had better lie down.' Ture lay down but put out one leg through the slit of the gong. Man-killer cried 'Ture, people don't lie in it like that!' Ture asked him 'How then am I to lie?' Ture then lay down again in the gong but put out his hand. Man-killer said 'That is not the way to lie in it.' This man was insisting how Ture should lie in order to kill him. Ture knew it and was just fooling about. Again Ture lay inside but put his head outside. He said to Ture 'People don't lie in it like that.' Ture did all sorts of things, lying with his ears out or putting out one eye, putting out his nose, and putting out his buttock. Ture asked him 'Eh, how then do people sleep in this gong of yours? You show me how to lie in it.'

So this man entered the gong to show Ture how to lie in it. He lay down and gathered himself inside it properly. So Ture took the big plank with which the mouth of the gong used to be closed and then closed the gong after Man-killer. Ture then carried this big gong with the man inside it and wandered with it all over the countryside and to the homes of all sorts of people. Ture would arrive at some place and declare 'Here is the man who used to kill your relatives.' Each person would take his spear and spear him with it. So all kinds of people speared this man over the countryside. They were very happy as they were avenging their kinsmen. They said 'Had it not been for Ture, who would have caught him for us? What a clever man is Ture!'

35. *Ture, Frog, and the river Baku* (G.)

THERE was a man who begot a very beautiful daughter. He said that the person who might marry his daughter was the one who would go and draw water from the river Baku and bring it to him. The same would marry his daughter. Ture said 'I am going to draw water from the river Baku and come and marry her.' He went and fetched only dirty water on the way and brought it. They refused him the hand of the girl.

Frog said he was coming to marry the girl, and they said to him 'Go and draw water from the river Baku and first bring it and then you can marry the girl.' Frog got a bottle-gourd and went on his way. He went on until it became dark on the way, and he made a mud shelter as his hut and spent the night in it. Next morning he started off again, walking on and on until it became dark again, and he made another mud shelter to spend the night in it. Next morning he started off again, and as he walked on and on he sang thus:

'*Kpafu*,[1] *kpafu* Frog, brother Frog is going,
Frog sees that stretch of country and overcomes it before he goes to spend the night.'

Frog went on until he was getting a bit nearer to the river, which was as far as from here to the stream Ndingbo.[2] He could hear the sound of the river saying

'*Nzenge nzenge* river Baku I have a good cause as the Aabini people,
Nzenge nzenge river Baku, as the Abandia people and the Aabini.'[3]

When Frog heard this he sang his own song, saying

'*Kpafu, kpafu* Frog, brother Frog is going,
Frog sees that stretch of country and overcomes it before he goes to spend the night.'

Frog set off from there and walked till he reached the river. Frog first leaped up so as to see the water of the river. He saw the very wide river, extending as from here to the river Mari.[4] Frog got the big bottle-gourd and drew the water with it until it filled that big bottle-gourd. Then he began to return home with this water. He walked on and on. On the seventh day he reached home. The father of the girl said 'Splendid!' They poured out the water, and they gave the girl for wife to Frog.

[1] The sound *kpafu* represents a frog's jumping movements.
[2] I cannot identify this stream or the river Baku.
[3] The sense is not clear.
[4] 'Here' is probably the Government Post of Yambio. The stream Mari is said to be about five miles from Yambio.

36. *Ture and a man's fish* (G.)

TURE went to the home of a certain man who used to find his fish for his meals right in his home. He had hollowed out a very big tree and inside it he put fish and bred them to eat. Ture came and sat down, and the man told his wife to cook for him. Ture said to himself that right now he was going to find out the place where the fish were. The wife went behind the hut and no sooner had she gone than she was back with fish, and she cooked them as a flavouring for the porridge, and she gave the meal to Ture.

Ture ate the food, and when it was finished he vanished and went behind the hut where he saw the fish in the hollowed-out tree. He carried it on his head and went home with the fish. He went on and on and on, and when he arrived home he told his wives to come and help him get the load down. They tried to get it down in vain, it stuck very firmly to Ture's head. Ture told them to collect sticks and stones to break it with them on his head. The women collected all these things and beat the wood, but they did not succeed in breaking it. It stuck to Ture's head so firmly that when they beat it it seemed as though they were striking Ture's head itself. He died from it, and they sent a message to the man whose fish Ture had stolen. When he came they related the whole story to him. He just took out his (magic) ash and rubbed some of it on Ture's head, and Ture recovered from death.

'I was just having a walk when I met a man beating his wife. When I tried to calm him he hit me hard, and when I cried out he took the thigh of a chicken and gave it to me. I put it over there. Boy, go and fetch it.'

37. *How Ture brought out his intestines* (R. M.)

THERE was once a man called Bakusireru.[1] This man used to eat like other people, but every now and again he would go to

---

[1] The name means 'one who brings out his intestines'. It is of interest to note that the text sometimes has *bakusireko*, the personal pronominal suffix *ko* instead of the animal one *ru*. See p. 26.

a pool and smear his belly with his (magic) oil extracted from
bulbs which was always with him. The belly would then open
easily.[1] He would then take out all his intestines and wash them
thoroughly and then put them back, and when he smeared his
oil again on his belly it closed up as it was before. In the course
of Ture's wanderings he came across this man washing his
intestines. Ture went close to him and said 'My friend, what a
wonderful thing you are doing. So while my intestines become
black in my body, you clean yours often. O friend, can't you
reveal this cunning to me? I shall bring you a woman, man!'
Bakusireru agreed to show Ture the secret for nothing. He
rubbed his oil on Ture's belly and it opened up. Ture took out
his intestines and began to wash them, rejoicing meanwhile:
'Ha! those ugly women at home with their dirty intestines. I
shall really jeer at them today.' Ture brought out his intestines
and washed them twice and twice smeared his belly with the
oil and twice it closed. When he begged Bakusireru for some of
the oil he gave it to him in a small horn. Ture would travel a
short distance and then sit down and rub the oil on his belly,
and when his intestines came out he would examine them and
then put them back again and continue on his way.

He once more brought out his intestines under a big tree.
While he was examining them, turning them in his hand, a
(strong) wind came and blew down the horn, and all the (magic)
oil that was in it was spilt on the ground. Ture's intestines
remained outside. Ture put them back into his stomach and he
smeared his belly with ash from any tree,[2] but it would not close.
He rubbed it with this-and-that leaf, in vain, and he rubbed it
with this-and-that bark, in vain. Ture tried every kind of
little thing: dung of birds, blood of toads, everything he could
lay his hands on. Meanwhile Ture's intestines were drying up
and beginning to pain him. Soon after, Ture burst out wailing
and his cries could be heard far off:[3]

> 'Ture, my intestines have remained outside ooo,
> My friend run to me with the oil ooo,
> O Ture, you have been suffering many things ooo.'

[1] *Teee* indicates the ease and grace with which his belly would open and close.
[2] This means magic paste made by mixing the ash of burnt woods (medicines)
with oil. Ture did not know the right wood (medicine) to use.
[3] Lit., 'Ture's screams were coming from the sky'. They hit the sky and rever-
berated.

When his friend Bakusireru heard this cry he said 'Oh, I thought so, I knew Ture would get into trouble today.[1] Was he told I wash my intestines as often as he tries to do?' Bakusireru rushed to his aid with the oil and some water in a gourd with which he wetted Ture's intestines, and when he rubbed the oil on Ture's belly his belly closed up after his intestines. Ture then went straight home without thinking of washing his intestines again.

38. *Ture's sons and the* kpengbere *elephant* (R. M.)

AMONG the children of Ture there was one whose mother had died and he used to be called Orphan. He was very thin and the others used to beat him. Ture said to his children 'That animal called *kandu* (rat),[2] no child is ever to eat it, it is my meat. If you eat rats you will then have to go and kill that animal which has much fat, the *mbara kpengbere*.'[3] Thus Ture used to go and dig up his rats, and his wives cooked them wrapped in leaves for him, (thick) like thighs, and they took up most of the fire. When Ture ate them his children ate other things.

One day when all the people had dispersed to the cultivations Ture's sons went and dug up rats in large numbers and came and cooked them in leaves, and they took up most of the fire. After that they ate up these rats and crumpled up their leaves and threw them into the bush. They (the leaves) appeared and lay right in the courtyard, and they shone with oil. They trod them into the rubbish heap, and they appeared and lay in the courtyard, shining with oil. They threw them into a stream,

---

[1] Lit., 'I already said something will see Ture right today'.

[2] The *kandu* is a rat noted for its fat (or oil) and is a great delicacy. The point of the story is to some extent dependent on this fact.

[3] *Mbara kpengbere* would appear to be an imaginary animal, but in the story it is some kind of elephant (*mbara*). I cannot attach any meaning to *kpengbere*. Lagae and Vanden Plas (*Dictionnaire Zande–Français* (1925), p. 86) give the word in their form of Zande spelling, *kpwengbele*, as meaning a plain with many stone-flats (Bandiya dialect) and as an adjective, 'ouvert', 'dénudé', but as this makes doubtful sense in the context I leave the name of the beast in Zande. That it conveyed no precise meaning to the writer of the text is suggested by his sometimes writing (which I have corrected) *kpekpere* instead of *kpengbere*.

they appeared and lay in the courtyard, shining with oil. They were still doing this when Ture appeared and saw these leaves of the rats. He said to them (the children) 'Oh, have you eaten the rats which I said should not be tasted by any of you? Go at once and kill only the animal which is so oily, the *mbara kpeng-bere*.' Ture's sons collected their spears and went into the bush. They would kill an animal, open its belly, and search there in vain, and then another animal, open its belly, and search there in vain.[1] When they were going into the bush Orphan wanted to follow them but they beat him and threw him into the bush, saying 'You useless thing, stop following us.'

They walked on and on till they found *mbara kpengbere* where it had made a (hollowed out) place for itself and lay in it. The eldest of the brothers speared it and it rushed out and cut him in two with its tusks. The second-born of the brothers speared it and it rushed out and cut him in two with its tusks. It did the same with Ture's sons till they were finished, except for Orphan. When Orphan saw this he was puzzled to remain alone in the wilderness amid the corpses of his elder brothers. Orphan dug a pit until it was large enough for him to fit into it. After that he looked for a rock and tried it on the mouth of the pit and it fitted it. He then gathered his elder brothers' spears and went after that animal. He speared it, and when it rushed out to cut him in two he ran and fell into his pit and closed the entrance after him with the rock. That animal ran towards him and hit its tusks on the rock and broke one of them. It went back to its place. Orphan went again and speared it and ran to his pit and closed it with the rock. This animal came and hit its remaining tusk on the rock and it broke. It returned to its place. Orphan then came out from his pit and went and speared that animal until it died. He gathered its tusks and flew until he hung them up very high and took a small drum and put it beneath them. After that he descended.

But he did not know what he should do about his elder brothers. So he arose and wandered all over the place until he met an old woman who had swellings on her body. He said to her 'O grandmother, I came with my elder brothers but an animal has killed them all, leaving me only by myself. I do not know what I can do to save them.' She said to him 'Only a

[1] For the fat (or oil).

person who can draw water and put it on the fire and then, when it is hot, pierce all these swellings on me, to him I would reveal my medicine for reviving people.' Orphan went and drew water and put it on the fire, and swept all her place and he gathered firewood for her. Then he pierced all her swellings with his teeth, washed her, and anointed her with her oil. So she went and gave him a drip,[1] telling him to go and drip it on his brothers.

Orphan came and dripped it on to his brothers and they all stood up in a line and started to argue among themselves, each saying that it was he who slew that *mbara kpengbere*. Orphan turned away and sat by himself afar off. Then they said 'What shall we do that our father may hear that we have killed *mbara kpengbere*?' They called all the birds by their species. They said to guinea-fowl 'Since you are speckled, you will arrive and say what?' It said 'I will arrive and say *ke ke keere*.'[2] They said 'You go away.' They said 'Cuckoo, you will arrive and say what?' It said 'I will arrive and say *tuutututu*.' They chased it away. They said 'Dove, you will arrive and say what?' It said 'I will arrive and say thus:

"Will this willowy tree break today?
Will this willowy tree break today?"'[3]

They chased it away. They tried all the birds and when they came to the hammerhead stork it said 'I will arrive and say thus:

"*Zaa zakiringi*, your sons have killed a big beast,
Zaa zakiringi, take big pots,
Zaa zakiringi, gather big baskets,
Zaa zakiringi, your sons have killed *mbara kpengbere*,
Zaa zakiringi."'[4]

They said 'Fine! Stork, you go.' The stork flew on its way and wherever it rested it sang its song. While it was still far off, Ture's

---

[1] *Togo* is a common type of Zande magic. An infusion from vegetable matter is dripped on whatever the rite concerns.

[2] The reply of the birds is how their cries sound to Azande in Zande sounds. I have discussed this elsewhere (*Man* (1961), no. 7).

[3] I do not mean 'a willow', but a thin tree which easily bends to wind or pressure.

[4] *Zaa zakiringi* has, I believe, no meaning other than the cry of the hammerhead stork.

little daughter heard its song and cried out 'Mother, birds are saying

"*Zaa zakiringi*, yours sons have killed a big beast,
Zaa zakiringi, take big pots,
Zaa zakiringi, gather big baskets,
Zaa zakiringi, your sons have killed *mbara kpengbere*,
Zaa zakiringi."'

Her mother dashed out of a hut and seized her and beat her and rubbed her with chickens' dung and cast her out (of the courtyard), saying 'Child, why do you joke about my children who long ago died in the wilderness?' A little while later the same girl heard the song of the stork and told her mother, and her mother beat her again and took her and threw her out (of the courtyard). The stork came right ahead and perched on the stick with which the mother of the girl was stirring porridge in a hut. It said

'*Zaa zakiringi*, your sons have killed a big beast,
Zaa zakiringi, take big pots,
Zaa zakiringi, gather big baskets,
Zaa zakiringi, your sons have killed *mbara kpengbere*,
Zaa zakiringi.'

Ture's wife cried out, saying 'O my daughter, what you said was indeed true.' She washed the chickens' dung off her and anointed her with oil.

Ture and his wives and many people carried baskets and pots and axes and big knives and went for the *mbara kpengbere*. While they went on foot the stork flew above and showed them the way. They went and arrived at the *mbara kpengbere* and there saw Ture's sons sharpening their spears. The people asked them who had killed it. One said 'It was I who killed it.' The others all spoke likewise. Orphan for his part sat afar off in his little ragged barkcloth and said nothing. Ture then asked where were the tusks of this animal, the person who hid its tusks was the one who killed it. They told the eldest to go and fetch its tusks. The eldest balanced himself and jumped so high that his tracks were lost sight of. The people therefore said that it was he who killed it. Afterwards he came down with nothing in his hands. The next son jumped yet higher than the first, he went on and

on and disappeared. The people said '*Ee*, he will really return
with the tusks of this animal.' But he came down with nothing
in his hands. The same thing happened to all Ture's sons. The
people said 'Who then killed this beast? Eh, you, Orphan,
come here, since you have been sitting all the time today.'
Orphan said 'Sir, could a person like me do anything?' He
then removed himself from his place, thin and with his little
piece of tattered barkcloth, and he came and jumped so low
that he scarcely left the earth and fell down again. He then
began again to jump and he jumped so high that he disappeared
from sight. When they heard the sound of a drum above they
said 'Bravo, it was surely Orphan who killed this beast.' After a
little while Orphan alighted with the tusks of *mbara kpengbere*.
Everyone was speechless. They washed Orphan and anointed
him with oil and gave him (new) barkcloth. The people
prepared (cut up) this animal and carried the meat and fat of
it and returned home.

That is why people say 'Who does big things is not himself
big (in body).'[1]

39. *How Ture used his eye as fish bait* (R. M.)

THERE was once a man who used to fish with his eye as bait on
the hook. He had his (magic) ash left to him by his father when
he was dying lest his son might suffer from lack of meat after his
death. When he went fishing he would rub this ash on his eye
and it would come out of its socket, and he would then fix it on
his hook and as soon as he dropped the hook into water a fish
would hurry and swallow the hook and he would then pull it
out. No fish could escape with his eye because of the power of
his medicine. When he had caught enough fish he would rub
his ash on to his eye again and it would return to its socket.

One day Ture too went fishing. Whenever he dropped his
hook into a stream, using worms as bait, he caught only worth-
less fish which he threw back. Ture persisted, but to no purpose;
and when he was annoyed he threw the worms into the water
and was about to return home when he met this man on the

---

[1] A well-known Zande proverb: one must not judge a man's capacity by his
size.

bank, catching very big fish. Ture went up to him and said 'My friend, what do you do to catch these big fish? I have been catching only little fish myself.' The man answered 'I don't use worms as bait, my eye is my bait.' Ture then went closer to him to inquire about this skill. He disclosed it to Ture and Ture cried out that he should give him a little of the ash also. It made Ture almost mad. He went along the river and began to catch fish as though his head was on fire. He would put his eye back and decide to go, but as soon as a fish struck the water with its tail Ture would rub the ash again on his eye, bring it out, and catch fish on that spot also. When Ture's bag was full he was throwing some away and catching others in their place. Meanwhile his ash was diminishing fast. When he had finally decided to return home a very big fish opened its mouth wide on the surface of the water at that moment and Ture could not resist the desire to catch it. In great haste he rubbed all the remainder of the ashes on his eye, brought it out, and threw it into the stream on the hook. This fish came and swallowed only Ture's eye on the hook and went off with it, because there was no longer any ash to keep his eye on the hook. When Ture brought the hook out of the water he looked in vain for his eye. Ture fluttered round and round on the bank.[1] Leaving the fish and the bag, he ran, wailing, with all speed to his friend. He burst in upon this man in his home and fell to the ground weeping with tears for his eye. When this man asked him, he said 'A big fish pulled me into the water, that is why my ash was spoilt in the water.' This man accompanied Ture to where the fish had escaped with his eye. He rubbed his ash on his eye and when he dropped it into the water on a hook this fish came and swallowed it, and he pulled it out and cut it open and brought out Ture's eye from its belly and put it back in its socket. Ture then asked him to give him some more ash, but the man refused. So Ture abused him and went home with his fish.

That is why people say, if somebody shows some new skill or device, do not use it too much.[2] Use it as you have been taught to do. If Ture had been more economical with his ash he would have continued eating fish for a long time, just like that man.

---

[1] The shock of losing his eye made him run here and there in great agitation.
[2] *Nguru* here has the sense of excess of enthusiasm.

40. *Ture and how it began with an egg* (R. M.)

One day Ture went to riverside forest to cut his grass (for weaving) and he brought it home and put it down under Nanzagbe's verandah. A cockerel went and laid its very small egg[1] in the grass. Ture's children went hunting lizards, poking them out (of their hiding-places), and when they looked they saw this cockerel's egg. They ran and told their father about it, saying 'Father, ah, a chicken has laid an egg in your grass!' Ture went and took up this egg and turned it in his hand, admiring it and wondering what sort of egg it was that was so small. He then knew at once that it was a cock's egg because hens' eggs are not so small. Ture dropped it into his bag and forgot about it.

One morning Ture slung his bag over his shoulder and went roaming over burnt country[2] as was his habit. He went on and on and met some buffaloes playing their game with a fruit of the *dama* tree.[3] When Ture saw it he was greatly amazed. So he said 'My friends, I have here a very good thing, much better for your wonderful game than that just ordinary rough *dama* fruit you are playing with. Look at it!' Ture then brought out the egg and showed it to the buffaloes. They begged him for it and he gave it to them. The buffaloes started to play their game with it and it was a fine sight to watch. Ture put down his bag and sat down to watch this wonderful thing. One buffalo would throw it and another would catch it and throw it back to the other. In this way they played without dropping the egg. The game went on until one buffalo who was left-handed tried to catch it and it fell and broke. So Ture began to sing a song, saying

'I went and cut grass, cut grass,
Cock scattered it and laid its egg in it,
Cock took its egg oo,
Cock gave it to me ooo,

[1] That is to say what we would regard as an egg laid by a hen with secondary sexual characteristics of a cock.
[2] *Ngaragba*: an area in which the grasses have been fired and new grass has begun to sprout among the scorched trees and undergrowth. People wander in it in search of honey and reptiles and small animals.
[3] *Sarcocephalus esculentus*.

Buffaloes have taken it from me, buffaloes have broken it e,
Hi where will you turn Ture?
Hi where will you turn Ture?'

The buffaloes consulted among themselves and cut off the tail of the left-handed one and gave it to Ture in the place of his egg. Ture threw it into his bag and went ahead. Ture went on and on until he met a big *tutue*[1] fanning its bellows with its bottom.[2] Ture said to it 'Friend, if your buttocks scorch, what will you say? Take this fine animal's tail and fan your bellows with it.' The *tutue* took the tail eagerly and began to fan its bellows with it and started to beat out many iron instruments. When it wanted to fan the fire again with it, it slipped from its hand and fell into the fire and was burnt, leaving only the bony part. Ture sang

'I went and cut grass, cut grass,
Cock scattered it and laid its egg in it,
Cock took its egg,
Cock gave it to me oo,
Buffaloes took it from me, buffaloes broke it e,
Buffaloes took their tail o,
Buffaloes gave it to me oo,
Tutue took it from me, *tutue* has burnt it,
Hi where will you turn Ture?
Hi where will you turn Ture?'

Tutue looked about and picked up an axe and gave it to Ture. Ture put it in his bag and went on his way. Ture went straight ahead till he met a woodpecker pecking[3] wood with its beak in search of honey. Ture said 'O my friend woodpecker, if your beak splits open on the tree what will you say? Take this axe there to split the wood with it to get at the honey.' The woodpecker cried 'That's a good idea Ture! O friend! I am quite

---

[1] *Tutue*: this is said to be a black insect which stings people. It lives in homesteads, where it steals seeds of grain, sesame, and dried termites. The Lagae and Vanden Plas dictionary gives 'variété de termites'. In another version taken down by myself the insect is *tuse*, a small black ant, as well as *tutue*. I do not know whether this was a mistake on the part of the narrator or of myself, or whether, possibly, they are the same insect.

[2] Blowing or fanning the bellows should probably be taken to mean that it was fanning the fire with its bottom instead of with bellows. The version referred to in the footnote above seems to make this clear.

[3] *Se anyege*: cutting into a hollow tree to expose the honey.

exhausted with pecking for honey with my beak. Oh you are so kind!' The woodpecker took Ture's axe and began to cut into the wood for honey. The man (the woodpecker) took out honey and it filled containers as if it had no owner. When the wood-pecker tried to cut the wood again Ture's axe slipped from its hand and fell into the hollow of the tree. Ture said

> 'I went and cut grass, cut grass,
> Cock scattered it and laid its egg in it,
> Cock gave it to me e ooo,
> Buffaloes took it from me, buffaloes broke it,
> Buffaloes took their tail oo,
> Buffaloes gave it to me e oo,
> *Tutue* took it from me, *tutue* has burnt it,
> *Tutue* took this axe, *tutue* gave it to me oo,
> Woodpecker took it from me, woodpecker lost it ooo,
> Hi where will you turn Ture?
> Hi where will you turn Ture?'

The woodpecker went and gave Ture a heap of honeycomb. Ture wrapped it in big leaves and dropped it into his bag and went ahead.

Ture travelled till he found himself on a river bank. He heard women ladling out water (in fishing) *vuuvuuvuu*.[1] Ture went up to them and met their children all crying their heads off. They begged Ture to calm the children for them so that they might go on ladling out the water. Ture collected these children and took them a little way downstream. He said to their mothers 'I am going to feed your children with honey. You won't hear the cry of a child again.' Ture ate his honey and then put just the comb (without honey) into the children's mouths. They were so full of honeycomb that their bellies were bloated. In the evening when Ture knew that the women had come out of the stream and were cutting up the fish he took the remaining honey and smeared the children's mouths with it, and their breasts, and they were in a mess all over. He then took them to their mothers. This affair delighted the women. They said to one another 'Had it not been for Ture today how would we have caught our fish with these children's beastly whining?'

---

[1] *Vuuvuuvuu*: the sound of water being ladled out in wooden bowls to get at the fish when most of the water is emptied out.

They cut up all their fish. One would offer fish to Ture for him to take home and Ture would just look up at the sky. A woman would bring good fish to Ture and Ture would just look up at the sky. They asked Ture, saying 'What do you want then Ture?' Ture would just look up at the sky. They therefore got up and took their children and told Ture that they were going, since he refused to accept fish from them. They were ahead and Ture behind them. They asked Ture where he was going to. Ture heard it as though he had no ears. They said among themselves 'We will see this day where Ture is going to.'

When they reached their homestead they separated, each going to her own hut. They were, however, living in one big homestead while their husbands were out fighting. Ture carefully noted the one who appeared to him to be a widow and followed her. Ture went and sat at the edge of the courtyard. She made a fire in the courtyard and invited Ture to come and sit by it. Ture said 'In my home, when Nanzagbe makes a fire she carries me to sit by it.' She shouted to her friends, saying 'Girls oo, just listen to this! He says that in his home they always carry him to the fireplace!' They replied 'You brought Ture from his place, so you carry him to the fireplace!' She lifted Ture and put him down at the side of the fire. She cooked fish and porridge and gave them to Ture. He said that in his home they put food into his mouth. She shouted again to her friends, saying 'Girls oo, Ture says that in his home food is put into his mouth!' They replied 'Well, you brought Ture from his place, so you can put food into his mouth!' She made a bed for Ture in her hut but Ture said that in his home he was carried to bed. When she told her friends, they said to her 'You dragged Ture from his place, so you can carry him to bed!' When they got to the bed Ture said that in his home his wife undressed him before he lay down to sleep. When she told this to her friends, they said 'You carried Ture from his place, so you can undress him!' Ture told her that in his home Nanzagbe lifted him to her breast. She screamed, but when she told it to the others they told her to lift Ture to her breast, since she had dragged him from his place! After a short time she called all her friends to come and see what sort of a man Ture was.

So Ture lived with these women as their husband. The women washed and dressed Ture and brushed his feet with maize cobs and trimmed his toe- and finger-nails and fed him like a baby and carried him to bed. One evening as Ture lay across the women's thighs they were cracking their finger-nails on his head and his eyes were closed.[1] A small boy asked his mother to inquire of Ture about their empty honeycomb: 'Hasn't he collected some more?' His mother questioned him closely in the kitchen about the honey which Ture said he had fed them with. The child said 'You see, when Ture ate his honey he gave us only the honeycomb (he spat from his mouth)! After that he smeared our mouths with honey.' She hurried to the fireside and broke the news to her friends. The women rushed against Ture with their mortar pestles. He fled with all speed from them at night.

After a long time Ture sought some cunning whereby he might go again to visit those women. So he went and dressed leaves over his barkcloth and looked like a woman. He gathered flowers of spear-grass and rubbed them into his hair and his hair was very white with them like that of an old woman. Ture rubbed ashes on his face so that it was just like that of an old woman. When he took a staff in his hand to lean on it (stooping) nobody could believe it was Ture. In the evening Ture hobbled into the women's courtyard supported by his staff. The children ran to welcome him, rejoicing, saying 'Here comes grandma, here comes grandma, there is granny, there is granny!' Ture came and collapsed by the fireplace, and the women surrounded him, making a lot of fuss over him, thinking that he was their old mother who had come. They gave food to Ture. He ate it and then went in and lay down to sleep. The children lay beside Ture cheek-by-jowl, believing that it was their grandmother. Early in the morning Ture came out and sat under the granary, as is the way with old people. The women dispersed to prepare food and only the children gathered round Ture while he told them stories of the old days. Ture sat carelessly (his private parts were visible). One of the children saw his parts at the corner of his barkcloth and went to her mother, singing thus:

---

[1] Women crack their finger-nails—not their fingers, that is something different —on the heads of children. This soothes a child and sends it to sleep. It is an endearment. A woman may do the same with her lover. It is called *fo ba kpe* from the sound made.

'I have seen Ture's testicles in the corner of my eye,
I have seen Ture's fat (testicles) in the corner of my eye,
I have seen Ture's testicles in the corner of my eye,
I have seen Ture's fat (testicles) in the corner of my eye.'[1]

Her mother seized and beat her and rubbed her in chickens' dung and chased her away, asking why she was speaking ill of her grandmother! The child returned and sat down and sang the same song. She was beaten in vain, the child persisted in saying the same thing. The women came together and decided to go and investigate this matter. However, Ture had already heard the child's song. When the women were near, Ture sprang up and landed far off, saying 'It is I, I am the son of Ture's father! I have been fooling people all my life. I have got the better of you. I have eaten up all your food. What will you do to me now?' When they made for him with their mortar pestles Ture fled with all speed.

So when somebody does something very naughty like deceiving people we say 'Even Ture who did many things, did he ever do that?'

41. *Ture's fight with a man and his sister* (G.)

THERE was a man with his sister. They went and found their cave which they cleaned for sleeping in as their hut. It was not their custom to eat. They had a certain way of dancing which they danced and which saved them from hunger, for they were satiated. They became fat from this dance as though it were their food. He had inherited a shield and his sister's heirloom was a buffalo tail. These things belonged to their grandparents, which, when their parents died passed to them. He inherited his father's shield and she inherited her mother's buffalo tail. Each of them would take these things and dance waving them. The shield sounded like a bell, and when the man danced and waved it, it sang, saying

'*Bangbaguma paranga nzanga bangbaguma kinzikinzi.*'

---

[1] Mr. Mambia here comments that a child would call them by some term according to the manner they were peeping out at her. They seemed to be 'smiling' at her.

His sister danced with the buffalo tail in her hand. It sounded as they danced. So they acted, because if they left off dancing they would become thin from hunger and die from hunger.

Then Ture went and met this man and his sister. He hid himself to watch them dancing. While they were dancing Ture rushed to them to take away from them the shield with its fine sound which was like a bell. He chased them and they fled into their cave and remained there. When Ture went home they came out again. Ture went to the *Atari* oracle to consult it. He said to the oracle 'What can I do to take away the fine shield from those people?' The oracle told him 'Go and collect the sap of a creeper and make the entrance to the cave very slippery with it. Then go and chase them so that when they try to run inside they will fall to the ground and you will take those things from them.' Ture went and did what he was told to do. He went aside and wanted to test the trap. He ran inside and fell. He then went to them and began to chase them. When they tried to run inside they fell at the entrance. He came and took the shield and the buffalo tail. He ran home with these things, and he possessed the shield. He made a very big feast for the shield. Ture made a big feast and many people came to the feast. Ture thought the shield would make the sound it made when it was with its owner. He took the shield and waved it, but it made no sound at all. Whoever took it, it made no sound.

The owner and his sister came to attend this feast of Ture's. They came and stayed nearby in the cultivations. They were very thin, only their bones remained, without flesh on them. They were thin because Ture had taken away their shield, which was their food and with which they danced and became fat. Since Ture took away this their shield—but oh no! All the many people who attended the dance tried it and it would not sound. They saw the man with his sister and did not know that they were the owners. The people said 'Call that thin man over there with his wife and let them try it.' When the man and his sister heard this they were very glad. Ture said 'You ugly thin man, do not touch my shield.' The people said to Ture 'Let him try it', but Ture said 'What does that thin man know? Do not give my shield to him or he will touch it with his dirt.' People begged Ture, saying 'All the people have touched it except this man. Why don't you want him to touch it?' Then they allowed him to take it. When they were coming towards it, he and his sister, they became very happy. When they got nearer to the shield they became fat. Their flesh was restored, because when they had the shield they used to dance with it and become fat. Ture did not know that they were those from whom he had taken the shield. The man got the shield and his sister got the buffalo tail. When the man touched the shield it began to sound, saying

'*Kinzikinzi.*'

The people wondered, saying 'You see! That is the true man.' When he waved this shield it sounded, saying

'*Bangbaguma paranga nzanga, bangbaguma kinzikinzi,*
Bangbaguma paranga nzanga, bangbaguma kinzikinzi.'

His sister was dancing after him with the buffalo tail. The sound of the shield so much resembled that of a drum than it attracted crowds of people to come and dance. The man and his sister while doing this became fat as they were before. The people danced so much that they were black with sweat. The man and his sister became very fat from their dance. While people were dancing strenuously the man and his sister ran away with their shield and their buffalo tail. They ran with them into their cave. The dance at once was spoilt. The people said 'What a thing is this! The man and his sister, before they took the shield were very thin, and after taking it they at once became fat.' Ture said 'If I had known they were the owners I would not have let them have it. If they had not taken their shield they would have died of hunger, from thinness, for they do not eat food, their only food is their dancing.'

42. *Ture and Yangaimo's feathers* (R. M.)

THERE was once a man called Yangaimo. When his father died he left Yangaimo his many-feathered hat. These feathers had great power, very great indeed. Whenever Yangaimo's wives began to lack meat he would put on this hat and say to his wives 'Women, you sweep the courtyard and clean the pots and bowls, and gather up all the baskets, open-wove and close-wove.' After that he would put on his hat and then jump up on high, singing his song which his father had taught him, which is

> '*Yuu* Yangaimo, *yuu* Yangaimo,
> Yangaimo, you come to take feathers.'

While Yangaimo was dancing on high between heaven and earth, birds from all over the world would fly and fall in the courtyard of Yangaimo's homestead. Whole flocks of birds would fall in his home, so that a man could not see his companion on account of the birds. Yangaimo's wives would kill these birds, and all their receptacles would be full, and the granaries and huts also. After that his wives would cook them in big pots, and people would flock to Yangaimo's home to eat his meats which came down from on high. That is why he was so much liked, people were never lacking in his home.

The fame of Yangaimo spread over the whole countryside; and Ture for his part heard it also. So Ture picked up his elephant-hide bag, hung it over his shoulder, and began to go to Yangaimo's home to witness this wonderful thing. After Ture had seen Yangaimo doing this thing he said 'O sir, my mother said that if I wandered and found a person doing such a thing I should understand that he is my maternal uncle. O uncle, how I have been searching for you, it is the ghost of my grandmother that decided I should find you today.' Yangaimo replied 'So be it, my sister's son, eat this meat of which those who are not kinsmen have been eating so much.' Ture spent many days at his uncle's home and then one day he said 'Uncle, I shall leave tomorrow.' Yangaimo agreed, saying to him 'Give my greetings to your mother.' Very early in the morning Ture took Yangaimo's feathered hat from where he used to hide it, stuffed it into his bag, bid Yangaimo farewell, and departed. As Ture was on his way a feather broke off (from the hat) and fell near Yangaimo's home. Ture, as soon as he arrived home, incited his wives to burn all their ground-nuts and sesame because they would never lack meat again. Ture said to them 'Sweep the courtyard and collect close-wove and open-wove baskets and bowls and stand them in the courtyard.' Ture then put on Yangaimo's feathered hat and burst into song, saying

'*Yuu* Ture, *yuu* Ture,
You come and see me with feathers, *yuu yuu* Ture.'

When Ture jumped on high a swarm of birds fell in Ture's home. Ture's wives killed birds till everything was full of them. Ture was so pleased with himself that he remained above shouting while birds were falling down in heaps.

While this was happening, Yangaimo looked in vain for his hat. He at once knew that it was Ture who had stolen it. So he got up and followed Ture. He advanced but a little way when he saw that little feather that had fallen from Ture, and he took it and walked on till he reached Ture's home and saw what was happening. Yangaimo then also for his part sang his song, saying

'*Yuu* Yangaimo, Yangaimo,
Yangaimo I have come to take feathers.'

Then Yangaimo jumped and flew up on high until he met Ture. He met Ture still glorying in himself with dancing. So Yangaimo flew higher than Ture and when he descended he snatched his hat from Ture's head. The birds stopped abruptly. The power of dancing on high left Ture, so he fell down to earth and died. Yangaimo descended to earth and came and met Ture's wives wailing for him. Yangaimo had pity on them so he smeared his medicine-ashes on Ture's lips and Ture rose from death. Yangaimo said to him 'My sister's son, never steal my hat again; if you want meat, just come to my home.' When Ture's wives began to get at him for their ground-nuts and sesame which he told them to burn, he wandered away from them to let their anger subside.

43. *Ture, the youth, the old woman, and the ripe fruit* (R. M.)

ONE day Bachelor went out to hunt guinea-fowl. When he reached a certain cultivation he shot a guinea-fowl with his arrow. This fowl flew until it fell in an old woman's fallow-ground. This woman killed it with the handle of her hoe and hid it under a heap of grass. Bachelor went in search of his

guinea-fowl and came to the old woman and found her hoeing
her cultivation, and he asked her 'Have you seen my guinea-
fowl here?' She replied 'No, I haven't seen a guinea-fowl.'
Bachelor said to her 'If you don't bring out my fowl you will
see something right now!' Being afraid, the old woman brought
out the guinea-fowl from under the heap and gave it to him.
But Bachelor gave this guinea-fowl back to this old woman,
saying 'You go and cook it while I am hoeing your garden.' The
old woman went home with it. When she reached home she
roasted first some manioc so that he might eat it while she was
preparing the meal. The old woman cooked animal meat,
cooked the guinea-fowl, and cooked manioc leaves, and she
prepared porridge and took these things to Bachelor in the
cultivation. When she got there she gave them to him, and he
took for himself the meat and manioc leaves and the porridge,
but the guinea-fowl he left for the old woman. When he had
finished his meal he told her that he was going home. She said
'All right, but when you are on your way home you will see
some ripe fruits; pick the small one, and continue on your way
with it until you reach where the path forks and there split it
(by knocking it) on the ground.'

Bachelor went and found the ripe fruits on the way and he
did what the old woman had told him to do. Bachelor continued
on his way and when he looked back he saw a very pretty
blooming girl following him. When he stepped on one side to
allow her to pass she said 'You are leaving the way to no purpose, you are my husband. My mother said I should go with
you to your home.' Bachelor went with his wife and arrived at
Ture's home. When Ture saw this very pretty girl behind him
Ture asked him 'O my friend, whose wife is that beautiful
girl? *wo wo* my younger brother, where did you find her?'
Bachelor related to him how he had acquired this pretty girl.

When Ture heard this he plunged headlong into his hut and
gathered up his bow and arrows and dashed out. After which
he chased away his wives, saying 'Eh, you ugly old women,
leave my home here because I am going to bring today a pretty
blooming girl.' Ture then went in search of guinea-fowl as if
his head was on fire. Ture shot a guinea-fowl and it flew until
it fell in the old woman's fallow. She came and killed it with the
handle of her hoe and hid it under some grass. Ture then went

in search of his guinea-fowl until he came to the old woman
and he asked her, saying 'Have you seen my guinea-fowl?' She
replied 'No, I have not seen a guinea-fowl.' Ture said 'If you
don't bring out my fowl you will see something today.' So the
old woman gave Ture his guinea-fowl. Then Ture returned
that guinea-fowl to this old woman telling her to go and cook
it with porridge while he was hoeing her cultivation. The old
woman went home, roasted some manioc, and brought it to
Ture so that he could eat it while she was cooking the food. The
old woman cooked the guinea-fowl and some animal meat and
also leaves of manioc, and prepared porridge, and she took these
things to Ture. Ture kept the guinea-fowl and the meat and
gave only the manioc leaves to the old woman. When Ture had
eaten up all these things he said he was about to depart. Then
she said to him 'You go, and on your way you pick the fruit
which is big. When you reach where the path forks, break it on
the ground.'

Ture ran with full speed and did as he was told hurriedly.
Ture smashed the ripe fruit on the ground and when he looked
behind him he saw an extremely ugly old woman dashing at
him with a big knife. Ture took to his heels and bumped into a
man's home and found him carving his drum. Ture pleaded
with the man to save him from the old woman. This man told
Ture 'Just enter my hut, you will see my people there.' When
Ture entered the hut he found only lions. The old woman
appeared with the big knife in her hand and asked for Ture.
The drum-carver replied 'I haven't seen Ture.' She said 'If
you don't reveal Ture's whereabouts it is you I shall kill.' He
said to her 'Ture is inside there.' When she plunged into the
hut the lions caught her and killed her. Thus Ture was saved
from that old woman.

44. *How Ture burnt Leopard all over*[1] (R. M.)

ONE day Leopard went and dug out some rats and tied them in
a bundle the size of a thigh and put them by the side of the fire
and lay down beside them. Ture wandered until he came across

---

[1] *Ndakpita*, the word used here, means 'to cover all over with wounds'.

Leopard and saw his rats near the fire. A longing for them was itching Ture. Ture broke off some resin[1] and tied it into a bundle the size of a thigh and put it near Leopard's rats. When Ture's resin melted and was dripping into the fire, Ture said to Leopard 'The fat of my rats will be finished by the fire. Let one of us lie on his back with his mouth open so that the other may feed him.' So Leopard lay on his back and Ture said to him 'Open your mouth properly.' Leopard opened his mouth wide and then Ture took his burning resin and smashed it against Leopard's mouth, and it spread all over Leopard's eyes and all over his body. Leopard was burnt all over in many spots. Ture then snatched Leopard's rats and ran away with them. Ture ran until he burst in upon his wife Nanzagbe and said to her 'Woman, get up, let us escape up above from Leopard.' Ture went until he found a big forked tree on the bank of a river and there he built his hut, and he twined a thick rope by which Nanzagbe could pull him up.

Whenever Ture returned from his wanderings he used to sing this song to Nanzagbe, so that she might know he was Ture:

'Nanzagbe, you pull me up,
Uwa Leopard's head is burnt since I burnt up Leopard,
Spots, spots, Leopard's head is burnt.'

Nanzagbe would then throw down the rope to Ture and would pull him up with it.

Leopard was very ill indeed from his burns. After some time Leopard recovered, but the marks of the resin-fire remained on the body of Leopard, spotted as he is right till today. Leopard went and knocked the *Atari* oracle on the head, and *Atari* fell into the fire and began to melt, and then Leopard began to run away. Then *Atari* said to him 'Didn't you come for oracular consultation?' Leopard came back and said 'What shall I do to find Ture?' *Atari* said 'Go after Duiker, he will show you where Ture is hiding.' Leopard went to Duiker and Duiker revealed the whereabouts of Ture in the tree. Duiker also taught Leopard Ture's song. Leopard went and arrived under his tree while Ture was away. Leopard said

---

[1] *Baro* is a torch made of resin.

'Nanzagbe, you pull me up,
Uwa Leopard's head is burnt since I burnt up Leopard,
Spots, spots, Leopard's head is burnt.'

Nanzagbe threw down the rope to Leopard, thinking it was
Ture, and she was pulling Leopard up when she looked and
saw Leopard, and then she wanted to throw him into the water
below. But Leopard opened his eyes wide to her and said 'If
you throw me down now I will seize just you.' Fear of Leopard
seized Nanzagbe and she pulled him up. Leopard lay there on a
branch and waited for Ture.

Ture went on wandering and then decided to return home
and when he arrived he raised his voice,[1] chanting

'Nanzagbe, you pull me up,
Uwa Leopard's head is burnt since I burnt up Leopard,
Spots, spots, Leopard's head is burnt.'

Nanzagbe threw the rope to Ture and began pulling Ture
upwards. When Ture glanced round and saw Leopard he
began to scream, saying 'Woman let me down! Woman let me
down! Woman let me down!' Leopard said 'If you let him
down, right now I will seize you.' Fear of Leopard overcame
Nanzagbe so she pulled Ture up to face Leopard. As soon as
Ture got there he rushed to Leopard saying 'O my friend, it is
a long time since we parted, have you been here long? Nanzagbe, you cook porridge for the son of my mother's brother and
be quick about it, woman!' Leopard said to himself 'I will eat
my meal first and then I will seize Ture.' Nanzagbe said there
was no meat, only elephant hide. Ture then went to Nanzagbe
and said (softly) 'Just bring that elephant hide and place it on
the branch on which Leopard is lying and I am going to cut it
with an axe, but whenever I bring down the axe on it (the hide),
pull it away.' Nanzagbe placed the elephant hide on the branch
on which Leopard was resting. Then Ture came to cut it in
pieces, but whenever Ture aimed at the hide Nanzagbe pulled
it back. Ture cut only into the wood. So Ture cut the branch on
which Leopard was resting so that it broke off and fell together
with Leopard into the river. Then Ture congratulated himself,

---

[1] *Ti ku ngba ko yo*: lit., 'he fell into his mouth'.

saying 'It is I, the son of Ture's father, I have dealt with you.'[1]

Leopard swam across the river to the other bank and ran to the *Atari* oracle again. *Atari* said 'Just make a feast,[2] you will see Ture. When the dance is started, fix a pole in the centre of the dance and gather dry leaves around its base and hide among them. When Ture approaches, you can catch him.' Leopard gave a big dance and everybody went to drink beer and to enjoy the dancing. When Ture heard about Leopard's feast he said to himself 'What shall I do to attend that dance?' He ran to *Atari* and hit *Atari* on the head, and when it fell into the fire and began to melt Ture took to his heels. *Atari* shouted to him 'Didn't you come to consult the oracle?'[3] Ture returned and related why he had come. *Atari* said to him 'Go and make yourself a big knife. When you come to the homestead of the dance go straight to the centre of the dance to the side of the pole there with dry leaves at its base. When you get near it just raise your big knife, then you will see Leopard.' Then Ture said 'You stupid thing! did I not know this already?' Ture went home and took his big knife and dashed off to Leopard's dance and went straight to the pole Leopard had erected in the centre of the dancing ground and at the base of which he was hiding amid dry leaves. Ture then raised his hand with his big knife, and Leopard lying under the dry leaves saw Ture's knife flashing, and he was scared, thinking that Ture wanted to cut him with that knife. So Leopard sprang up from under the dry leaves and fled from the homestead of his dance. Ture congratulated himself on how he had dealt with Leopard.

45. *Ture and Duwainga* (R. M.)

THERE was a man called Duwainga who was Ture's neighbour. Ture said to him 'My friend, whenever you hear me talking in my home that means my wife has prepared food for me, so just

---

[1] *Mi fu ti ro*: a form of boasting when you have defeated or outwitted a person, lit., 'I have smelt on you'.

[2] *Wari* is 'to brew' (beer), and hence 'to give a feast'.

[3] *Iwa* is the rubbing-board oracle, but the word is used here with the general sense of 'oracle'.

drop in and we will eat it.' Duwainga waited a short time and then he heard Ture's voice in his home. When he went there Ture said '*Wo wo* my friend! Why didn't you come earlier, for I have eaten all the food?' Duwainga replied 'Never mind my friend.'

Two days later Duwainga invited Ture for honey in his home. When Ture went there Duwainga gave Ture honey in the comb, and Ture ate it all. After that bees developed in Ture's stomach and were making a terrific sound. Ture took to his heels and as he ran he threw down his bag. Ture then went on a bit further and threw away his feathered hat. Ture ran on a little further and took off his barkcloth from his waist. Then Ture thought it was his loin-string troubling him, so he loosened it off. Whenever Ture tried to stop, bees would buzz in Ture's stomach, *guu*. Ture dashed forward again with all speed, singing this song:

'*Ya ya ya*, a man has deceived me wife of Ture oo,
Ya ya ya, what shall I do oo my wife oo?
Ya ya ya, where shall I go to o Ture oo?
Ya ya ya.'

After that Ture's wives sent a message to Duwainga to come and save Ture. Duwainga came and warned Ture: 'Never again deceive me about food. I have been kind to you, I could have left you to die.' Duwainga then said 'Ture, you go to the mouth of a hollow in a tree.' Ture went to the entrance of a hollow, and the bees left Ture's stomach and went into the hollow. So Ture was saved, and he never fooled Duwainga about food again.

'As I was walking this evening I found my uncle barking at his wife and when I tried to mediate he sent me off with a blow on the head. When I wept he consoled me with what was left over of a chicken he had been eating in the afternoon. I ate some of it but brought back one leg which I hid on the lintel of the doorway. Anybody may run and help himself to it.'

46. *Ture and Eye-bee*[1] (G.)

TURE went to lay a snare for animals. Eye-bee came and got caught in the snare. Ture came and disentangled him from the snare and took him home. He gave him to his wife Nanzagbe and told her to roast him. As she was about to roast him he began to sing, saying

> 'Nanzagbe wife of Ture do not roast me at all,
> It is Ture who snared me against my mouth,
> That is why I have been caught o.
> Since I have been going about as an animal,
> Somebody has untied me as an animal.'

When Eye-bee sang his song Ture thought he would go and see what was happening. Eye-bee caught Ture and rolled him over with his tail and flew away with him. When he reached the country of crabs he put Ture down and told him 'You get down and collect crabs for me.' When Ture got down he left the crabs and ran away. He played a trick, picking fruits of the Kaffir apple and putting them in his eye-sockets and climbing up a tree. Eye-bee came and when he looked up he saw Ture but did not recognize him. He asked 'Have you seen Ture?' Ture played a trick and said his name was Tanga. He said 'When I look down everybody dies.' When Ture was about to look down Eye-bee ran quickly away, and Ture came down and went home and was saved.

47. *Ture and Bakureako* (R. M.)

THERE was a man called Bakureako[2] behind whose home mushrooms used to grow. Nobody knew the whereabouts of these mushrooms. Whenever people came to his home it was only he who used to pick them so that they might be cooked for his guests. Even his wives also, they did not know the place of them. Those mushrooms were abundant.

---

[1] The Zande word is *banvunvuranvu*. I believe this to be the eye-bee. See footnote to no. 13.

[2] *Bakureako*: lit., 'his blood-brother' or 'his friend', but in the story it is rather a name and is so presented.

So people told Ture about this man. Ture went to this man's home and said to him 'Bakureako I have come to eat mushrooms.' He replied 'Ture, just wait a bit, you will eat mushrooms today till you are sick of them.' After that he took a basket and went round to the back of his hut, Ture watching him closely so that he saw the way to those mushrooms. When he returned with the mushrooms they cooked them for Ture. He ate them and found them very delicious and he said to himself 'If my wife Nanzagbe were to cook these mushrooms, oh! they would be so delicious!'

Ture said to Bakureako 'I am going home, I have eaten well of mushrooms.' Ture, instead of going home, went behind Bakureako's huts and came across the path to the mushrooms. Ture ran along it till he got to the mushrooms and found them covering an entire termite mound.[1] So Ture picked them till his bag was full. When Ture wanted to return, the mushrooms seized him and kept him on the top of the mound. Whenever Ture tried to lift his foot to depart, oh no! The mushrooms tightened their firm grip on him. Ture tried to bear the pain in vain and soon he burst out wailing.

Bakureako heard Ture's cries and went after Ture and when he found Ture he beat him, saying 'My friend, as you have already eaten mushrooms, why did you come to steal more of them?' After that he said to the mushrooms 'Let Ture go.' The mushrooms then let Ture loose. Bakureako took almost all the mushrooms in Ture's bag, leaving only just a few in it.

Ture went home and came to his wives Nanzagbe and Nangbafudo and said to them 'My wives, I have found mushrooms nearby covering a whole mound, here are a few I picked. I came to you for you to cook them and then, after eating them, we can go and fill baskets with some more.' They replied 'Ture, since you are always fooling, maybe you are just deceiving us.' Ture said 'O you! Cook these mushrooms quickly and then we can go and pick some more.'

After eating these mushrooms Ture led the way for them and they went after him, but when they were approaching the mushrooms Ture said to them 'There are the mushrooms you see on the termite mound. I am going to the bush.' Ture then disappeared.

[1] *Kengerekengere* indicates an enormous number (covering the mound).

His wives came upon the mushrooms and when they saw them they were out of their minds with delight,[1] and they picked them till their baskets were full. But when they wanted to leave, the mushrooms pulled them on to the mound until they cried out in pain.[2] Bakureako came running and found only Ture's wives crying from the mushrooms. He asked them who had shown them the place of his mushrooms. They said 'Ture.' After that he told the mushrooms to release them, and they let them go. When Ture's wives were about to run away he called them back, saying 'Don't run away leaving your mushrooms which are in your baskets. You take them with you, but don't let me see you here again.'

Ture's wives set off for home, threatening him on the way. When they got home they found that Ture had gone away so that they might forget, and then he would return.

48. *How Firefly cheated Ture* (R. M.)

WHEN rain fell which makes the termites fly, Ture went early into the bush to clean before his termite mounds. When he had finished cleaning before his mounds he was very hungry, so he made for his home in a great hurry to (his wives) Nanzagbe and Nangbafudo. He met Firefly on the way, who was also returning from cleaning before his mounds. He said to Ture 'Friend, why are you sweating so much? Where are you running to?' Ture answered 'Don't bother me man, don't you see that I am very hungry?' Firefly replied 'As your home is far, come let us go to look for that old wife of mine for some manioc she might have broiled.' Ture insulted him, saying 'Who wants your wife's bad food?' Ture went on his way, running to his home like one whose head is on fire.

What Ture had said to Firefly displeased him deeply. So he went to his home and in the evening he paid Ture a visit. He found Ture binding together grass-stalks in bundles for torches in collecting termites. There was fire of ghosts near Firefly's home under a fig tree of which only he knew what it used

---

[1] *Bangiri yo ki su*: lit., 'their eyes popped out (of their heads)'.
[2] *Kpe yo ki gba*: lit., 'their cries shot up'.

to do to anyone. Firefly said to Ture 'Man, are you still tying up grass-stalks? I don't gather up grass-stalks for torches. I have my fire which when I light it, stays alight near all my termite mounds. I just sit around and my termites flit into the holes by themselves.' Ture threw away his grass-stalks and begged Firefly to show him the secret of this fire: 'O my friend, I am tired of gathering grass-stalks every year. So these termites you have been collecting so much, this is what you have been doing! Man, show me this cleverness quickly.' Firefly showed Ture the place of the fire of the ghosts and told him to go and look under the fig tree when it was dark and he would find this wonderful kind of fire there.

Ture took away her torches from that wife of his Nanzagbe and threw them away into the bush, saying to her 'Woman, you, whom are you going to follow with your torches? Don't you know that I have already discovered a wonderful new kind of fire that will collect my termites for me?'[1] When he went to Nangbafudo she lost her temper with him, saying 'Hey, you madman! Return from where you came with that nonsense of yours, or I will beat you right now with my mortar-pounder!' When it was dusk Ture said that he was going to get this wonderful fire of his that Firefly had told him about. He went to under the fig tree and saw fire burning on a fire-log. When he tried to take it, the log with the fire on it jumped on him and burnt him all over, up to his head. Ture fled and when he was near his home he stopped running and came slowly and sat down as if nothing had happened. He sat for some time and then sent Nanzagbe, saying 'My wife, go and collect our fire under the fig tree which is near the home of Firefly over there.' She went and when she reached the tree she looked around and saw this fire on a log. When she touched the log the fire jumped on her and burnt her all over, even her head, and she ran home making straight for Ture.

Before she arrived Ture had already fled to the bush where his termite mounds were, and there he found Firefly (happily) collecting his termites. Ture hid himself and stalked Firefly on and on, and when he was about to gather up his termites into his baskets, Ture jumped on him, saying 'If you move, I am

[1] The sense is: 'when I put the fire over my termites-hole I can go away and return to find the hole full of termites. I shall not have to mind the fire.'

going to spear you right now, man! Why did you deceive me and let me be burnt by your terrible fire? Now, give (all) your termites to me so that I may take them to my wife who has been scorched by your beastly fire.' Firefly said 'I deceived you because you despised my wife's food. Let us divide the termites and go home in peace, but never again in your life despise the food of anybody's wife.' So they shared the termites and Ture poured his into his bag and took them to Nanzagbe's door where he left them and disappeared till her anger had subsided, and then he would return.

Nangbafudo in the morning jeered at Nanzagbe, saying 'You always accept Ture's foolishness, and so you will always suffer at his hands.'

49. *How Ture killed his father* (R. M.)

TURE arose and started wandering and he found a man called Bambiro[1] who had taken out his medicine-horn[2] into his courtyard and sat near it saying

> 'O my father's ashes, when I look over there
> May porridge appear.'

When he looked he saw indeed porridge appearing. He said again

> 'O my father's ashes, when I look over there
> May a beautiful lady appear.'

When he looked he saw a most beautiful lady coming. Then he said again

> 'O my father's ashes, when I look over there
> May beer appear.'

When he looked he saw a pot of beer standing. Ture was speechless with surprise.[3] Ture drew near to the man and asked 'O my friend, how clever you are! Who taught you this wonderful thing? Oh you show it to me.' Bambiro said to Ture

---

[1] Bambiro means owner of magical paste (made by mixing oil and ash).
[2] This kind of medicine is kept in a horn container.
[3] Lit., 'Ture's mouth went cold'.

'It is my father whom I did not insult; I did not beat my mother; I always honoured my father and mother. So when my father was dying he said "When I am dead, my son, burn all my body and grind the ash into a horn, it will do many good things for you."' When he heard this Ture plunged into a run and ran until he bumped into his father, sweating up to his neck and breathing heavily. He said to his father 'O my father, what a bad person you are! Other fathers have done many good things for their children. What good thing have you ever done for me?' So Ture speared his father, burnt him, and ground the ash into a horn. After that Ture dashed home and incited his wives to burn down all the huts and granaries. When they tried to argue Ture threw a bundle of stalks into the fire and set everything on fire with it. Ture then said to his wives 'You sweep the courtyard very clean to stand aside and see the good things I am going to bring out for you right now.' They did as Ture bid them. Ture took his father's ashes (in the horn) and stood them in the middle of the courtyard and sat beside them. Ture's wives drew near to him to see what would happen. Ture then opened his mouth and said

> 'O my father's ashes, when I look over there
> May porridge appear.'

Ture looked and saw nothing. Ture's wives looked and saw nothing. They said 'Ture, we want to see today why you burnt all our food. We have had enough of your wantonness.' Ture cried again, saying

> 'O my father's ashes, when I look over there
> May beer appear.'

When he looked he only saw a spear appear suddenly and begin flying towards his belly. Ture jumped up and took to his heels. His wives and children then suffered greatly from lack of food and shelter. They said 'We will never again heed Ture's foolishness.'

50. *The fathers of Ture, who were Bambasi and Bangirimo* (R. M.)

THERE was once a man called Bambasi who married a woman who conceived and gave birth to twins, and Bambasi named them Ture and Nanzagbe. They married when they grew up. When they were babies Bambasi said to his wife 'Cook a chicken for feeding the babies.' She cooked the chicken and left it to cool while she went to fetch water. Bambasi for his part went out hunting.

While Ture's mother was at the stream Ture got up and looked down the path after her, and then he called his sister and they ate up all the chicken, and then went and lay down in sleep as babies.

When Bambasi's wife returned she looked in vain for the chicken, and she complained angrily, saying 'Who has eaten my children's chicken? Oh, people are very bad, how could they steal from babies?' Bambasi returned and she told him about it, and he was very angry about it.

After that Bambasi told her to cook another chicken the following day, but the same thing happened as before. The third time Bambasi hid behind the hut while his wife went to collect firewood. To his astonishment he saw Ture get out of babyhood, look towards the path, and say 'Sister, come let us eat our chicken.' Bambasi sat quietly watching Ture and his sister eat the chicken. After finishing it they again went and lay down as babies.

When his wife returned he said 'O my wife, these people are not babies. Those chickens you have been cooking, it is they who have been eating them. Get up and let us depart from them.' Bambasi thundered like thunder, and when the heavens opened he disappeared into them with his wife, leaving Ture and his sister in the world.

Bambasi was a terrible man, he used to descend from the heavens and kill his buffaloes and return with them to on high. Ture and his sister grew up and they did not often meet people. So Ture married his sister and she became his wife Nanzagbe.[1]

---

[1] See also footnote on p. 53.

They lived for a long time, and then Ture heard the renown of that man who used to sound like thunder and descend to the earth to kill buffaloes. So Ture journeyed to that part of the world where he used to kill buffaloes. When Ture heard something sounding like thunder, and he looked, he saw his father descending to kill buffaloes. Ture rushed to him saying 'O my father, where did you go, leaving me? I am going with you.' His father said 'O Ture, I am not going home with you because in the sky the king there does not want people to praise women (for their beauty) there. And there is no adultery there and people do not steal there.' So he only gave Ture a buffalo and went home and Ture did not see him again.

Ture ran to the *Atari* oracle to consult it about how he could go with his father to the sky. *Atari* said 'You go and tie a rope to your leg and bind the other end to one of his dead buffaloes when he comes again.'

Ture went and hid in the place where his father used to descend. It thundered and Bambasi descended and he killed many buffaloes. When he went to rest Ture tied his leg to the biggest buffalo. Bambasi burst again like thunder, and when the heavens opened he flew there with his buffaloes and Ture also.

When Bambasi reached his home his wife said '*Hu*, who smells like a person of earth? I smell a person of the earth.' When Bambasi went to search among his buffaloes he saw Ture hiding under one of them. He pulled Ture out, saying 'O Ture my son, as you have come here give up all the things you do on earth. There is a terrible king here called Bangirimo,[1] we will not be saved from him.' They then hid Ture in a hut.

When Bambasi went again to earth to kill buffaloes Ture came out and sat under the granary. After that, Bangirimo's wives passed by, going to draw water. When Ture saw them he was struck dumb by their beauty. Ture dashed out from under the granary and said 'O Ture, what lovely women, *wowoo!* Whose wives are so lovely?'

Bangirimo's wives went home and reported that there was a man in Bambasi's home who praised them. Bangirimo was very angry and he sent his young warriors to Bambasi's home

[1] *Bangirimo* means 'father of', or 'big', 'lake' (or 'lakes'). The story later accounts for this name.

to go and bind that man and bring him. The young men invaded Bambasi's home and found Ture sitting under the granary. They said 'You there, is it you who praised the king's wives?' Ture said 'I am the one.' They seized Ture and tied him up properly. They then carried Ture to Bangirimo's court, while Bambasi and his wife fled to hide in fear.

When they arrived with Ture Bangirimo urged them to tie him up again tightly. They tied up Ture till he could hardly breathe. Bangirimo beat on his gong and all his subjects came except Bambasi and his wife. Bangirimo said 'I summoned you to come and see the man who praised my wives, since women are never praised here.' Bangirimo told them to throw Ture into his big lake which was right there. Ture spoke once, saying 'O master, since you are a great king, so I also on the earth was an important person, so I want you yourself to throw me into the water.' Bangirimo therefore got up and went to Ture's side, but when he tried to lift Ture and throw him into the water the rope (with which Ture was tied) broke completely. Ture landed at the side of Bangirimo and pulled him towards him with great force.

Bangirimo was very annoyed at the thought of somebody's coming to contest with him in his realm where he had mastered everybody. Ture and Bangirimo pulled each other from side to side. Bangirimo got a foothold and tried to lift Ture to throw him into the lake, but Ture was too strong for him. Then Ture got a foothold and crouched to be rid of Bangirimo into the water, but Bangirimo was like a rock. What was happening greatly shocked Bangirimo's people: what manner of man was it who could get the better of Bangirimo? Bangirimo gathered Ture up, but when he tried to throw him into the water Ture clung to Bangirimo's head and then plunged it into the water. Bangirimo died by drowning.

The people applauded Ture because he had rescued them from Bangirimo's bad rule. They altered their allegiance and agreed that they would make Ture their king. But Ture refused and put his father Bambasi as king instead of himself. Ture then descended to earth to his wives and children.

'I went over there and found Bairagene beating his senior wife. I asked him why he was trying to kill his wife. When I spoke thus he left off beating his wife and came and struck me hard over the head with his spear-shaft. When I cried out in consequence he gave me some left-over cooked eggs. I ate some and hid the rest on a shelf in the hut. Somebody go and fetch them.'

51. *Ture and his mother-in-law* (R. M.)

THERE was once a man called Ture. He had a wife called Nanzagbe. One day his mother-in-law came to his home to visit her daughter, his wife, and her son-in-law, the man himself. After that the season of termites arrived. Everybody throughout that district prepared their termite mounds.[1] So Ture also prepared his, he and his wife Nanzagbe. They then tied stalks as torches for collecting the termites. Now Ture and his wife owned two termite mounds. One was near their home and the other was far away in the bush.

When it was evening Ture said to his wife 'O my wife Nanzagbe, as it is like this what will happen tonight?' One thing was that Ture was thinking of his mother-in-law as a woman.[2] That is why he told Nanzagbe to remain at the mound which was near the home, and he and his mother-in-law would go to the mound in the bush. He said to his wife 'O my wife, stay with our termites which are near the home, because they swarm plentifully. You know their habits. But I am going with my mother-in-law into the bush.' Nanzagbe agreed to this. His mother-in-law agreed also. At once Ture got up, gathered his spears, and tied the torches together, and his mother-in-law carried them and also a basket, and they set off. When they reached the place in the bush they made their fire. After that he broke off some tender leafy branches and prepared with them sleeping-places on each side of the fire for himself and for his mother-in-law.

When it was dark Ture examined the mound by torchlight. The termites had perforated the mound properly. But lust for his mother-in-law was in his heart like the love of a sesame grinding-stone in the heart of a dog.[3] So after inspecting the

---

[1] Cleared round their mounds.   [2] He desired her.
[3] A dog likes to lick the stone.

mound he lay down at once. His mother-in-law was also lying on the other side of the fire. After a while he said to her 'O mother, there is one thing, that is, since we are in the bush leave that side of the fire and come and lie behind me, because there are many animals around. We can also make another fire on that side.' She said to him 'Yes, my son, what you say is very true.' She got up and lay behind him. He said to her again 'O mother, don't lie with your back to me, an animal might pluck out your eye.' She said 'Yes, my son, that is true.' She turned over to him. He said to her again 'O mother, don't lie with your barkcloth on, it might catch fire and burn you.' She said 'Yes, my son, that is true.' She took off her barkcloth. He spoke again: 'Ah, so, I am taking mine off also, I might get burnt with it.' So he took off his barkcloth. He said to her again 'O mother, put your arm over me because it is very cold, so we can't sleep far apart.' She stretched her arm over him. He stretched his arm over her also. So then they at once embraced. When things were like that his mother-in-law fell asleep, and he began to ravish her. When she awoke she discovered what was happening. However, she liked it very much. They went on doing it, forgetting all about the termites. The termites all escaped that night while they were having adulterous congress. When they awoke in the morning they found only their wings in heaps in their courtyard.[1]

Ture said to his mother-in-law 'O mother, what shall I say to Nanzagbe? There is one thing we can do, we can sweep aside the wings and when we return we will tell her that they did not swarm.' So they swept aside the wings, and then they started to return. He gathered up his spears, put them over his shoulder, and, looking quite innocent,[2] walked off briskly. They went on and on, on and on, till they arrived at a certain homestead. Its owner said to Ture 'O my friend, it is sad that you are lacking termites. However wait for some to eat them.' Ture sat under the granary while his mother-in-law sat in the kitchen-hut with the women. The mistress of the home fried termites and gave Ture his and gave his mother-in-law hers. When they started eating them Ture's private parts blurted

---

[1] *Sukubusukubu* indicates great quantities lying at random. By 'courtyard' is meant the space cleared in front of the mound.

[2] *Mbakadi ngba ko*: 'looking as though nothing bad had been done by him'.

out 'Oh dear! Ture, are you eating termites when, while you were sleeping with your mother-in-law, the termites escaped?' His mother-in-law's private parts replied 'Do you say it is a lie?' The people of the home were shocked. Ture and his mother-in-law were very ashamed. Ture ran off in shame and poured the termites into his elephant-hide bag, for he was a wanton fellow. They went and arrived home to Nanzagbe. She asked 'You there, where are the termites, as you return with only an empty basket?' Ture said 'They did not swarm. I think that their time has not come yet.' They sat peacefully.

Anyhow, Nanzagbe had collected plenty of termites. She made porridge and cooked them to go with it, and when she gave Ture his share and her mother her share, and they at once began to eat them, Ture's private parts blurted out 'Oh! So you are eating termites, you who were just sleeping with your mother-in-law while they were flying away!' His mother-in-law's private parts answered, saying 'Do you say it is a lie?' Nanzagbe was shocked and she was enraged against Ture and his mother-in-law, her mother. She took hold of her stick and chased them with it. Ture took the porridge and the termites and dropped them into his elephant-hide bag and fled with his mother-in-law.

52. *Ture, Nanzagbe, and the toad* (A. B.)

TURE told his wives that he was going to hunt in the bush, so let them grind him some flour for the journey. His wives ground him flour into a big elephant-hide bag and ground some sesame into a big calabash. Ture gathered up all these things and went off to the bush to hunt. When Ture was in the bush he did not kill many animals, only a reed-rat and a hare which he ate up completely, without keeping any meat for his wives. He tried to hunt again to get some meat to take to his wives but he failed again to kill any animal. So, lacking anything, he decided to go home.

He started on his way home and on a stone-flat he met a toad on the path, such a big toad. He took the toad to rub it clean on the surface of the stone-flat to take it home to eat, since he had got nothing from his hunting. He took it to the surface of the stone-flat and sat down to scale it. Just as he was about to rub the toad a second time it turned him over as one turns a porridge-stirrer and started to rub him on the surface of the rock with its buttocks. Ture tried to push the toad away, but in vain. Oh no! He started to shout, and Ture's blood was flowing on the rock as if it was nothing. When he was near to death it released him and only his dead body rose to stagger. He could not go home, so he returned to the bush to treat his wounds with hot water that they might heal. In the meantime the flour he had with him was all finished and he was just living on wild yams. Ture spent some two months in the bush before his sores healed.

He went home at last, having nothing like meat or anything else from the bush. When he reached home his senior wives asked him, saying 'Where is the meat?' He answered them 'I met my brother-in-law in the bush, the brother of Nanzagbe, and we consumed the meat I had with him. Oh, my brother-in-law, the brother of Nanzagbe, how could I pass him by with meat?' Nangbafudo said 'O Nanzagbe, my friend, if you see Ture talking like that it means that something has happened to him.' Nanzagbe suspected her of envy and said 'O madam, since he is telling the truth when he says that he came across my brother why are you talking like that? Are you saying it because he is not well disposed towards your relatives?'

That night Ture slept in Nanzagbe's hut. Very early in the morning he told her to chase a chicken and catch and cook it and fetch also some beer, so that they might go with it to her brother. Nangbafudo told Nanzagbe again 'You are taking this matter lightly but you will see the consequences later.' Nanzagbe lost her temper with her again and insulted her. So Nangbafudo for her part kept quiet. So Nanzagbe brought out some beer and prepared a meal with chicken and said to Ture 'Let us go to visit my brother.' Ture dashed inside the hut and put on his feathered hat and took his two spears and led the way. Nangbafudo said again to her 'I know something is going to happen, you will see for yourself later. I know Ture only too well. I am sure something will come of this.'

Ture and Nanzagbe went on their way and reached the stone-flat. Ture said to her 'Your brother is very fond of toad meat, let us look out for some toads here and if we find one we can scale it and take its meat to him. This is the place where we used to catch toads with him. Put down the food first and then go to beneath that big tree over there and search for toads.' When she had gone Ture sat down to the chicken and beer and consumed them all, leaving only bare porridge on the ground. Then he got up and fixed his feathered hat firmly on his head and stood laughing. Meanwhile Nanzagbe went under the tree which Ture had pointed out to her and found a toad there, such a big toad, and she took it and came with it. When she was just approaching Ture he told her to take it over there to the rock and scale it quickly so that they might be on their way, for they had a long way to go. Nanzagbe took it to the rock and sat down to rub the toad. She rubbed the toad once, and then a second time, and when she was about to rub it a third time the toad lay on the ground and pulled at her legs and she fell heavily like a cocoa-like fruit; and it turned her over and rubbed her with its buttocks. When Ture saw it rubbing her he began to dance, singing

> 'Big toad is rubbing Nanzagbe,
> Toad is irritated by Nanzagbe,
> Big toad is rubbing Nanzagbe,
> Ture is irritated by Nanzagbe,
> Big toad is rubbing Nanzagbe,
> Ture is irritated by Nanzagbe.'

In this way the big toad rubbed Nanzagbe till she was near to death. Ture for his part wandered off and went home. At last the toad released Nanzagbe, more dead than alive. It returned again to its place under the tree. Nanzagbe sat for a while and her eyes began to clear. All the things she had brought, porridge and beer and fowl, she did not find them, for Ture had eaten them up. She started to cry in a loud lamentation. When she reached home Nangbafudo was shocked to see her condition. She said 'My friend, what happened there that you are covered with blood?' Nanzagbe started to relate what Ture had done to her and finished it.

53. *Ture and Civet Cat* (R. R.)

CIVET CAT waited till there fell the big rain which makes the termites rise. Everybody went to collect termites, and Ture also. But for his part Civet Cat did not go after the termites because he did not own one of their mounds. When the people returned with their termites Ture gathered up his also in great numbers. Civet Cat rose to send a messenger to Ture's home; he summoned his son and said to him 'Go to Ture's home and ask him to give me some termites, for I have not caught any termites at all. But child, when you go to repeat my words to Ture, pay attention to what he first says and come and tell it to me.'

The lad went and arrived at Ture's home, and he said to him 'My father said you give him termites, because he lacks them altogether.' Ture then spoke thus: 'Oh that somebody! Though he knows how nice termites are he excretes into their holes.'[1] Then he quickly turned his speech and said 'All right, child, you wait a little to take them to him.' However, the child had already heard what Ture had first said about Civet Cat, that he excreted into termite-holes. Ture then gathered termites for him in large quantity. The lad went home to his father, Civet Cat. He gave him the termites, but Civet Cat first asked about Ture's first words. The lad said to him thus: 'I went and arrived at Ture's home and I gave him the message you sent me with. But the first words he spoke were "Oh that somebody! He knows how tasty termites are so he goes and excretes into their holes." These were his first words.' Civet Cat was for a time silent, and then he said 'All right, since he says thus, that I excrete into the holes of termites, no matter, I will get even with him.' When a certain day came the termites-rain fell upon the earth, and everybody went after termites. For his part Civet Cat arose and went and arrived in front of Ture's termite mound and, not seeing Ture anywhere around, he proceeded to excrete into all Ture's termite-holes, for there were many of them; and then he returned to his home. Ture came and arrived in front of his termite mound; and the termites arose in flight in great numbers. As Ture began to

---

[1] The holes dug for the termites to fall into.

gather them up he put his hand into Civet Cat's dung, for wherever the termites were the holes were full of Civet Cat's dung. So he lacked termites just as Civet Cat did. So Ture returned home; and that is the end of the story.

So a man gives of a thing freely to another, for if he is a poor man he asks him for it. People give things to others, for it is not good to refuse a man a thing. How do you know that when you are in sore need of something and you ask him for it he will give it to you? However, if you don't oblige him you will ask in vain for the same and he will not give it to you, because you first did the same to him with your things. Azande say in their roundabout way 'They crush termites into the pots of others.'[1] This is as though one were to say that a man is generous to a man who has been generous to him. For if a man is not generous to you, you are also not generous to him. That is 'They crush termites into the pots of others' in a proverbial manner of speech.

54. *Ture, his mushrooms, and Death* (R. R.)

TURE arose and went to collect his mushrooms. He went and found them in quantities on a termite mound. He plucked them and his large elephant-hide bag was filled with them. Then he returned home and appeared there where his mother was. He called to his mother to bring a large pot, a really big one. He put the mushrooms in it and they filled it, bulging right over the top of it. He told her to take it and go and cook them for him. She washed them well and put them on the fire, and they boiled for some time. They sank in the pot to half-way down it, for they are soft things and even if they fill a thing, when you put them on the fire they diminish until they are quite small things. She cooked porridge to go with these mushrooms and she brought the meal before Ture. When he looked into the pot he saw that the mushrooms only half filled it. He began to scold his mother, saying that it was she who had eaten his mushrooms, for they had completely filled the pot. He began to beat his mother and drove her from him.

---

[1] One of the best known and most quoted Zande proverbs.

On a certain day he went again to the bush and filled his elephant-hide bag as he had done before. He returned home with it and gave it to Nanzagbe (his wife) and she sat right beside him and put the mushrooms in the pot, and they filled it. Then she went with it and put it on the fire. They boiled for some time and they sank down right to the bottom of the pot; and she cooked porridge to go with them and brought it to him. When he looked into the pot he saw his mushrooms right at the bottom of the pot. He went straight to Nanzagbe and beat her and chased her at once from his home.

A man called Death heard of him and of his tricks. He arose, saying that he wanted to go and kill Ture. He went on his way and arrived where Ture was. He said to Ture 'Ture, I want you to beat someone for me with a throwing-knife.' In vain Ture considered this proposal, it did not seem that he could beat a man with a throwing-knife. He went to, and arrived at, where his mother was and told her the words Death had spoken. His mother replied 'What can I do about it, since you have already driven me into the bush? Moreover, I am merely a woman, so what can I do for my part?' Ture left her and went to the *Atari* oracle and he struck the top of the oracle and it popped (as in fire), and when it was settled, when it was settled, Ture said to it 'O my blood-brother, a man came to kill me who is Death, he wants me to beat a man with a throwing-knife. I have sought in vain for some way to escape from him.' The oracle was for long silent and then it said to Ture thus: 'You go and take two pots, big ones, and take them and give them to Death, and say to him that one does not beat a man with a throwing-knife, but one beats a man with tears. Let Death summon his people to come and weep into these pots, and if their tears fill these two pots, then you will beat the man with a throwing-knife.'

Ture went on his way and appeared at Death's home. Then he took two large pots and placed them before him and said to him thus: 'Master, Death, one does not beat a man with water, I beat a man with tears. It were well that you should summon your people to come with you and they can weep into these two pots, and if you and your people's tears fill them I will beat your man with these tears as a fine throwing-knife, one so beautiful that you will not be able to put it down.' Death then summoned all his people, those who came with him. They bowed their heads over the pots and they wept in vain, for their tears did not at all fill the pots and scarcely covered the bottoms of them. Death rose with his followers and returned to his home, for Ture had got the better of him. Death had told Ture that he must beat a man with a throwing-knife for him; if Ture did not do so he would kill him right away. However, Ture got the better of him by trickery.

55. *Ture, Leopard, and Cricetus* (R. R.)

THERE was once a man called Leopard, who had a cultivation of ground-nuts. Now he went to the cultivations where he found Cricetus and thought it was Squirrel. So he seized him, and when he struck him he showed his teeth. When Leopard saw them he asked 'Who sharpened your teeth?' He replied to Leopard 'I myself sharpened them.' Leopard said 'Sharpen mine please.' He replied 'When I sharpen (teeth) the person lies down on his back and I hammer (stakes into) him. After that I sharpen his teeth.' Leopard said 'All right, I want you to hammer (stakes into) me.' So Cricetus began to hammer (stakes into) Leopard. When Cricetus had hammered Leopard he wandered off without doing the sharpening. So Leopard stayed on the ground for many days. Then he saw Iguana, who was searching for his snails, and he said to Iguana 'O my friend, release me.' Iguana released Leopard.

After that Leopard gave a feast. Everybody came to it. Now Ture for his part went there also. On his way he saw Cricetus. So Cricetus said to Ture 'O my friend, you hide me in your bag, because Leopard hates me.' So Ture put him in his bag. They went to the feast. As they arrived there the people started to dance vigorously, and Ture danced also for his part. As he danced he sang this song:

> 'Drum, Cricetus, bag,
> Drum, Cricetus,
> What is Cricetus who split bone
> *Kamuruka*?'

So they danced vigorously, and Ture danced with Cricetus in

his bag, and as he danced Cricetus sounded in the bag *kpusakpusa kpusakpusa*. So they said they would kill Cricetus. So when the time came Cricetus began to eat through the bottom of the bag, and when they came to kill Cricetus he jumped down from the bag. They chased Cricetus hard. Cricetus ran and ran and jumped into a hole. So they asked 'Who is going to wait at the entrance there?' Now they said that Owl should wait at the entrance to the hole. Now Owl was eating his salt. Cricetus said 'O master, give me salt for me to eat, for when I come to die they will give you my guts, and you will find that it has increased.' So Owl gave it to him, and he ate it. As he was eating it Owl opened his eyes. Cricetus then spat the salt into them, and as Owl fell back Cricetus rushed out of the hole. When they came and found Owl waiting at the entrance they dug into the hole but looked there in vain. They said to him 'Owl where is Cricetus?' Owl kept silence. So he flew on to a mahogany tree, such a huge mahogany tree. They started to chop it down, they chopped and chopped, and their hands were worn away, and they all died.

56. *Ture and Bativogo* (R. R.)

THERE was once a man whose name was Bativogo. He called himself thus because his home was in the midst of many *vogo* trees.[1] But this man had no wife at all, he just lived by himself. However, when guests came to his home he gave them hospitality. He left them in his home and went to beneath his *vogo* trees, for he had already swept everywhere beneath them. He came and arrived beneath his *vogo* trees, and he began to sing his song which he used to sing. Then all foods appeared before him. This is that song:

'You swing from branch to branch on the top of the *vogo*,
You swing from branch to branch on the top of the *vogo o*,
Bativogo o bewails his father,
Swing on top of the *vogo*.
When I look up *vogo* fruits break, falling *kpa*,
Swing on top of the *vogo*.

[1] A very tall tree found by streams.

It falls into my eyes, my eyes break up,
Swing on top of the *vogo*.
I i i i, swing on top of the *vogo*.'

When he had finished this song one of the fruits of the *vogo*
broke off above and fell straight into one of his eyes and bruised
it and water gushed out of the eye. When he looked behind
him he saw many foods around him, cooked porridge and fine
meats, because he lay on his back on the ground and looked
above, singing his song. When the fruit at once broke off to
injure his eye, then, as he glanced behind him, he saw all the
foods he desired. He arose and collected this fine porridge and
those fine meats and took them to his guests, since he had no
wife to prepare food for him. This astonished the many people
who came to visit him. Many people knew about him and
heard about this affair of his. Some people went by stealth to
beneath the *vogo* trees and attempted in vain to do what
he did, for no food whatsoever appeared for them. People
assembled at his home every day to eat there plenty of food.

Then Ture heard about him. Ture slept, and at crack of
dawn he went and arrived at Bativogo's home. He saluted Ture
and offered him a stool and he seated himself upon it. Then he
went and arrived beneath his *vogo* trees, and he lay on the
ground with his chin pointing upwards, and he began to sing
his song as I[1] sang it before. A *vogo* fruit broke off above and fell,
fell into his eye and blinded it, and then when he looked behind
him he saw many foods. However, his eye was not blinded for
good. It soon became sound again. He collected together these
things and took them to Ture. Ture said to him 'O my mother's
brother, you teach me the medicine with which you do this
thing.' He replied to him that he would do so, but let him eat
his meal first. Ture ate his food quickly. He then said to him
'O my mother's brother, you give me this magic.' This man
replied to Ture 'Let us go to look for the medicine.' The two of
them went off together. Then he told Ture that he should halt
in a certain place. He halted. This man then dug up the
medicines for Ture and gave them to him, and also taught him
all the song. Ture returned home. He said to his wives that they
should all come to see this marvellous thing he had brought

[1] The narrator.

back from his maternal uncles. They all came to see what Ture wanted to show them. He lay on his back on the ground and he sang that song he had heard on the lips of Bativogo. He sang it in vain, for a *vogo* fruit did not at all break off and injure one of his eyes. His wives then chased him away. He fled to Bativogo's home and spoke thus to him: 'O my maternal uncle, what have you done to me thus? Why did you not give me good medicines?' He replied to him, let him come to get other medicines to return home with them. So Ture summoned all his wives to come and watch again. He lay on his back on the ground and sang his song bravely. When he stopped singing, a *vogo* fruit at once detached itself above and struck him in the eye and blinded it; but he did not turn correctly,[1] so he looked in vain, for no food appeared at all, just his eye remained blinded. His wives then chased him from home, telling him that he was a cheat and was never to come there again. So Ture at once fled, and he wandered off to a different country. That is the end of the story.

57. *How Ture was saved by his dogs* (R. R.)

THERE was a woman who bore a daughter. Now many men came to marry her, for she was very beautiful. But her mother summoned men for her work, and when a man had come she sharpened her big knife to a keen blade, and then when he fell asleep she cut his throat with her big knife, and when he was dead she cut up his flesh and cooked it and ate it all up. Then Ture arose also for his part to go and take (marry) this girl from her mother. Now he collected his two dogs, one called Karawandikiri and the other called Ngbanguru. Now this woman summoned Ture for work. He went with his dogs. So she prepared a meal for him and told his wife to make ready a hut for sleep. She swept beneath a new hut and built up a fire in it. When it was dark Ture went inside with his dogs and his wife. When all chatting had ceased this old woman got up in her hut, took her big knife, and came and entered Ture's hut. Then his dogs sprang at her to chase her and bit her buttocks, and she fled and fell into her hut.

[1] He should have turned his head very quickly as Bativogo did—hence no food.

Then when it was light she said to him 'O husband of my child, my honey which I have found, go and get it out for me.' So Ture got up, his wife got up, and his mother-in-law got up and took her axe. Now when Ture's dogs got up she said to Ture that he must take them back because they disliked her. Then she told Ture that he must shut the door firmly and tie it up against them. Ture did so, and then they went into the bush. They arrived at this nest and she pointed out to him the tree, a tall one. When he had climbed up this tree and got high up on it the old woman began to chop it down, saying 'I chop the tree, chop the tree, *rokporokpo*.'[1] So Ture called to these dogs, saying 'Karawandikiri o, Ngbanguru o, my father's dogs I am dying.' So they tore down the door of the hut quickly and ran with all speed. Now when the woman heard Ture calling his dogs she set to with a will at the tree, and she put another axe in the hands of her daughter, and as her daughter chopped at the tree she cried out, saying

> 'I chop a fine man with my hand,
> I chop a fine man with my hand.'

The dogs ran and ran and when they saw her chopping down the tree they tore her to pieces, and so Ture's wife was saved. Then Ture began to climb down and he took his wife and his dogs, and he and his wife returned home. So Ture married this girl whose mother was always killing men on her account. And that is the end of the story.

58. *Ture and Leopard's fruit* (Kamanga–E-P.)

TURE arose and took his bag and wandered off on and on and went to find Leopard's fruit, and, avoiding Leopard, he climbed up and picked it into the bag; and he went on picking it and then rose and went home, on and on till he reached home. His mother cooked the fruits in water and when she had cooked them she poured out Ture's portion and gave it to him. She then ate her portion and left what was left over in the pot. The mother of little Cricetus arose and came to Ture's home and came and looked into the pot and saw the food there, and she

---

[1] The sound of the axe on the trunk of the tree.

took it and ate it and then wrapped up (in leaves) what was
left over and went home with it and appeared before Cricetus
in the home. When she put it down, little Cricetus jumped up at
his mother and tore open the leaves and took it from her and
ate it. His mother said 'You eat it! Is it not your friend Ture
over there who picks it?' He replied 'Mother, you be quiet, I
shall go tomorrow morning to my friend to pick it.'

So as it became light he arose, did little Cricetus, and went on
his way, and when he arrived at Ture's home he took his big
billhook, and Ture took his. They went on their way to a rock.
Ture took his and sharpened it, and little Cricetus sharpened
his. Ture then said 'Oh!' Ture then said again to him 'My friend,
your mother is calling.' Little Cricetus departed with all speed,
and then Ture, in his absence, took his billhook and went to
blunt the edges of it on the rocks. He blunted the edge of his
billhook altogether. Little Cricetus then came running up.

They went on and on and on and arrived there. Ture said
'My friend I cut mine *nzi* and take it to the hole (in the tree),
and you cut yours *gbu*[1] sitting on the tree to drop it into the bag.'
Leopard came and saw little Cricetus. Ture had before told
him 'My friend, when we come I cut mine *nzi* and take it to the
hollow, you cut yours *gbu* and sit with it on the tree. If Leopard
comes and questions you up above you tell him that you are
alone.' So Leopard arrived and asked him up above 'Who are
you who eat my fruit?' When Leopard asked him little Cricetus
replied that it was he. Leopard said 'You climb down.' Cricetus
climbed down and down and down till he reached Leopard,
who sprang at him and seized little Cricetus and began to eat
him and he went on eating him. Then Ture stood up above and
said 'You eat him but cut off the head for me and I will bring
another one tomorrow.' Leopard ate him but cut off his head
and gave it to Ture. Ture got up to take it home and he returned home and entered it and put down his fruit, and then he
went to the home of the mother of little Cricetus and said to
her 'My friend has gone to inspect his game-hole, and he asked
me to bring back this animal's head.'[2]

So his mother took it and then kindled a big fire and took a

---

[1] *Nzi* is the sound of the well-bladed billhook, *gbu* of the blunted one.

[2] *Kerepai* is the head of an animal with *bingba* grass tied round it as a sign that it
is claimed by a blood-brother of the owner of the beast.

pot and put it on the fire and began to slice off the meat into it. As she sliced it he said '*Hu!* The woman slices her son's head.' She said to him 'What is that sir?' Ture said to her 'Nothing, mother of my friend, I was just saying how well the mother of my friend knows how to cook meat.' It boiled and then she took it off the fire and put in some salt and then tasted her son's head and ate it. Ture said 'The woman eats her son's head o!' She said to him 'What is that sir?' He replied 'Nothing, mother of my friend, I was just saying how well you know how to cook meat.' Then she put a pot of porridge on the fire and then divided her son's head, and when she had taken her portion she tied up (in banana leaves) Ture's; and she cooked the porridge and broke off her portion and broke off Ture's. She took Ture's and brought it and placed it before him. Ture washed his hands and sat down and waited by the side of his portion. She broke off some of hers and tasted the flesh of her son's head and put it in her mouth. He said '*Hu!* the woman eats her son o!' She said to him 'What is that sir?' He replied 'Oh, I was just saying does not the mother of my friend know how to cook meat!' She broke off some more porridge and tasted it with some of her son's head, and then Ture at once jumped up saying loudly (not as before in a whisper) 'The woman has eaten her son's head o!' As she cried out and wailed loudly Ture dashed forward and stole her food. He then dropped it into his bag. So Ture made off with all speed, dashing to his mother's home where he sat down to a meal of little Cricetus's head and he went on eating it till he had finished it, and then he got up again and went after these fruits and picked them into his bag and brought them home. His mother cooked them.

The mother of little Bushbuck arose and came and arrived at Ture's home, and she took them off the fire and ate them, and she wrapped what little was left and returned home with it. Little Bushbuck snatched it from his mother and sat down to eat it, and as he ate it she said 'You just eat it while your friend over there is always picking it.' Little Bushbuck said 'Be quiet mother, I am going tomorrow after Ture to pick the fruit.'

Early next morning he took his billhook and went on and on until he arrived at Ture's home, and he said to Ture 'Let us be going to pick our fruit.' Ture got up and they went on until they reached the country in between streams. Ture brought out his billhook, and little Bushbuck brought out his from his bag. Ture said 'Oho!' He said 'Friend, your mother is calling you.' Little Bushbuck said 'What could my mother be calling me about, since before I left I told her that I was going after my friend, going to pick our fruit?' They got up from the rock and continued on their way, when Ture said again 'O friend! your mother is calling you.' Little Bushbuck said 'Friend, you are being nasty with me today, for I already told my mother I was going on a journey.' Ture said to him 'O friend, you are determined to be angry with me today in the bush.' They resumed their walk and went on and on till they arrived. Then they climbed up on high. Little Bushbuck took his bag and filled it at the side of the tree. Ture said to him 'I cut mine *nzi* so I will sit with them in the tree hollow, you cut yours *nzi* and will sit at the side of the tree.' Little Bushbuck said 'Not at all, you cut yours *nzi* and you go with it into the hollow, and I cut mine *nzi* and I shall sit with it at the entrance to the hollow.' Ture said 'O friend, what an unpleasant character you have!' Ture said to him 'When Leopard comes to inquire, whom will you tell Leopard you are up with?' Little Bushbuck replied that he would tell him that he was up above with Ture. Ture said 'O friend, so! I knew about your tricks before.' Leopard came and asked 'Who are you who eat my fruit?' Little Bushbuck said it was he. Leopard then asked 'Whom are you with up there?' Ture said to him 'Friend, say that you are up above by yourself.' Little Bushbuck said 'I am up above with Ture.' Ture said 'Friend, what trickery!' Leopard said 'You and Ture descend.'

Little Bushbuck got up and climbed down the side of the trunk of the tree and so Leopard seized him. When Leopard seized him he snarled. When Leopard saw his very white teeth Leopard said 'Who filed your teeth?' He replied that he himself filed them. Leopard asked him to file his. He told Leopard that when he filed his he went to cut big stakes and hammered them into his hands. Leopard told him to do the same to his. He went and cut the stakes. Little Bushbuck then brought them and hammered one into Leopard's front paw and then he hammered another into his other front paw, and then he hammered one into his hind paw, hammered it into his hind paw, and hammered another into his other hind paw also, and then ran away from Leopard as fast as he could and went on running till he reached home.

Tortoise arose, he and Iguana, and they wandered off. Tortoise said 'Iguana o, when you find mushrooms call me Iguana o.' Iguana for his part said 'Tortoise o, when you find snails call me.' They went on their way and found Leopard as little Bushbuck had hammered his paws. He asked Tortoise to come and pull these things out of his paws. Tortoise came and pulled the stake out of his paw. Then he scratched Tortoise. Tortoise cried out '*Hu u!* You are scratching me.' Leopard said 'My friend, my paw hurts.' He pulled out another stake. He pulled out one in his hind paw and then the one in the other hind paw. Leopard thanked Tortoise and ran off; and Tortoise fell into a pool.

Leopard went by the side of the river and caught the leg of Tortoise. Tortoise said he had not caught his leg but a shadow. So he let go of his real leg. Leopard then got up to go home and went on his way till he reached home, where he told his wives to take up bowls. They collected bowls. They arrived at this pool and began to bale out the water and after baling for a time they saw Tortoise and took him. Tortoise said let him hear what he had to say. Tortoise said to Leopard that he should take a pot and sit with it downstream: 'Take a big knife and put it on your leg.' Leopard took Tortoise and put him on his leg and raised the big knife on high. But as he was about to chop into Tortoise, Tortoise jumped into the water again and Leopard cut into his thigh and sustained a nasty wound, and he cried out to the women at the side of the river that they should not draw water, it was his blood. The women desisted. Leopard returned home with his wound.

59. *Ture and Kpikoro*[1] (R. R.)

THERE was a man called Kpikoro, who possessed many termite mounds. Now when morning rain fell he went to clean his mounds. Now Ture came for his part also and found that Kpikoro had prepared all his mounds, so Ture asked him 'O

[1] See footnote on p. 75.

son of my mother's brother, will you please give me just one
mound?' So Kpikoro gave Ture some three termite mounds.
When night came they went after the termites. Now Kpikoro's
termites swarmed in great numbers. But when Ture looked at
his they had hardly perforated the mound at all. So Ture began
to detest Kpikoro. So when the termites came out of their runs
Ture thought to pick a quarrel with Kpikoro. So he began to
pull Kpikoro's head round (to provoke him). So it got worse
and they hated each other. Then Ture snatched up his big
stick and hit Kpikoro with the head of it. Kpikoro fell with
deceit to the ground like a corpse.

Then Ture was afraid because he thought Kpikoro might be
dead. So Ture went to fetch water to wash Kpikoro's face, but
he did not revive. So it was; and as it terrified him he picked
up his bags and baskets and started off with all speed. He ran
for a very short while and then Kpikoro began to revive. So
Kpikoro told his wives to wail. When Ture heard the wailing
of the women he made off as fast as his legs could carry him. As
soon as he reached home he said to Nanzagbe 'O my wife, I
have killed their husband Kpikoro at the termites.' Now while
Ture was doing these things Kpikoro was catching his termites.
After Kpikoro had finished catching termites he began to
gather the termites into a basket. When they were all in the
basket he carried them home. Now as he walked quickly his
feet sounded *zizizizi*. Ture called his wife Nanzagbe and told
her to question that man who was walking outside. When she
inquired, saying 'Who are you who walk outside?' Kpikoro
himself replied to her 'It is I who am going to the home of the
dead Kpikoro. Ture killed him before the termite mound.'
Then Ture excreted (in fear) on Nanzagbe's mat and it smelt
horribly. He said to her 'O my wife, hide me.' She placed a
basket over him. Now after a short time Kpikoro came again
with his termites and the sound of his feet sounded *zizizizi*,
and when Ture's wife inquired of him, Kpikoro replied again,
saying 'I am he who is going to the home of the dead Kpikoro;
Ture killed him at the termites.' So Ture dashed off with all
speed and removed everything and also what was in the
granaries. So early next morning Ture saw a man coming from
Kpikoro's home. Ture inquired of him, and he told Ture that
Kpikoro was not dead, he had deceived him. So Ture lacked

termites. So it was that Kpikoro was a cheat. That is why he was called Kpikoro.[1]

60. *Ture and the Orphan* (R. R.)

THERE was once an orphan, and he set many snares in the fallow of cultivations. Then Ture came along and saw these snares with many birds in them and he took them all. Early the following morning Ture came and saw many birds caught in the boy's snares. While he was loosening them from one direction, Orphan for his part was loosening them from the opposite direction, and when he and Ture met he asked Ture 'Why are you collecting my guinea-fowl?' Ture abused him, asking him what he thought he was doing there. They quarrelled. Then the boy put his hand in his bag and took out his little (magic) whistle, which was an animal's horn.[2] When he blew it Ture began to fly upwards. Then, when the boy stopped blowing the animal's horn, he sang this song:

> 'Wa zagbo, wa zagbo, wa zagbo,
> Wa zagbo, wa zagbo, wa zagbo.'[3]

As he spoke these words Ture fell down on to a tree-stump and sustained a nasty wound.

When the boy became silent Ture darted off to run to Nanzagbe, who was that wife of his who knew trickery as well as he. He said to her 'O Nanzagbe, go quickly and collect our animals from the snares.' In such a manner he was always deceiving Nanzagbe. Nanzagbe arose and made herself ready and she painted herself carefully with red dye. She went and arrived at the snares and she saw many birds caught in them. She bent down to loosen them. The owner of the snares saw her loosening the birds. He said to her 'Hey you, woman! What are you loosening my birds for?' He went after her and abused her. He took his little (magic) animal's horn out of his bag, and as he blew it Nanzagbe flew up on high right away. When he ceased to sing this song, which is

---

[1] The name has the sense of somebody who appears to die easily.

[2] An animal's horn is frequently used in magic, often, as here, as a magical whistle.

[3] *Wa zagbo* is the sound made by something falling to the ground.

'*Wa zagbo, wa zagbo, wa zagbo,*
Wa zagbo, wa zagbo, wa zagbo',

she came down with her rump on a tree-stump and she was wounded just as Ture was wounded.

Ture told the children of the homestead that when Nanzagbe came home they were to shout, saying 'Mother is coming, mother is coming.' She came on her way and when she arrived at the bank of earth around the courtyard the children cried out 'Mother is coming.' Ture bounded out of his hut and departed in all haste. She chased him in vain, for she lost sight of him.

61. *Ture and Nguali*[1] (R. R.)

THERE was once a man whose name was Nguali. Now there was a river so great that no one could swim across it; but on the other side were many yams. Nguali arose and stretched his entrails over this river and they reached the other side. Ture arose and went with Nguali, and so they went and Nguali said to Ture that he should take hold of his entrails and they would together soar above the river. Ture took hold of Nguali's entrails and they soared above the water and landed on the other side. They dug up many yams and their bag was full. Then Nguali stretched his entrails again as before and they soared above the water and went home.

Then Nguali sent his son to Ture, saying to him 'When you go, tell Ture to come early tomorrow morning, but should he say anything, whatever he first says, you come and tell me the same.' So Nguali's son went and spoke what his father had said, saying 'Father said you are to come tomorrow to go with him to dig up yams.' Ture replied to the boy thus: 'That stinking gut of your father, tell him that I will come tomorrow.' So this boy returned home to his father and said to his father 'Father, Ture said "that stinking gut of yours, he will come tomorrow".' Nguali took great offence at this remark.

So when day broke they began to go after their yams. Nguali stretched his intestines over the water and they soared to

---

[1] *Nguali* is a name for the vulture.

beyond it. When Nguali arrived on the other side he dug up
his yams quickly and his bag was soon full. After that he began
to excrete and, having excreted, to bury the dung, saying to it
'If Ture calls out it is for you to answer.' So Nguali went home.
Ture dug up his yams and his bag was full. Then when he
called out, Nguali's dung answered him. He began to call, crying
out, saying 'Nguali, my friend, where are you?' Only the dung
of Nguali went on answering. When it was like that dusk fell
and Ture could find no fire anywhere, and there were only
raw yams in his bag. So when it was light he went and arrived
at the home of a man called Thunder. His daughter was there,
for she was unmarried. So Ture hid among the banana trees.
This man Thunder, people did not visit his home. Therefore
Ture hid himself in the midst of the banana trees. Then Ture
sent a grasshopper to this woman. The grasshopper flew and
arrived and settled on her ear, and she struck it, and it flew
away. Another one came and tapped her on the head and then
also flew away to where Ture was. This woman began to go to
where Ture was hidden. So she saw Ture, and he much
pleased her.

Now, because this man Thunder used to kill people, she gave
Ture thunder medicines. Now Thunder had been in the cultivations and when he returned and was near the home he smelt
Ture, a smell just like a man on earth here. He said 'Who is it
who smells just like a man on earth?' Then he exploded just
like a gun and he lifted up Ture on high and threw him violently
to the ground. Ture broke into small bits; and then Ture
lifted Thunder up on high and threw him violently to the
ground. So when Thunder understood that Ture had eaten
their medicines he left him alone. So it was that Thunder said
about it to Ture 'This daughter of mine, I have said that only
that man who comes here and does not die, the same can marry
her.' Her father said to Ture thus: that for two days he would
let him go with his wife to his home. Thus her father spoke to
Ture: 'When you return with your wife, this drum here, when
you return, as soon as you descend to the earth you must beat
the drum.' So Ture donned his feathered hat and his wife
carried a basket and they descended, and as they approached
the earth Ture began to beat the drum. After that this woman
returned on high again. Ture descended just by himself, for

he was not able to rise on high again. That is the end of the story.

62. *Ture's failure with his termites* (L.)

TURE and Nanzagbe settled down in their homestead as they had done before. They led their daily life together, and the season of termites arrived. Nanzagbe departed and made ready her termite mound, and Ture departed and made ready his mound also. The rain of termites fell and Nanzagbe went and broke off her stubble (for torches), and she swept clean the front of her mound. When that was finished she tied up her stubble and carried it on her head. So she came with this stubble and returned home, and she dried it in the sun, and while it was drying she sat down.

Ture got up and departed and cleaned the front of his mound also. He broke off his stubble also. When he had done that he bound up the stubble and brought it home with him and poured it on the ground in the sun, and while it was drying he sat down. He and Nanzagbe waited till evening came. Then as Ture bound up his torches Nanzagbe bound up hers also; they bound up all the stubble. That being finished, they waited.

Dusk came and they remained outside for a long time. When the time approached for the termites to swarm Nanzagbe said to Ture that she was going after her termites. Ture replied that he was also going after his. Nanzagbe bound up her torches and carried them, and she took a basket, and she took a fire-log and she went on her way. Ture also bound up his torches, and he took his bag and hung it over his shoulder, and he carried his torches, and he took a fire-log and held it in his hand.

Ture went, arrived, and appeared before his termite mound. He put his torches on the ground and he lit a fire which flared up. He lighted his torches from the fire and went and inspected the holes made by the sentinels of the termites in preparation for their exit. They were indeed about to swarm. He put out his torch and he put some wood on the fire and when it flared up he went and broke off some leaves and spread them on the ground and he lay down on them. Sleep overtook him and he slept well.

While he was asleep all his termites escaped. When he awoke from sleep the termites had dispersed. He blew up the fire and it flamed, and he took a torch and lighted it, for he did not know that all the termites had flown away. So when Ture lit up to inspect the termites he saw only their wings strewn all around. Ture asked himself what he should do about this affair. Ture extinguished the torch and he went to the fire he had made. Ture took his bag and shouldered it and he took the path. He went on his way, went down into a stream and got wet through in the water, as did also his elephant-hide bag. He came out of the water and shook himself. When that was finished he continued on his way and arrived and appeared in the home where Nanzagbe was.

When he arrived home he called out strongly to Nanzagbe and Nanzagbe answered. Ture said '*Hi hi hi!* Nanzagbe, kindle a fire for me quickly, rain has saturated me on the other bank in truth.' Nanzagbe said nothing. Ture said further to Nanzagbe, did her termites not swarm? Nanzagbe replied to Ture 'Those termites you went to wait for, where are they?' Ture said to Nanzagbe thus: 'My termites did not swarm, they made their tunnels, I waited for them (to rise), they all made ready to swarm; and I thought they were about to swarm (take wing) when rain came down and they refused (to come out). So rain saturated me on the other side in truth. Look at my body as it is, I am completely soaked.' Nanzagbe heard it but said nothing.

They waited some time. Then another termites-rain rained, and Nanzagbe went and prepared her mound. That being done, she went and broke off her stubble, bound it up, and carried it; she came home and put down the stubble on the ground, and she undid the cord binding the stubble and spread it in the sun. Ture went and prepared his termite mound also. He broke off stubble and bound it up; he brought it home with him and he dried it in the sun, and when it was dry he waited. They waited till evening came, and then Nanzagbe tied together her torches, and when that was done Ture also tied together his torches.

They continued to wait. It became dusk and then people went after their termites. Nanzagbe said to Ture 'Since people have dispersed after termites, let us go after ours.' Ture said to

Nanzagbe 'Let us go.' Nanzagbe rose and took her basket, bound up her torches and carried them, and took a fire-log and held it in her hand. And so Nanzagbe went after her termites.

Ture rose and took his elephant-hide bag and put it over his shoulder. He went, arrived, and appeared before his termite mound. Ture put down his torches on the ground. He blew the fire on to the stubble and it flared, and he went and examined the termite-runs with it. The termites were indeed piercing their way out. He put out his torch and he put some wood on the fire and it flared fiercely, and he plucked leaves and spread them on the ground and lay down. Ture went on sleeping and while he was asleep the termites swarmed and indeed they flew. Then Ture awoke from sleep and he lit a torch and ran with it to the place of swarming. He raised the light in his hand and when he looked he saw the runs of the termites and the wings of the termites were there thick in the place of swarming. Ture said 'Now what shall I do?' Ture was most upset. Ture came before the fire which he had built up; Ture took his elephant-hide bag, put it over his shoulder and went on his way, and continued on his way and descended into the stream. Ture saturated himself in the water and then went on and crossed to the other side.

Ture continued on his way and arrived home where Nanzagbe was. Ture said to Nanzagbe that she should build up a fire for him quickly, rain had saturated him on the other side of the stream. Ture said further to Nanzagbe 'Did your termites rise?' Nanzagbe said to Ture 'You might well ask me, those termites, people are roasting them right now. How can a man ask about termites right now?' Ture said to Nanzagbe 'If it had not been for the rain I indeed would be roasting them now.' Nanzagbe said to Ture 'Since this rain of termites fell everybody is roasting termites, only you lack them, how did you wait for yours?' Ture replied to Nanzagbe, those termites, he had not gone to their place of swarming again because rain had made him miserable at their mound. Nanzagbe heard what he said and said nothing. They just sat around. This story is now finished.

63. *Ture and Wilimbia*[1] (R. R.)

THERE was a man called Wilimbia. Now the rain of termites began to fall heavily. So Wilimbia went after his termites. Now Ture also for his part went to await the termites. Now Wilimbia, after preparing his mound, curled himself up in a ball. When Ture saw him he raised his stick on high and hit Wilimbia with it. Then Wilimbia got up from the ground and raised his big stick and struck Ture hard with it. Then Ture raised his stick and struck Wilimbia hard with it. Wilimbia then raised his stick for his part and struck Ture with it. Then Ture lit a big fire and put Wilimbia in the fire. Then Wilimbia was all burnt. Then, when Ture took him out of the fire, he stuck to Ture's mouth, and Ture dashed off with all speed. Wilimbia chased him hard. So Ture wandered off. Wilimbia went to wait for his termites to swarm. And that was that.

64. *Ture and the two brothers* (R. R.)

THERE was a man who had two sons, the elder of whom married after the death of their father. Now their father was killed by buffaloes. So when the elder went to his in-laws he gave baked bread to his younger brother and told his younger brother to climb up to the granary. So when the younger climbed up into the granary his elder brother tied up the granary behind him, saying 'Child, child, let nobody deceive you; if anyone calls you, keep silent.' His younger brother agreed.

After his elder brother had departed after his wife as far as from Yambio here to Meridi,[2] Ture came to where this child was and called him in a whisper 'Son of my mother's brother.' The child kept silent. Then he started to entreat the lad, saying 'O son of my mother's brother, there is porridge, come let us go and eat it.' The lad kept silent. Ture then said 'I am going to set fire to that granary with you in it.' So the boy climbed

---

[1] *Wilimbia* could mean either 'little stone' or 'kidney'. The first is the more likely meaning.

[2] Yambio and Meridi are government posts, some eighty miles apart.

down from the granary, and Ture said to him 'Go to the track of the buffaloes, I am going to hunt them for you.' So the boy agreed. Then Ture began to shout at the buffaloes and when they started off with speed Ture cried out to the boy, saying 'O son of my maternal uncle, they are coming there, you spear one of them well.' But when the boy tried to spear one of them, a left-handed one, it took hold of him and ran off with him, and Ture tied up his leg with *ndakari*[1] and cried out, saying '*Ndakari*, let me go, the son of my uncle is dying! *Ndakari*, let me go, the son of my uncle is dying!' Then this buffalo went off with the boy as far as the Bodo river, and the boy cried out in appeal to his elder brother Kirinzoro, saying 'Kirinzoro, Kirinzoro, *ayana*[2] Kirinzoro, big buffalo has gone with me, Kirinzoro *ayana*.' Kirinzoro heard the cry of his father's son and set off with all speed, taking his spear in his hand. The big buffalo went off with the boy as quickly as it could to their lair where they lived. Kirinzoro ran at full speed and as he got near, it also approached their lair. Now when it arrived and was about to enter the lair with the boy the elder brother bounded forward and tried to spear it but missed, and it entered into its den, and his younger brother jumped down from its head. So Kirinzoro took him and they returned to their home.

Then the elder brother again baked bread for him and again set out to visit his in-laws. So he said to his young brother 'Don't let anyone deceive you again.' The younger agreed. So, when he left, Ture turned up again for his part and said to the boy 'Son of my maternal uncle, come and let us go and eat our hens' eggs which I have, I son of Ture's father.' The boy climbed down to go after Ture again. So Ture said 'Go child, to the buffaloes' tracks, I am going to hunt them for you, and you spear one of them hard.' So Ture went and shouted at the buffaloes and when they ran towards the boy Ture cried out to him, saying 'They are coming there, son of my maternal uncle e!' When the boy tried to spear one of them with his spear it took him up on its head and went off with him, and the boy cried out, yelling, saying 'Kirinzoro, Kirinzoro,

---

[1] *Ndakari* is a plant in which people's legs get entangled. Ture was just pretending to have got entangled so that he had an excuse for not helping the boy.

[2] *Ayana* is a cry of distress.

Kirinzoro *ayana*, Kirinzoro, big buffalo has taken me away, Kirinzoro *ayana*.' So Kirinzoro ran till he was exhausted, and when Kirinzoro got there, it was entering its den. So, they cut up this child.[1]

65. *Ture and the old hoe* (G. 1926)

TURE went to prepare his termite mound and found a hoe in a hole there. He took this hoe and threw it into his bag and went off with it. The owners of the hoe came and did not see it. They called out to the hoe, saying 'Worn-out hoe o! Where are you?' It replied 'I am with Ture o!' Then Ture beat his breast and said to it 'Don't talk.' They called out to it again and it shouted back as before. Ture said 'Ha! Ha! Don't talk.' When it went on talking Ture started to run as hard as he could and ran and ran. The owners of the hoe called out again, saying 'Worn-out hoe!' And it cried out 'I am here!' Ture hastened to throw it away and then went on running to get away. Then the owners of the hoe took it and went away with it.

Ture then went again and saw a man who was an orphan who was eating red ground-fruits. He said 'My nape, my nape, my nape, I have swallowed with a gulp, I scraped the back of my head, it sounded *waa* (fizzy), I have swallowed with a gulp.' And as it was delicious to him so it was delicious in the throat of Ture. Then Ture cried out loudly, saying 'You give it to me, how sweet it is!' Orphan said to him 'I am a poor man, you eat yours, I am only eating mine.' Ture then got up and chased him vigorously and he ran away hard and jumped into a hole in the ground.

Ture then went to consult the poison oracle and asked it 'What shall I do to take this good thing?' The poison oracle answered 'You make just a slippery thing at the entrance to his hole.' When he had gone to eat food Ture did as the witch-doctors[2] told him. Then Ture went and saw him eating

---

[1] The sense here seems to be that the boy was dead and they cut him up for meat, like an animal. It is not clear who 'they' were; probably the buffaloes. The word *mbakada* could have the sense of 'restored'.

[2] There appears to be some confusion here. The poison oracle is not usually mentioned in the tales. Also, we have just been told that Ture consulted the poison

something, and Ture said 'You bad thing, always eating a good thing. I am going to spear you.' Ture then chased him vigorously. Orphan ran hard and reached his entrance and as he fell his salt fell to Ture and all his nice things.

66. *How Ture saved a child who fled from Man-eater* (F. G.)

THERE was an old woman named Man-eater and with her her brother's son Orphan, a small child whose parents had died long ago. She had taken care of him. The home of the old woman was beyond a great river in the wilderness and no one lived near her. All her life her meat was only the flesh of children who strayed from their parents and went and appeared in her home. She would take such a child and look after him till he was grown, when she cut his throat with her large knife and then ate the child with her oil of *kpagu*[1] and *bangumbe*[2] and *detiro*[3] and sesame. Such were her oils (for cooking). That large knife of hers was as long as two paces and its blade was as sharp as a razor's edge; if a fly were to settle on its edge it would have its legs cut off.

A little girl strayed from her parents and they searched for her in vain and they forgot about her, thinking that she must be dead. This child went on and arrived there where this old woman was and she said to the child 'You are my child.' The child lived with the old woman for four years. Then the old woman thought the time had come to eat the child without the child's knowing that she ate people. The day came and she collected the oil-bearing cucurbit *kpagu* and gave it to the child to shell, and she collected the oil-bearing cucurbit *bangumbe* also for her to shell, and she collected *detiro* and sesame for the child to pound and refine. The girl did all these things and it was finished. Other things, thus. Then the old woman collected eleusine and gave it to this child to dry over a bottomless pot and then pound it and winnow it and grind it into flour for making porridge. The old woman left the child with this work

oracle (*benge*), so the reference to witch-doctors (*abinza*) is not clear.
[1] *Lagenaria vulgaria.*   [2] *Luffa* sp.   [3] *Citrullus vulgaris.*

and went to her cultivations, which were a short distance away, to work in her cultivations.

No one was allowed to go round to the back of the hut of this old woman, that is to say, those children she was wont to eat, lest they might see the bones of their fellows which she used to throw there, for then they would take flight and she would lose her meat.

The child put the drying-pot on the fire, gathered up the eleusine in a flat basket and put it on top of the pot to dry, and then she would pound it. That orphan who lived there was hungry and he took a switch and went to beat his insects, grass-hoppers, to bring them back and roast and eat them. He went and struck them down and brought them back, and he scattered a little to the side some of the embers beneath the pot and poured the grasshoppers on them. The girl scolded him, saying 'What are you scattering the fire for beneath my mother's eleusine?' She gathered up the grasshoppers from the fire and threw them into the grass. Orphan was very sad and bowed his head, just looking down at the ground in his sadness for his insects, thinking that he might have eaten them to assuage his hunger. He raised his head and looked into the face of the girl and saw her and bowed his head again towards the ground, and he spoke to her in a soft voice, saying to her 'Ah! Well! What I might tell you I will not tell you because you have killed me by throwing my food into the grass when it might have saved me.' When the girl heard what he said she ran quickly to the grass into which she had thrown his insects and when she found them she gathered all of them up and brought them and roasted them and when they were cooked she removed all the husks, added salt to them, and gave them to him. Then he ate them and ate them all and drank water and belched, *bouu*. Then he said to her 'Those seeds of *kpagu* and *bangumbe*, it is oil for you, that with which they are going to eat you; that *detiro* and that sesame you are pounding and refining, it is oil for you; that eleusine you are drying, it is porridge for you, with which they are going to eat you. If you think I am telling you a lie go and have a look behind the hut, you will see skulls there of people we have eaten with grandmother and have thrown there.' When the girl heard this speech she got up, leaving the eleusine over the fire, and went behind the hut, and when she

looked she saw people's skulls thick on the ground and bones
of their legs and arms were all over the place. She came back in
haste from the back of the hut to where Orphan was and said
to him 'I am going to collect some dry twigs for the eleusine
and will be right back to pound the eleusine and winnow it and
grind it to flour.'

The day advanced quickly, whew (*wuu*)! The girl escaped
with all speed to the side of the river. Now this old woman had
a cock which stayed in the chicken-house and did not go outside. She fed it on human flesh, right in the chicken-house. This
cock looked outside for the girl in vain, for it did not see her, and
it did not hear so much as a word from her, and so it knew that
the girl had gone off for good. It cried out, opened its beak and
shrieked

'That head of yours, ah! I wish I had eaten it!
Those ears of yours, ah! I wish I had eaten them!
Those eyes of yours, ah! I wish I had eaten them!
That mouth of yours, ah! I wish I had eaten it!
Our person has escaped oo!
Kokoryoko, koo, ah!'

The words of the cock most softly[1] reached the ears of the old
woman. The old woman left off her work and stood straight up
and turned her ear to the message. While she listened again the
cock cried out

'That heart of yours, ah! I wish I had eaten it!
That belly of yours, ah! I wish I had eaten it!
Those thighs of yours, ah! I wish I had eaten them!
Our person has escaped oo!
Kokoryoko, ah!'

The old woman now heard it correctly. She took her large
knife and dashed from the cultivation and as she almost flew
to get on top of things she leapt with such giddy speed as she
had never known! Not even speech could keep pace with her
precipitation to her home, and she asked Orphan in a high
voice, saying 'That girl who was here, where is she?' Orphan
said 'She went to get firewood at the side of the river there.'
The old woman began to run in truth to chase after this girl as

---

[1] The Zande word is *firifiri*, which Fr. Giorgetti translates *sottilissimamente*.

though she was shaving the earth. When she looked ahead she saw that the girl was running with all speed, far, far, in a cloud of dust; and when the old woman saw her thus she strove with all her strength after the girl and as she approached her she raised her large knife on high to cut into the child, to sever her with a single stroke. The child at once moved and threw herself into the water and escaped under the water, and the old woman did not see her again. The old woman flipped her fingers in fury, *guda*, *guda*, *guda*, and then she went home with this speech in her mouth: 'Alas! Alas! I indeed lack meat. That child is the child of a wild cat (witch). No matter! I will find another person in her place.'

The child went on and on, always under the water and when she was far away she came out of the water on the other side of the river near her country. Having got there she sat in a stream-side wood (gallery forest) near water there and began to think about the matter thus: 'Where shall I find a person among those people of the country there? What shall I do to find a person? Alas! What shall I do by myself in this riverside wood?' While she was reflecting on the matter thus, Ture was thinking about cord for his net; how he might cut it at the side of that river, that is, the cord called *wido*.[1] He, Ture, came and began to cut his cord at the entrance to this riverside wood in which the child sat. Ture cut his cord, *gbuu*, *gbuu*, *gbuu*. The child heard the sound of a person and she thought to herself 'Who has caused a person to cut wood here? What good fortune is thus mine!' She opened her lips and cried out

> 'Cutter of *wido* o! Cutter of *wido* o, sir!
> Cutter of *wido* o! Cutter of *wido* o, sir!
> Cutter of *wido* o!
> Tell my mother I am saved.
> Cutter of *wido* o!
> Tell my father I am here.
> Cutter of *wido* o!
> Tell my kinsmen I was lost.
> Cutter of *wido* o!
> Why when I speak
> Do you keep completely silent, without a word?'

[1] A plant of the *Euphorbiaceae–Manniophyton africanum*. Cord is made from its bark.

Ture heard this speech and moved ahead and cut his cord, *gbuu, gbuu, gbuu*. The child cried

'Cutter of *wido* o! Cutter of *wido* o, sir!
Cutter of *wido* o!
Tell my mother to cook (porridge).
Cutter of *wido* o!
Tell my mother to roast (manioc).
Cutter of *wido* o!
Tell my mother to prepare (food) for me.
Cutter of *wido* o!
Why when I speak
Do you keep completely silent, without a word?'

Ture moved further ahead because he wanted to see the person who sang this song, and he cut cord, *gbuu, gbuu, gbuu*. She cried out again

'Cutter of *wido* o! Cutter of *wido* o, sir!
Cutter of *wido* o!
Tell my mother (to cook) sweet potatoes.
Cutter of *wido* o!
Tell my mother to cook (meat).
Cutter of *wido* o!
Tell my mother to cook (food).
Cutter of *wido* o!
Why when I speak
Do you keep completely silent, without a word?'

Ture came quickly to beside the girl and seized her hand vigorously and asked her 'Where do you come from into this riverside wood here?' Complete silence. The child did not speak. Ture asked her again, saying 'Ah, child! Whose daughter are you?' Complete silence. 'Where do you come from?' Complete silence. 'Who is your father?' Complete silence. The child did not speak again. Ture took her and went with her to his home and gave her food. While she ate it he wandered off over the countryside to ask people about which person had lost a child. He went round questioning thus many times until he found the parents of the child. They came and saw her and recognized her, and they took her and returned with her to their home to feed her with every kind of food. Meanwhile her parents questioned her about where she had gone away to. The child was altogether silent, never a word.

Getting nothing out of her in speech her father went off to the *Atari* oracle and struck the oracle on the head. The oracle fell into the fire and boiled over frothily.[1] The child's father was terrified and he fled with all speed. When he fled the oracle shut his anus with its potsherd[2] and said to him 'Man, since you run away why did you come in the first place?' The child's father came back from his flight and came to it. The oracle asked him what he wanted. The child's father said to the oracle 'My daughter was long lost to me, years ago, and I thought she was dead; however, Ture found her in a riverside wood and took her to his home. I went and took her and brought her to my home. She has not spoken a single word. What can I do to hear her voice?' The oracle said to him thus: that he should go home with her and gather sesame on a potsherd and put it on the fire and go away, leaving just the child near it. Then he would hear her speak. The child's father went home and went and told it to his wife, the mother of the child. She acted accordingly and went away from the sesame on the potsherd, leaving just her child near it, and she went round to the back of the hut. The sesame began to crackle, *ketekete, ketekete*. In vain the child looked round for someone to stir the sesame on the potsherd and she cried out 'The sesame is burning.' No one came to stir it. She cried out again 'People o! the sesame is burning.' But no one came. She cried out 'O mother o! Mother o! Your sesame is burning. Where have you gone to? The sesame is burnt!' Her mother then came from there to take the sesame off the fire. The child spoke from then on, spoke with people and recounted the story of what happened to her with the old woman. Her parents then made a feast to celebrate her recovery. Her kin came from all over the country and her mother's people also, together with the people of the country-side. They came to see her, for if she had died there they would not have seen her again. That is the end of the story of the child.

---

[1] Fr. Giorgetti gives a metaphorical rendering: '*L'Oracolo avvampò come fuoco e bolliva e schiumava (nel suo animo).*' The Zande is '*atari ki ti ku wiyo ki fuko kakpuu*'. See p. 36.

[2] This sentence is not clear to me. The Zande is '*atari ki diko ngbadarako yo na gayo kpakamira*'. Fr. Giorgetti translates this '*l'Oracolo gli chiuse l'ano col suo coccio*', with a note: '*che per lo spavento non se la facesse addosso*'.

67. *Ture and the hypocritical mother-in-law* (A. B.)

THERE was a man who had a daughter. This girl was a virgin and she was as beautiful as a woman could be. Her father and mother said that whoever wished to marry this child of theirs must first kill a bushbuck and bring it to them and then they would give him her hand. The person who just brought marriage-spears and not a bushbuck whole with its stomach, he would not marry the girl.

Many men began to come with spears for the girl's hand but her parents refused them, saying that they wanted only a bushbuck. Then Ture heard about this girl. He prepared himself, put on his feathered hat, and went there with a single hoe and said that he had come to marry the girl. Her parents told Ture that it was only the man who would kill a bushbuck and bring its dead body to them who would marry the girl. Ture said to them 'O my in-laws, it is the simplest thing to kill a bushbuck. As for me, there are in my home as many bushbuck as grass, I breed them like poultry. Please accept my hoe and put it after this girl. She is my wife, let no one marry her, and I shall bring a bushbuck this very evening.'

Ture's in-laws accepted him to marry the girl and told him to go and bring a dead bushbuck. Ture then left for home. When he reached home he started to lay traps to catch a bush-buck in them. Meanwhile, however, while Ture was still away, Leopard came to his in-laws and said he had come to marry the girl. The girl's father told him that this girl was not to be married with spears, it would only be the man who brought a dead bushbuck, only he would marry her. However, a man had come already, called Ture, and said he was going to bring a bushbuck that evening, and let nobody marry the girl. Leopard said to them 'Where can Ture find a bushbuck so quickly, since he does not know how to kill an animal? In the whole life of Ture has he been able to kill an animal that he could kill a bushbuck today? Who else except me, Leopard, who does not miss a day in killing an animal? Take away your child from that thing called Ture and give her to me. I am going to bring an animal right now.' The girl's father said 'That may be so, where will Ture be able to find a bushbuck? Whereas Leopard kills bushbuck every day. Ture is a bluffer, he will not bring any animal quickly.' The girl's mother said 'Oh, though Ture is a bad fellow, since he left his hoe here what can we do?' Leopard said 'My mother-in-law speaks the truth. But now I want my mother-in-law to lie in a hut and say she is sick. Then a boy will be sent to tell Ture to come and visit her in her sickness. As for me, I will wait over the door inside the hut and when Ture arrives and tries to enter to see his mother-in-law in the hut I shall fall on him and break his neck from behind.' Ture's in-laws agreed to this proposal entirely. Ture's mother-in-law lay inside the hut and pretended to be sick. They sent a small boy, the brother of this girl, to go and tell Ture that his mother-in-law was seriously ill, let him come the same day to visit her in her sickness. The boy went running and ran until he reached Ture's home. When Ture looked towards the path he saw the boy and asked him, saying 'Son of my in-laws, is it bad news in your mouth?' The boy stood panting and said to Ture 'Yes, my mother is very sick and that is why my father sent me to tell you that you should come at once to visit her in her sickness.'

Ture got up and said 'What a bad thing to happen to my mother-in-law.' He went into Nanzagbe's hut and took what was left over of porridge together with pounded termites mixed with oil and brought them to the boy. When the boy was eating them Ture told him that he was going to dress up so that they might go. Ture went and entered the hut of Natagbinda,[1] his wife junior to Nangbafudo, in order to put on his (best) barkcloth. The boy ate for a short time and then he said 'Oh! Ture, my kind in-law, is going to be killed by Leopard today.' From inside Ture heard this faintly and he asked 'What? What is it, boy?' The boy said 'No, I was just remarking that our home is far off and shall we be able to reach it today?' Ture came out of Natagbinda's hut and went to get his hat in Nanzagbe's hut. The boy said, in the (pleading) voice of an orphan, 'Oh, Ture, my kind in-law, when I come he gives me my pounded termites with oil. Leopard is going to kill him today.' This time Ture heard it properly and he said 'What? What is it, boy?' The boy replied 'It is nothing, just a small thorn pierced my foot, and I was saying who would take it out for me today?'

Ture now understood that there was something behind it, that something bad awaited him, as the boy was saying. He

---

[1] Ture's third wife, little heard of in the tales.

decided to go and consult the *Atari* oracle. He said to the boy
'Please, son of my in-laws, I am coming back right now.' He
went beyond the cultivations and there struck the head of the
oracle. The oracle fell into fire and boiled over. Ture ran away
as fast as he could out of fear of the oracle. The oracle cooled
down and asked Ture if he had come to make a fool of it. Ture
returned and said 'Not at all, I have come to consult you
about my journey.' The oracle told him to go and fetch two
witch-doctors and go with them. When he reached his in-laws'
homestead he should not enter his mother-in-law's hut. Let him
call for a drum and say he had brought witch-doctors to dance
about his mother-in-law.[1] Before the oracle could finish Ture
told it to shut up, he knew all that already. Ture went home
and summoned witch-doctors, who were the birds Pigeon
together with Honey-sucker, and told them to accompany him
to the home of his in-laws. Pigeon and Honey-sucker, also Ture
and the boy, set off for Ture's in-laws' home. Ture took a big
billhook and sharpened it as sharp as could be. While they
were on their way Pigeon stumbled with his unlucky left leg[2]
and he became apprehensive and said 'O Ture, my friend, it is
not good where we are going to.' Honey-bird then appeared
high up in the sky and came down and broke wind like the
blast of a whistle, and he said 'O Ture, there is trouble ahead.'

When they reached his in-laws' home Ture said he would
not enter the hut until he had discovered the witch killing his
mother-in-law. Let them bring a drum right then for there
were present witch-doctors all ready to dance about her. Ture
told them to beat gong and drum right then. A youth with
skill started to do so and all were alerted. The gourd-rattles
sounded high, not to speak of the hand-bells. Pigeon and
Honey-sucker dressed up in their wild cats' skins and were
dancing as stylishly as a red duiker in a small bush of ground-
fruits. As for Ture, he was jumping up as high as half the
height of that tree over there and landing down with his billhook in his hand, singing a song, saying

'My mother-in-law oo, mother-in-law of deceit,
My mother-in-law oo, mother-in-law of double-talk,
My mother-in-law oo, mother-in-law of deceit,
My mother-in-law oo, mother-in-law of lies.'

[1] To discover the witch causing her sickness.   [2] A bad omen.

While this was going on, as I am telling you, sir, the young man was banging away at the drum. All the old people stood up leaning on their staffs and shaking their heads. All of a sudden Ture dashed inside the hut and cut off one leg of the bed on which his mother-in-law lay, and it broke, leaving only three legs, and Ture was out again in a moment. He joined the witch-doctors in their dance, singing at the top of his voice

'My mother-in-law o, mother-in-law of deceit,
My mother-in-law o, mother-in-law of double-talk,
My mother-in-law o, my child, mother-in-law of lies.'

He dashed inside the hut again and cut off another leg of the bed and then dashed out. When Leopard saw that billhook in Ture's hand, very sharp-edged, he was afraid and could not do anything to Ture. The third time Ture dashed into the hut, instead of cutting a leg off the bed under his mother-in-law he turned towards the door after Leopard and cut into him good and proper, and Leopard started to cry out to the name of Ture's in-laws, saying what bad people they were, they had deceived him so that Ture might kill him. Ture's in-laws said 'What! Was it we who started this affair? Was it not you, Leopard, who said we should send for Ture so that you might kill him? Did anyone put it into your head?' Before they could finish what they were saying Leopard died. Ture took his wife and went home with her without bringing them a bushbuck. Shame overcame his in-laws and they were speechless.

68. *Ture and Bangbangate* (R. R.)

TURE was there, and he went to a man's hunt which the man had arranged. His name was Bangbangate. A certain old woman went after leaves of all kinds and plucked them all into her large pot; and she then went and sat on the way to the hunt which Bangbangate had arranged. Bangbangate said to Ture 'All these many people coming, some of the leaves the woman has cooked, each coming should scrape out some of the mixture and eat it and sing this song and then come after me to the line of the hunting fire.' The woman had cooked it nicely and had thrown her block of salt into it. A man came and scraped out some of the mash, and she sang, saying 'Bangbangate, this your hunt I am coming to attend, may nobody die.' The man answered her, while scraping out a handful, '*Depuru kina re kpio dengbanga.*' She replied, saying '*Gude gude beru ze ga re kporo bomonzimi kporo saka ngba ro gbisigiri saba ango da no gbisi e dano.*'[1] That man passed on. She gave him her (magical) paste (made from the leaves she had burnt) which she had put in a horn. The man went on and came to a rock which blocked the way to the hunt, and he rubbed the paste on the rock, saying 'Rock, you get out of the way for me please, so that I may pass to the hunt.' The rock moved out of the way. Everyone did likewise.

Ture started to follow when everybody had gone to the hunt. He found the woman on the way to this hunt, and he asked her 'Where do we go to the hunt?' She told him to come and scrape out some of this broth and eat it. Ture scraped out a handful and when he ate it he found it very delicious. He sang the same song. Ture passed on. Ture said 'What a wonderful woman! How delicious her broth is! What is it she has cooked it with?' He hid his hat at the side of the path so that the woman might not recognize him. He came back again and sang the song to her and again took some of the broth, and then he passed on. He went on his way once more and collected his hat.

While Ture delayed beside the nice broth the hunt ended. As he was about to go to take up his hat to put it on, a man came by with an animal. He said to him 'O my mother's son, give me a foreleg and I will help you carry it.' The man replied to him 'Ture, just go there, there are lots of animals lying on the ground there.' When Ture went he came up against the rock which blocked the way. As he looked he saw the remains of the paste left on the side of the rock. He took them and rubbed them on the rock and it moved out of the way. He went on till he met another man coming with a dead animal. He said to him 'Give me a thigh and I will help you carry it.' The man replied to him 'Ture, Bangbangate has said that all those many people, since they came and killed many animals—every kind of beast—each should take away only one animal. Even if a man should kill five animals he should take only one for himself. That is why they took only one each.'

[1] I can make no sense out of these sentences left in Zande.

It was a vast tract of burnt land, as far as from here to Wandu's kingdom.[1] All of it was strewn with dead beasts. Ture went on and when he reached there he surveyed the mass of these animals extending far. Ture erected a drying platform as far as from here to Wandu's kingdom and he began to cut up these animals, putting them on the platform till it was full and their fat was dripping from it. His companions said to him 'Ture, Bangbangate said that everybody should leave the burnt tract.' Ture thought that they were just deceiving him; it was because they saw his meat, that was why they were deceiving him. He told them to go and tell his wife Nanzagbe to bring a big basket, together with Nawondiga and Nangbafudo;[2] all of them should bring big baskets. So they came and met the woman who cooked the mash. She told them to go back because Bangbangate had said that everybody should take only one animal for himself.

Next morning Bangbangate started far away, as far as from here to beyond Mongala, and came to see the burnt tract of land stretching as far as Yambio here.[3] He came in great anger, shouting loudly 'That man I find there, I will eat him.' When he looked around he saw Ture. Ture said 'O my mother's brother, where do you come from?' Bangbangate said 'Ture, do you know me? Who is your mother's brother? I will swallow you right now!'

The people ran away from the burnt bush because Bangbangate was intending to swallow all those animals into his stomach, for his mouth was very wide. He swallowed all the animals and then he started to chase Ture, saying to Ture

'Ture, where did you see me?
How could you see me when my sisters have not seen me?
Where did Ture see me?
How could Ture see me when my fathers have not seen me?
Where did Ture see me?
How could Ture see me when my grandparents have not seen me?
Where did Ture see me?'

[1] A considerable distance.

[2] Ture's wives. Nawondiga is perhaps the same person as Natagbinda of no. 67.

[3] Mongala and Yambio were administrative centres. A great distance is indicated.

The chase continued till Ture climbed the big rock he had rubbed paste on. They climbed the rock together. Bangbangate then swallowed Ture. Ture spent three days in his stomach and then he changed into (the insect) *kpikoro*. Now when Bangbangate went to defecate these animals, he defecated Ture in the form of *kpikoro*. After that, Ture changed back again into a person, and he collected his feathered hat again and set off for his home.

But all that was happening to Ture, his wives were not aware of it. They thought that Ture was going to bring back baskets of meat. But when Ture's wives asked him where the meat was, Ture told them that his mother's brother had taken all the meat from him.

69. *Ture and Bakumeme*[1] (R. R.)

TURE went off to dig for rats. He went and arrived at a man's home in a little battered old hut. This man's name was Bakumeme. Ture looked at him and saw just an ordinary bone lying on the ground, for Ture could not know that it was a man. He picked up some earth and when he threw it at him, this bone arose from the ground. When Ture realized that it was a person he said to this man 'O my father-in-law, where do you come from?' But this man replied not a word to Ture.

Ture sat on the ground and put his hand in his bag and drew out two rats. When that man saw them in Ture's hand he rose and came and snatched them from Ture quickly and swallowed them whole, and he saw Ture, flies hovering near his cheek, and he ate the flies near his cheek. Ture brought out more rats and he snatched them from Ture quickly and swallowed them whole. This greatly astonished Ture and he hung his bag over his shoulder. That man, he moved near to Ture. When Ture darted off he cut off Ture's buttock and swallowed it. As Ture jumped up again he cut off his other buttock. Ture continued in flight and arrived at where Nanzagbe was and he said to her 'O Nanzagbe my sister, I saw your brother over there and he complained strongly about you and said that when

[1] *Meme* means 'bone'. *Bakumeme* could be rendered into English by some such name as Barebones.

I saw you I was to tell you that you were to bring him food, for he was very hungry.' Early next morning she cooked porridge and she cooked a fowl and poured oil over it. She brewed beer. She went on her way and arrived at that little battered hut and there she saw just a bare bone lying inside it. This bone, it arose and seated itself. She put down her load on the ground and she crossed her hands at the back of her neck (in fright) and speech departed from her altogether; she did not utter a word. Bakumeme arose from the ground and snatched at flies and ate them, and then he looked at Nanzagbe with desire to eat her up. She took the porridge out of the basket and the fowl to go with it. As she was putting it on the ground Bakumeme was already on his way and, lifting up the porridge in his hand in one piece, he turned it over in the bowl and swallowed it in one piece, and he did the same with the fowl also. She brought out beer for him, and he bit the mouth of the gourd and broke it off, and the beer poured into his mouth in one stream. Then he looked intently at the woman herself. As this terrified her she dashed away from him with all speed. He jumped up together with her and cut off her buttock on one side. Then he severed her other buttock into his mouth and swallowed it. She continued to flee and when she was near home she broke off a big stake for her hand. She continued to flee, and when she arrived home and her children ran to meet her, saying 'Mother is here, mother is here', Ture got away as quickly as he could. When Nanzagbe saw him she ran as hard as she could but when she tried to spear him with the stake she missed him. Ture went on running and escaped.

70. *Two sisters* (R. R.)

[See Appendix I, p. 225.]

CHAPTER IV

SOME DIFFERENT VERSIONS

EXAMPLES of different versions of some of the tales—nos. 2 (A, B, C, D), 38 (E, F, G), 42 (I, J), 15 (K, L, M), and 4 combined with 48 (N)—are now given. The correspondence between one version and another is sometimes close, but they may vary considerably in details, and even in more than details, as the reader may judge for himself. The examples were selected because several different versions were available, rather than merely alternative ones. Other examples can be traced by consulting the Index of Tales in Appendix II. The story H (A man and his daughters Ingo and Kpoko) attached to the versions of the tale of Ture's sons and the *kpengbere* elephant is a quite different tale, and one in which Ture does not appear. It is included because it is a good example of how what is the plot of one tale may become an incident in others. N is an illustration of how two separate plots may be combined in a story.

A. *How Ture released the water* (R. R.)

AN old woman went and planted many yams. When a person came she cooked a yam for him and he ate it, but as there was no water he died of thirst. So Ture started to go also for his part, and he took his little water in a bottle-gourd and put a hollow grass-stem in it and put it in his bag. Now after he arrived at the home of the old woman she cooked a yam and gave it to Ture, and Ture ate it all, and drank his water, and waited, watching the woman starting to cook another yam for Ture. Ture ate it all and waited, watching. When the woman saw Ture swollen to repletion she thought from that that he was going to die; for those people who had eaten her yams, they died from thirst, and she ate them. So after Ture had eaten the yams, her little path which was there where she had dammed the water she drew, for there was no (stream) water and people drank rainwater only; this, her water, no man had ever seen it. So Ture began to depart and went to the entrance to her path, and she said to him 'Ture, there is no path there.' Ture continued on his way, and she said to Ture 'Ture, it is the path of excrements, you must not go there.' Ture just continued on his way. So he arrived beside that water she had dammed. Then he broke through it and said to it 'Water, you divide over the earth everywhere.' So it came about that the water divided thereby all over this earth.

B. *How Ture released the water* (Zakili–E-P.)

THERE was an old woman who rose and planted her yams, and the yams flourished into what big yams! When a certain man came she went and dug up one of them and put it on the fire. When it was thoroughly cooked she cut down a fine banana leaf and came and placed it before this man; but there was no water. She took this her yam and gave it to him. After eating for some time he became very thirsty and then she brought out her big knife, and as he was choking she cut his throat right away, and it was his corpse which fell. Another man came. She went and dug one up and put it on the fire and it was cooked thoroughly, and what a big thoroughly cooked yam! She went and cut down a banana leaf for him to sit on. She took this her yam and gave it to him. When he was dying of thirst she took her big knife and cut his throat with it right away.

Ture then heard about it, where he was. So after waiting a while he arose and went on his way until he saw her home, whereupon he walked away at the side of her home to walk about, and he went to see her water which she had dammed, very much water, as high as the crown of a hut. Ture took his bottle-gourd and drew water there, and when it was filled he arose and he continued on his way and he cut a hollow grass-stem and pushed it into his water in his big bag, and he brought this hollow grass right under his armpit, and then he appeared before her in the homestead and said to her, those yams, the renown of which he had heard, it was them he had come to eat. She cut down a banana leaf and gave it to him and then she went to find a real big one (yam) and dug it up to put it on the fire. It was thoroughly cooked, and what a fine thoroughly cooked yam! She took it and brought it. Ture cut into it and ate and ate. When it stuck in his throat he put down his mouth to under his armpit and drank his water. She beat her chest (in despair), saying (to herself) how could she deal with this man? Ture said to her, let him eat yams, those yams the renown of which he had heard here. It was them he had come to eat. She went again and dug up two (yams), such huge ones, and put them on the fire. They were cooked and she brought and gave them to him. He ate and ate. When it stuck in his throat he put his mouth down to his armpit and drank his water. She said, *he he he!* Men come to eat up her yams, what should she do? Ture told her that he had not eaten enough; those yams of which he had heard the renown at her home, it was those he had come this day to eat. She went again to dig one up, a real big one, and put it on the fire. When it was cooked she took it and gave it to him; and she sharpened her knife and came and stood behind him. He ate and ate, deceiving her by turning his eyes (as though dying). She thought by that that it was thirst and she snatched out her big knife and made straight for him with it.

Ture rose from the ground quickly and ran away swiftly, escaping by the path to her water. Although she cried out to him 'Ture, there is no way there, there is no way there', Ture ran straight ahead by it and went and fell on to the dam of her water and broke it down. She heard the sound (of rushing water) right in her home. The water began to spread, to flow to form little streams, and flow on. Water remained ever afterwards.

C. *How Ture released the water* (L.)

THERE was once an old woman who planted yams and these took so well that the fame of them spread over the whole country. People all knew about it and said there were yams in her home. When a man heard the fame of the old woman's yams he went to her home after them and arrived at her home and told her that he had come to eat of her yams. She replied

'All right, I have heard, be seated.' He waited a short while, and the old woman went and roasted a yam and scraped it well and brought it and gave it to whoever came to eat her yams. He ate it and finished it all and his throat was parched (cracked) with thirst. He asked her to give him some water to drink as, after eating the yam, his throat was parched with thirst. She answered 'There is no water.' When the man was near to death she cut his throat with her knife, and that man died. Another man came and said to her that he had come for her to cook him one of her yams, the fame of which he had heard, for him to eat. She went and cooked a yam for this man and he ate it. When he had finished it his throat was parched with thirst and he said to her that he was parched with thirst, let her give him water to drink. She answered 'There is no water.' When this man was near to death she cut his throat with her knife, and the man died. Thus this woman killed many men with her yams.

Ture heard about this old woman. Ture went and drew water into his bottle-gourd and put it in his bag. He cut a hollow grass-stem and put it in his bag. He appeared in the home of this woman. Ture told this old woman to cook one of her yams of which he had heard the renown that he might eat it right now. She went and cooked a yam and came and gave it to Ture. So Ture ate the whole of the yam, and he waited a little while until he was thirsty. He then took the hollow grass-stem and put it into the gourd and sucked up water through it. When it was finished he belched; and he said to her that he was not replete and that she should roast him another yam to eat. She went away and cooked another yam and came and gave it to Ture. Ture ate it all, and when he became thirsty he took the hollow grass-stem and put it into the gourd and sucked up water through it.

It was finished and he waited a little while. She said (to herself) what did this mean? Since men did not survive her yams, why did Ture not die? She was vexed. She went and entered her hut and took her big knife and came out with it with the intention of slashing Ture with it. Ture jumped up quickly. Ture avoided the (main) paths and fled by the path which led to her water. She cried out, saying to Ture 'There is no path there, it is the path to (the place of) excrements.' Ture paid no attention to what she said. Ture continued his flight and broke through (kicked down) the dam and it broke and water spread over the whole world.

Once upon a time there was no water, only the water this old woman hid. Ture went and showed men where it was, and because of this they learnt about water.

D. *How Ture released the water* (G.)

THERE was once an old woman who planted many yams and people came to work for her on their account. When people worked for her she cooked yams for them in a large pot, and as they ate them they became thirsty and the yams stuck in their throats, and while they were writhing in distress she cut their throats with her big knife. She killed many people in this manner.

Ture heard about this woman. She alone possessed water and she altogether hid it from people. Ture said 'It is I, Ture, I surpass people; that woman who has killed people with thirst, I am going after her.' He set out to go to her home and he begged work of her, and she gave him a task and Ture went to work and finished his task. Ture already knew beforehand that when a person ate this woman's yams he was overcome by thirst. So he had already drawn his water and put it in his bag, knowing that as he was going to work for her she would cook yams for him, and then, when he ate them, he could drink water afterwards. He broke off that grass-stem which is hollow inside and shoved it into this water in the bag so that he might drink it through it. She cooked a yam for him and Ture ate it and waited, and she thought Ture would be in distress with it. Ture waited again and ate it (another yam) and secretly drank his water through this hollow grass-stem, and he toppled to deceive her, making her think from that that he was about to die, and she stalked him with her big knife to cut his throat with it. Ture asked her 'Why do you stalk me, are you going to cut my throat? It isn't going to happen!' She was enraged with Ture.

Ture started off with all speed. Ture avoided all (the main) paths and went by just the narrow path leading to her water, that water she hid from people. She spoke thus to Ture: 'Ture, don't go there, there is not good, that path goes to a nasty place, the nice path is here.' Ture paid no attention to what she said, saying 'What has it got to do with you? I want to go by that path which leads to a nasty place.' As she cried aloud she went after Ture, and she was angry with Ture because he was going to see her water, for at that time there was no other water. She feared that Ture was going to disperse her water. Ture fled and kicked down the dam and water was dispersed everywhere, and he said to this water 'May you go all over the world.'

Once upon a time there was no water, only what this old woman hid. Ture went and disclosed its place to people and thereby they came to know about water.

'I came here and saw men quarrelling and as I went to calm them one of them made for me at once and hit me hard, and as I cried out he took a bit of meat and put it in my hand, and I brought it and placed it on top of the doorway here; child, go and fetch it.'

E. *Ture's sons and the* kpengbere *elephant* (G. 1926)

TURE had arisen then and taken his large bag and gone into the wilderness and dug up some field-rats, and they filled the bag. Then he returned with them and gave them to Nanzagbe and Nzagbe.[1] They then hastened to roast them, and as soon as they were finished they hastened to wash them, then picked leaves to cook them in the coals. They then arose to go for a walk.

While the Tures were away the sons of Ture took them and undid them; and the sons of Ture ate them all up. Then they hastened to take their leaves to go to throw them even there where the Tures had gone. And they went with them and put them into the grass, and they rushed from there oozing fat. Then they began to say among themselves 'How shall we manage the affair of these leaves of the field-rats?' Then they arose

---

[1] His wife and her daughter.

to go with them even there where the Tures had gone, and hid them in the water under the earth. Then they came out of the water and lay just in the eye of the path oozing fat. And they were astonished, and they hastened to tread them into the water, and hurried to run to the homestead. The leaves of the field-rats then came out and lay just in the middle of the path. And as Ture returned he saw them and they knew at once that here were nothing but the leaves of the field-rats. And he said to his sons they must go and kill an elephant, an elephant very large, and must kill one which was very fat, and come with it; even though they should kill an elephant, if it was not fat they must leave it.

And they went and met an elephant, very large and fat, and the eldest brother went out and speared it; then it charged and seized him and killed him. Then another one came and speared it, and it charged and seized him and killed him. Then another one speared it, and it charged and seized him and killed him. The youngest brother then dug out his rock and he dug it out, and as soon as it was finished he fitted its door; and when it fitted he shut it, and it was firm. Then he went out and took a spear and speared it with it, then it charged there to chase him. Then he ran and jumped into the cave and shut the door of it. As it stabbed at him one of its tusks broke. Then it betook itself back. Then he came out and went and speared it and it charged, and as it came to seize him it missed him, and he jumped into the hole. And as it stabbed at him it stabbed only the rock, then its tusk broke and it died. Then he came out from there and said 'What shall I do to restore my elder brothers?'

Then he saw a woman and said to her that she should show some medicine to him. And she told him to go to the stream; the plant which should say 'Drip, drop, drip, brother, brother, arise, let us go', let him pluck it and go with it and drip it on his elder brothers, they would awake. Then he went and plucked it and dripped it on them and they awoke. And one said he killed it and another said he did. But the youngest then took its tusks and climbed up with them and put them in the sky, and came down, and said 'Let us send a messenger after Ture.' And they said 'Who is going to tell it to our father?' Then they said 'Dove, you go.' And they said, 'Dove, you will arrive and say what?' And dove said it would arrive and say 'The sown

eleusine will die, the sown eleusine will die.'[1] Then they said
'Dove, go away.' Then they said to bulbul 'What will you arrive
and say?' And bulbul said '*Kpere, kpere, kpere, kpere*'; and they
said 'Bulbul, go away.' Then they said 'Guinea-fowl, what will
you arrive and say?' And guinea-fowl said it would arrive and
say '*Sukue, sukue.*' And they said 'Guinea-fowl, go away.' Then
they said 'Partridge, what will you arrive and say?' And
partridge said it would arrive and say '*Kukute, kukute.*' Then all
the birds came, and mocking-bird arose and came. Then they
hastened to come, and they said 'Mocking-bird, what will
you arrive and say?' And mocking-bird said 'I will arrive and
say "Take a big pot, *zaa zakiringi*, take a basket, *zaa zakiringi*,
take large baskets, *zaa zakiringi*, thy son has killed a large fat
elephant."' Then they said 'Yes, you go.'

Then it flew all night on and on and arrived and sat at the
top of Ture's clearing (cultivations) and said 'Take a big pot,
zaa zakiringi, thy son has killed a large fat elephant, *zaa zakiringi.*' Two months had passed since the sons of Ture had gone,
and they had been seeking only a large fat elephant. Now as it
cried at the head of the clearing, Nanzagbe was inside the hut
cooking a meal, and only Nzagbe was outside. Then mocking-
bird flew and came and sat on top of the doorway and said
'Take a big pot, *zaa zakiringi*, take a big pot, *zaa zakiringi*, thy
son has killed a large fat elephant, *zaa zakiringi.*' Then Nanzagbe hastened to go out, and they hastened to collect open-wove
baskets and close-wove baskets and very large baskets and all
these things, and hastened to go out thither.

And one said he killed it, and another said he killed it. Then
the youngest said 'Since they are arguing, where are its tusks?
Let them go and get its tusks, please.' Then one of them
jumped up to go and get them and he fell. Just the youngest
then took a shield and danced with it, and flew and went into
the sky, and plucked the tusks and descended with them.
Then they said 'The youngest killed it to clear the name of all
his elder brothers.'

---

[1] '*Urugu moru a kpi a kpi, urugu moru a kpi a kpi*' is what the call of the dove seems
to say. There can be other translations.

F. *Ture's sons and the* kpengbere *elephant* (G.)

THERE was a man called Ture. He went with his wife Nanzagbe to the bush to dig for rats. They caught them and brought them home and cooked them in leaves and left them for the morrow. At day-break they went again to the bush to collect salt, leaving the rats in the embers of the fire. Ture told his sons, who were five, that they were not to eat his rats, and they agreed. However, they did not listen to what their father had said; they agreed with Ture with words only. After that Ture left them all at home and went with his wife after salt.

His sons ignored what Ture had told them, all five of them, and they went into the hut and took the rats and ate them all. They said among themselves 'Let us hide their leaves in the bush.' They took their leaves and hid them in the bush. As they returned home their leaves came out of the bush and fell, oozing oil, in the courtyard of the home. They took them again and threw them into the fire, and they came out of the fire and oozed oil. They took them and trod them into the rubbish-heap and buried them, and they came out from there and fell right into the courtyard. They ran with them to a stream and trod them into the water. As they returned home they came out of the water and fell right into the courtyard, oozing oil.

They were with them when their parents returned. They saw the leaves of the rats right on the path, oozing oil. They went to look in the place of their rats, and they looked in their place in vain, and they summoned their sons to question them about them. Their sons came. One said another had cooked them; another said it was another. Their father knew it was they who had eaten them, and he said to them 'We don't want to see you in any circumstances until you kill only that elephant which is *kpengbere*, which is very oily.' The five of them wandered off into the bush, and they saw a buffalo and killed it, but they did not find oil in its belly. They went on further for many days; and the years passed without their parents seeing them. Then they found the *kpengbere* elephant. The elder sons were four, the youngest was the fifth. The eldest speared it and it seized and killed him. Another came and speared it, and it killed him. The third also speared it, and it

killed him; likewise the fourth one. The youngest sought for a
rock-hole and found it, and he prepared the inside of it, and
collected his elder brothers' spears and went after the elephant.
He speared it, and it chased him, and he fell into the rock-hole.
As it tried to pierce him with its tusks one broke on the rock. He
took it and hid it. He went and speared it again, and it chased
him and he fell into the rock-hole. As it tried to pierce him its
remaining tusk broke, and it died.

He went by the side of water and saw an old woman drawing
her water, and she had lumps all over her body, and he said
to her 'All my elder brothers are dead, what can I do all by
myself at the side of this elephant?' She said to him 'It is like
this, if you burst the pus in this big boil which is on my bottom[1]
with your teeth I will revive your elder brothers for you.' He
took a small stick and was about to burst it open with it. She
said to him 'You must not burst it open with a thing, only
with your teeth.' He burst it open with his teeth and the pus
spurted out. He squeezed it all out and washed all the pus off
her. And she gave him medicine to go and drip it on his elder
brothers. He sewed a leaf-funnel for it and went and dripped
it into the mouths of them all, and as he dripped it he said
'Drip, drop, *ii*, drip, brother, brother arise, let us go!' They
all woke up and saw the *kpengbere* elephant, that it was dead.
One said he had killed it. But he who had killed it, he had
already taken up its tusks and put them in the sky near the
moon. He said to them 'Since you say you killed it, you fly
please and show its tusks.' One of them flew, but did not
reach them. He (the youngest) for his part flew and took them
away from near the moon and put them on the ground. They
knew by this that he had killed it.

They said 'What shall we do to send a messenger after our
father and mother so that they may come to beside that elephant
which they demanded?' They summoned all the birds, and
said to francolin, since it was used to the dawn, it should go to
tell it (the news) to their father and mother. They asked it,
saying, what would it say when it arrived? It said it would
say '*Gurungbe sosooro!*' They chased it away and summoned
cuckoo and said to it that it should go because it was well used

---

[1] The Zande word is *baongodare*, a polite expression for 'my buttocks': *ba-ongoda-re*,
'the place of-resting-my'.

to the dawn, and they asked it, saying, what would it say when it arrived? It said it would say '*Tutuutuu!*' They chased it away also. They summoned all the birds, but they did not know how to speak the message. They summoned vulture and said to it, since it was used to flying high and far, it should go. They asked it, saying 'What will you say to father and mother?' It said it would say '*Kokokoo!*' They chased it away. Mocking-bird then came forward, and it said to them 'If it is not I who shall tell the affair to your parents who should tell it?' They said to it 'You say what you would speak to our parents.' It said 'I will arrive and say

> "Nanzagbe, Nanzagbe, your sons tell you to come,
> Arise, take large gourds, *zaa zakiringi!*
> Grind flour o, take pots,
> Grind out oil, *zaa zakiringi!*" '

They said 'That's fine! You are an excellent bird, you go after our parents.' It flew and flew and arrived near their parents' home and settled on a tree there, saying

> 'Nanzagbe, Nanzagbe, your sons said, *zaa zakiringi*,
> Come, arise, *zaa zakiringi*,
> Take big gourds, *zaa zakiringi*,
> Your sons have killed the *kpengbere* elephant, *zaa zakiringi.*'

A small sister of theirs, Nzagbe, sitting by the side of the hut, she heard this its speech and she said to her mother 'Mother, a bird says

> "Nzagbe, Nzagbe, your sons said, *zaa zakiringi*,
> Come, take gourds, *zaa zakiringi*,
> Your sons have killed the *kpengbere* elephant, *zaa zakiringi.*"'

Her mother took hold of her and beat her and rubbed her in the dust and pushed her aside, saying 'Since my sons are all dead, why are you troubling me about them?' The mocking-bird came and settled right on top of the entrance and cried aloud. Their mother heard it clearly, that her sons had said, let her come, let her arise. She took large gourds and ground flour, and she took pots and ground oil-seeds; her sons had killed the *kpengbere* elephant. After that she took her daughter and washed her and anointed her with oil. Then their little sister, Nzagbe, was happy. Ture and his wife and daughter and all the people of his home arose, and all took up baskets and bowls and collected things to go after their sons to their *kpengbere* elephant. Ture asked 'Who killed it?' All together said 'I killed it.' That youngest who had killed it kept silence. Ture said 'That man who can produce its tusks, the same is he who killed it.' It was the youngest who produced them, having killed it. Ture told them to fall to the ground to honour him. Ture was happy, but the elder brothers were not happy. They hated their youngest brother. Ture said 'You bear him on your heads to return home with him.'

G. *Ture's sons and the* kpengbere *elephant* (Kamanga–E.-P.)

TURE arose with Nanzagbe and they went into the bush to dig for rats. They dug up rats and caught rats in great numbers. They brought them home and roasted them and wrapped them in leaves, and they then ate some of them with porridge, and they took three (bound) bundles (of them) and put them in the drying-basket (for meat) and left their sons with them, of whom there were five, Orphan being the sixth.[1] He said to them thus: 'Children, I and Nanzagbe are going again to the bush. You stay with my rats lest a dog steal them.' They stayed there.

Ture went to the bush and spent two nights there. His sons arose and took the bundles of rats from the drying-basket. When they ate them they gathered their heads for Orphan; they kept on giving them to Orphan. The eating of them was finished. So they said to Orphan 'Child, go and throw the leaves of the rats into the bush.' Orphan went with them and threw them into the bush. He turned and came back, and the leaves of the rats rushed out of the bush and came and sat before them, shining with oil. They seized Orphan and kept on beating him, saying 'Child, you did not throw the leaves of the rats into the bush.' Orphan said that he had already thrown them away. They said 'It is a lie, as there they are.' Another

---

[1] The orphan, having been taken into the family, counted in this sense as a son.

took them again and went and threw them into the bush and
turned and came back. They rushed out again and sat before
them, shining with oil. They took them and went and dug a
hole and buried them in the earth. They beat down the surface
of the grave, all of it, all of it, all of it. As they began to go home
they rushed out all oily. They said *'Yuwu!* (exclamation of
astonishment) What shall we do with them?' They built up the
fire and took them and threw them in it. They rushed out of it
all shining. They said 'Alas! What shall we do with them?' One
of them said let them give the leaves to him here. He took them
and swallowed them. They rushed out of his anus, shining with
oil. They took them again and gave them to Orphan. Orphan
went and hid them together with the heads of the rats. They
remained there.

Ture was away for five days and then he began to return.
Ture returned and arrived home. The sons of Ture spoke
thus:

> 'Mother that comes from there,
> Father that comes from there,
> Mother that comes from there,
> Father that comes from there.'

Nanzagbe said 'O my children! You must be dying of hunger?
O my children! Alas! Alas!' For their part they replied 'O
mother, you have spent long away there.' Ture entered the
hut, he looked towards the hearth (the drying-basket) and saw
only three bundles of rats.[1] He said 'Nanzagbe, something has
happened.' Nanzagbe said *'Huwe!* (exclamation of surprise)
Ture, what is the matter? You tell me about it please!' Ture
said 'Nanzagbe, some of the rats are missing.' Ture said 'Nanzagbe, you summon my sons.' They were six in number. They
questioned the eldest. The eldest said thus, that they had
not eaten the rats. They questioned the next eldest. They
questioned all five of them, and they came to Orphan. Orphan
said 'Mother, we ate the rats.' Nanzagbe asked 'Who was it
who stole them?' Orphan said 'It was my elder brothers who
stole them.' They said *'Ehe, ehe, ehe he he he,* it is a lie.' Orphan
said about it 'Mother, with regard to the eating of them, since

---

[1] The narrator seems to have forgotten that it was only three bundles the
parents had left behind.

they deny it, the heads they gave me, I did not eat them.'
Orphan went to fetch them from where he had hidden them.
Orphan went and took them, the heads of the rats and the
leaves of the rats also, and he poured them out before his
mother. Orphan said 'Since they deny it, there are the heads of
the rats.' So Ture said thus: 'Alas! Have they not eaten my
rats?' Ture then began to give them all a good beating, save
Orphan. He then collected five spears and distributed them
among the brothers from the eldest downwards, and he told
them that they were to travel till they killed the fat elephant
which is the elephant *kpengbere*; let them kill the same in the
place of his rats as their reparation, before he, Ture, would see
them. Orphan said '*Ai!* I am going to accompany my elder
brothers.'

They went off. Nanzagbe was left alone with Ture. They
went on and on and when they were well away they arose
against Orphan and beat and beat him, beat and beat and beat
him. Then they let him alone and they went on and arrived in
the wilderness. They killed a waterbuck but it did not contain
much fat. They left it. They continued on their way and killed
a buffalo but it did not contain much fat. They went on killing
animals but there was no fat in them. They arrived at the place
of the *kpengbere* elephant. They started to spear it. It chased
him (the one who attacked it), but it did not catch him. It
turned round and went back to its lair where it lived. He stalked
it again and speared it. Then it rose again and chased him and
caught him, and it killed him. Another came forward and
speared it. It tossed him along with it and killed him. Yet
another came forward and speared it twice. It tossed him
along with it and killed him. Yet another came forward and
speared it again. It seized him and killed him. Yet another came
forward and speared it. It killed him also. Orphan arose and
gathered all the spears at the side of the corpses and took them
away in his hands. Then Orphan arose and dug his pit among
rocks, and it was ready. Orphan descended into this pit. Then
he fitted himself into it, fitted himself there, and his place was
fine. Then he tested himself by running a little way off and then
running and falling into his pit, but he did not come to harm.
Then he arose and took up his spears and stalked the elephant
in its lair. He speared it. It squealed at once, *woowoo wowowowo*,

and it chased him right away, and he fell into his little pit which he had dug. It came to seize him and struck its tusk on the rock, but did not catch him. It returned to its lair. He came forward again out of his pit and stalked it again and went and speared it. It leaped up at him again and chased him. As it came to seize him he dropped into his pit. It struck its tusk on the rock, and its tusk was broken. It again returned to its lair. He took this tusk and went and hid it; then he stalked it again, and again speared it. It chased him and came to seize him and struck its tusk against the rock again, and its tusks in its mouth were finished, that is, those great teeth (tusks). He took it and went and hid it.

He came forward again and stalked it and went and speared it. It chased him and he fell into the pit. It came to seize him and struck its tusks again, that is to say the place of its tusks. Then it returned again to its lair. He started again to spear it, and only two spears remained in his hands. He speared it with one of them, and it drove him back and came to seize him and struck its teeth on the rock. Orphan said 'Alas! What affair is it thus, since the spears are finished and I am about to spear it with this last one here? What shall I do later?' He stalked it and speared it in its trunk, and it beat the same on a tree, but it did not chase him any more. It fell to the earth to die just where it was. So, Orphan came out of his pit and gathered up his bones (tusks) and went and hung them up in the sky and left them there.

He came down from the sky and said 'What can I do now to wake my elder brothers from death?' He arose and went on and on and arrived at the home of an old woman. Nobody lived with her; she was all by herself. He spoke thus: 'O mother! My elder brothers are in the wilderness where an elephant has killed them all; you reveal to me a medicine so that I may wake them from death.' The old woman said 'I say thus, that person who lances into my pus, I will reveal the medicine to him.' She further said 'I am not talking about a person cutting into it with a knife, but about that person who cuts into it with his teeth, it is he to whom I shall reveal the medicine.' He then drew water into his mouth to wash it and then put his mouth into her pus. He cut into it with his teeth, and he cut it; it (the pus) flowed out on to the ground, and it was finished. He then took warm water and pressed the place of the wound. She seated herself. She said to him thus: 'What is your name?' He replied to her thus: 'My name is Orphan, I am one of Ture's sons.' She spoke to him thus: 'That medicine I am about to reveal, you must not reveal it to anybody else.' He said 'O mother! O mistress! I will not reveal it to anyone.' She said to him 'You go until you arrive at the side of a spring, that plant which you see growing at the spring and moving thus (narrator waves hand from side to side), pull it up.' So he pulled up this plant. She told him to scrape it and roll up a little leaf-filter thus and put the medicine in it and take it and go to drip it on them. He began to drip it on to them, saying '*Togo*[1] *ngi*, you wake my mother's son.' He dripped it on to this one and he awoke. He said 'I killed it, I killed it, I killed it.' Orphan was silent. Then he appeared at the side of another one also, and he said '*Togo ngi*, you wake my mother's son o', and that one awoke. He said 'I killed it, I killed it, I killed it, I killed this beast.' Orphan was silent. He dripped it on to another one: '*Togo ngi*, you wake my mother's son, *togo ngi*, you wake my mother's son.' He awoke. He said 'I killed it, I killed it, I killed it.' He moved over to another one and said '*Togo ngi*, you wake my mother's son o, *togo ngi*, you wake my mother's son o.' This one woke also. He said 'I killed it, I killed it, I killed it.' Orphan was silent. He went and dripped on to another: '*Togo ngi*, you wake my mother's son, *togo ngi*, you wake my mother's son.' He woke. He likewise said 'I killed it, I killed it, I killed it.' Orphan was silent. They began to dispute among themselves, the eldest saying that it was he who killed it, it was he who killed it, it was he who killed it, it was his beast. Orphan said thus: 'All right, since you all quarrel, you will in no circumstances see what is happening.' Orphan said 'That man who can fetch the tusks of that elephant from the sky, the same is the slayer of it.'

So Orphan said thus: 'My elder brothers, let all the birds be summoned to be asked, all of them, to find which one among them might speak about that affair to Ture, which is that we, his sons, we have killed the *kpengbere* elephant, so that when Ture hears it he will come, because if a bird is sent which can speak correctly then our father will come, who is Ture.' So they then summoned the birds. All the birds came. They said

[1] *Togo*, to drip.

'Bulbul, what would you go and say?' Bulbul said '*Geregada, geregada, geregada, geregada.*' They said 'Hm! bulbul, you get out.' They summoned cisticola warbler and said 'Warbler, what would you go and say?' Warbler just said thus: '*Ti, ti, ti, ti, ti, ti.*' They said 'Ah warbler! You can't speak properly, you get out of the way.' They summoned cuckoo. They said 'Cuckoo, what would you go and say?' Cuckoo replied '*Tu tu tu, tu tu tu tu tu tu tu.*' They said 'Ah cuckoo! Get out of the way, you can't speak properly.' They summoned swallow and said 'Swallow, what would you go and say?' Swallow said that he would say thus: '*Mbira mbira, mbira mbira mbira.*' They said 'Ah swallow! Get out of the way.' They then summoned vulture. They said 'Vulture, what would you go and say?' Vulture came forward in his turn and said he would go and say '*Depio ba ru a ru, depio a ndu ku dio.*' They said 'Ah vulture! You will not tell the affair.' They summoned weaver-bird and said 'Weaver-bird, what would you go and say?' Weaver-bird said he would go and say '*Zoga zoga zoga zoga goliiiiiiiiiiiiiii, if it were me, if it were me, maize ripens, geeeeeeeeeeeeee, it is not I, if it were me, if it were me, maize ripens, geeeeeeeeeeeeee, it is not I, it is not I, I was at my mother-in-law's.*' They said 'Weaver-bird, get out of the way.' They summoned laughing dove and said 'Dove, what would you go and say?' Dove said he would go and say 'The sower of eleusine will die, the sower of eleusine will die, the sower of eleusine will die.' They told him to get out of the way. They summoned another dove[1] and said 'Dove, what would you go and say?' Dove said 'I would go and say *rakataru, rakataru, rakataru, rakataru.*' They told him to get away. They summoned scaly francolin and said 'Francolin, what would you go and say?' Francolin said he would go and say '*Gurungbe sosoro, gurungbe sosoro, gurungbe sosoro.*' They said 'Ah francolin! You shall not tell the affair, get out of the way.' They summoned guinea-fowl and said 'Guinea-fowl, what would you go and say?' Guinea-fowl said he would say '*Sukue, sukue, ke ke ke ke nge, ke ke ke ke nge,* oh, people are bad! Oh, people are bad!' They laughed at him and then told him to get out of the way. They then summoned francolin[2] and said 'Francolin, what would

---

[1] *Rakataru* is, I believe, the same bird as laughing dove (*mbipo*). It changes its call in the dry season. The narrator appears to consider it to be a different bird. It may be the long-tailed dove.   [2] Another variety of francolin.

you go and say?' Francolin replied that he would go and say
'*Karu karu, karu karu, karu, karu,* where am I?' They said
'Francolin, you get out of the way.' They summoned that bird
which is zakiringi.[1] Zakiringi came forward and said

'*Ƶaa zakiringi,* your sons have killed the *kpengbere* elephant,
Ƶaa zakiringi, when you set forth take big axes,
Ƶaa zakiringi, when you set forth take big baskets,
Ƶaa zakiringi, when you set forth take big bottle-gourds,
Ƶaa zakiringi, when you set forth take big bowls,
Ƶaa zakiringi, when you set forth take big knives,
Ƶaa zakiringi, your sons have killed the *kpengbere* elephant,
Ƶaa zakiringi.'

They said '*U wu!* Oh, does not zakiringi understand things?' And
they cut off a big slice of meat and gave it to zakiringi and put it
in his bag, and he set forth. He went on his way and alighted on
his tree, and he said

'*Ƶaa zakiringi,* your sons have killed the *kpengbere* elephant,
Ƶaa zakiringi, when you set forth take big axes,
Ƶaa zakiringi, when you set forth take baskets,
Ƶaa zakiringi, when you set forth take big bottle-gourds,
Ƶaa zakiringi, when you set forth take big bowls,
Ƶaa zakiringi, when you set forth take big knives,
Ƶaa zakiringi,
Ƶaa zakiringi, your sons have killed the *kpengbere* elephant,
Ƶaa zakiringi.'

He went on and on and after three days on the journey he arrived
at Ture's home. He settled at the head of the cultivations and
said

'*Ƶaa zakiringi,* your sons have killed the *kpengbere* elephant,
Ƶaa zakiringi, when you set forth take big axes,
Ƶaa zakiringi, when you set forth take big baskets,
Ƶaa zakiringi, when you set forth take big bottle-gourds,
Ƶaa zakiringi, when you set forth take big bowls,
Ƶaa zakiringi, when you set forth take big knives,
Ƶaa zakiringi, your sons have killed the *kpengbere* elephant,
Ƶaa zakiringi.'

[1] Here the name of the bird is taken from its cry. In other versions it is either the
hammer-headed stork (*ete*) or the mocking-bird or Ethiopian thrush (*taramani*).

A child heard him at the head of the cultivations and the child ran home and told Ture thus: 'Father, there is a bird at the head of the cultivations which says thus: "*Zaa zakiringi*, set forth and take axes." Father, that is what he says thus.' He took hold of this child to give him a good hiding, saying 'Look you, the child is mocking, for my children long ago died in the wilderness and he says my children have killed the *kpengbere* elephant', and he seized this child and rubbed him with the dung of chickens and then threw him into the chicken-house. So zakiringi flew and settled on top of his hut and began to recite this speech to Ture:

'*Zaa zakiringi*, your sons have killed the *kpengbere* elephant,
Zaa zakiringi, when you set forth take axes,
Zaa zakiringi, when you set forth take baskets,
Zaa zakiringi, when you set forth take big bottle-gourds,
Zaa zakiringi, when you set forth take big bowls,
Zaa zakiringi, when you set forth take big knives,
Zaa zakiringi, your sons have killed the *kpengbere* elephant,
Zaa zakiringi.'

Now Ture said 'So! Thus this child, this child spoke the truth. I have heard news of all my sons at the beak of this bird. Has he not indeed spoken the truth?'

Ture called Nanzagbe and said 'Nanzagbe, take that child out of the chicken-house and wash his body, wash his body all over and anoint him with oil.' Ture rose and collected all the axes and baskets. Zakiringi went ahead to show Ture the way, and they went. They went on and on till they reached the elephant, and they cut up the elephant completely and dried its flesh. As they were putting down the dried flesh Ture appeared and seated himself and said 'My sons, that man who killed this elephant among these my sons, let him come forward and say that it was he who killed this elephant so that I may praise his prowess, for it is the debt of the rats.'

He who was the eldest said to his father 'By your limb, it was I who killed that elephant.' His younger brother then came forward and swore vehemently about the killing of the elephant, to boast to his father of having slain the elephant. Another came forward and spoke also in the same wise. Another came forward and told Ture that it was he who had killed it, sir. Then Orphan came forward for his part and said to Ture thus: 'Father, it was I who killed the elephant.' They all started crying '*Ha a a a!* Orphan, you did not kill the elephant.' Orphan came forward on this and said to Ture thus: 'Let our father give us a shield, let us soar with it beside those tusks of the elephant which are on high. That man who killed it, it is he who can soar to cut the rope of the elephant tusks on high so that they fall on top of his shield, and Ture will know by that which person killed the elephant without doubt.'

Ture said 'Orphan speaks well.' He took a shield and a ceremonial knife and gave them to his sons, saying 'That person who can soar to cut the rope of the elephant's tusks on high, I wait to see him in the presence of so many people, and I will know by it that he is that child of mine who slew that elephant.' They then began to take the shield to soar with the shield. That one soared with the shield in vain, soared in vain, soared in vain, for the elephant's tusks did not fall on to his shield. He put down his shield on the ground. They laughed and laughed at him. Another came forward and took the shield and soared with it but he did not cut the rope of the elephant's tusks. They laughed at him also. Another one came forward, and soared with the shield in vain, for he could not cut the rope of the elephant's tusks. Another came forward also, soared with the shield in vain, for he did not cut the rope of the elephant's tusks. Another came forward and soared in vain, for he did not cut the rope of the elephant's tusks. Orphan came forward and took the shield and soared and soared and soared and soared, and he held out his shield thus, and he cut the rope of the elephant's tusks on high and they fell on his shield. He put it down before Ture. They cried out in his honour '*I ye! ye! ye! i ye! ye! ye!*' Laughter sounded for those (elder brothers) with a great laughter.

Orphan then went and said to Ture thus: 'Since they disputed it, they did not kill the elephant. When we came and found the elephant with them, we started to spear the elephant, and the elephant killed them all; and I alone survived, so I arose and dug my little pit and then started to spear this elephant after their deaths, all having died, and their corpses on the ground. I dug my little pit and from there slew this elephant. I asked what I should do to raise them from death. So I went and found an old woman with her pus on her belly, and she said this: that if I were to cut this pus with my very teeth she would reveal to me good medicine with which I might revive my elder brothers. So this old woman gave me this medicine and I went and revived them with it. So sir, Ture, they did not kill the elephant.' They rose to anoint Orphan with oil, to dress him with fine barkcloth, and then they started off to go home.

'So I went on my way and we saw Siani beating his wife, and I said to him, "O Siani! What are you quarrelling about?" He took a spear-shaft and hit me over the head with it, and when I cried out *"i hii!"* he took a fowl and cooked it for me. So I ate it and took what was left over and came and put it on top of the doorway here; a child ate the remains of the flesh of the fowl. A child said "It was Kamsa."[1] I said "O that child! Does he not trouble me?" '

H. *A man and his daughters Ingo and Kpoko* (R. R.)

NOW Ture was there. A man begot two female children, the one's name was Ingo and her younger sister's name was Kpoko.[2] Ingo died leaving only Kpoko. Since she died her father and mother ate nothing. When her parents arose to go to the cultivations they left Kpoko at home by herself. After they had left Kpoko at home she began to cry, saying 'Oh, has not my elder sister died? Or she would have prepared a meal for us to eat, leaving father and mother in the cultivations.' Now she entered a hut to roast beans near the grave at the side of the hut. When she went to roast the beans she got burnt by the fire and as she turned round to cry she saw Ingo at the head of the grave and as soon as she spoke Kpoko recognized her voice. Ingo roasted beans for Kpoko and left them for her and moved off from her and climbed up to the granary to collect eleusine and dried meats and oil-seeds; and then she came down quickly and roasted it (the grain) and pounded it with all speed, and

---

[1] A name Azande have taken over from the Arabic word for 'five'.

[2] *Ingo* means 'cup-gourd' and *Kpoko* means 'the spine of a leaf'. Here, I think, they are simply proper names without association with the literal meanings, as we might speak of Rosemary or Violet.

she cooked the meat and put the pot off the fire with all speed; and while she was grinding the eleusine the porridge-pot was on the fire. As Kpoko cried she drew off the meat on to *kau*[1] leaves and gave it to her to eat. After she had eaten it she broke off portions (of the porridge) for Kpoko and herself and broke off portions for her father and mother, but Kpoko's portion was the largest since she saw her misery, for she was indeed emaciated.

When Ingo heard the voices of her father and mother she ran and fell into the grave. Her parents came and arrived and met Kpoko eating porridge, and her mother asked her, saying 'Child, since you could not have prepared porridge, who prepared this for you which you are eating here?' She answered, in the manner of speech of an orphan, 'Madam, have you not both ill-treated me since my elder sister Ingo died? My elder sister came out of the grave to cook my porridge.' Then her mother gave her a good hiding and smeared her all over with chicken dung and threw her into the bush. When her father came her mother took this porridge and placed it before him and she took hers and ate it, and she said to him thus: 'Look at this porridge. Kpoko says that Ingo cooked it.' He said 'Eh woman, what are you talking about thus, as though laughter had overcome me?' Her father went and tapped the top of the *Atari* oracle and *Atari* boiled over. As he departed in haste *Atari* said to him 'Look at his frayed buttocks! Have you not come to listen to advice?' He replied to the oracle 'Francolin pecks at termite and shakes itself in the dust.' Then *Atari* told him to go with her and her mother, singing this song, which is:

'My daughter for that, my daughter o! My daughter o!
Ingo, it is indeed I who call you,
Ingo, you are going to answer,
Ingo, the mother of another calls you,
Ingo, surely you will answer,
Ingo, it is indeed I who call you,
Ingo, you are going to answer,
Ingo!'

She who was Ingo for her part answered back, saying

'Mother for that, mother oo! Mother oo!
Ingo, the mother of another calls me,

[1] *Bauhinnia Thonningii.*

Ingo, surely I will answer,
Ingo, indeed it is you who is calling me,
Ingo, surely I will answer,
Ingo, o o!'

Her father came and sang, saying

'My daughter for that, my daughter oo! My daughter o!
Ingo, it is indeed I who call you,
Ingo, you are going to answer,
Ingo, the father of another calls you,
Ingo, surely you will answer,
Ingo.'

She remained completely silent. Her father dashed off to where
the *Atari* oracle was and tapped the top of *Atari* and *Atari*
boiled over, and as he was running away it rolled him over on
the ground[1] and it said to him 'You are wrong in the head,
have you not come to hear advice from me?' It said to him 'Go
and slay only that elephant which is the *kpengbere* elephant, and
when the gourds of its fat are numerous come with them and
hold a feast for all the people; then your daughter will arise
and appear.'

He went to search for elephants of every kind. But when he
killed an elephant it had no oil in it. He went on and on until
after six years he found the *kpengbere* elephant in the wilderness,
and he killed the *kpengbere* elephant, and it appeared that its
oil would require innumerable gourds. So he sent a great bird
to his home, and the great bird came and met his wife and
daughter hoeing the cultivations, and it spoke to her (the wife)
thus:

'You take large bottle-gourds, *zaa zakiringi*,
You take large open-wove baskets, *zaa zakiringi*,
Your husband has killed the *kpengbere* elephant,
Zaa zakiringi.'

So Kpoko spoke to her mother thus: 'Mother, listen, a bird
says thus:

"Father has killed the *kpengbere* elephant, *zaa zakiringi.*"'

[1] *Kpangario* is an adverb describing the act of something thrown down and
rolled over abruptly.

She replied 'What a child! What is the matter with you?' The bird spoke again, saying

> 'You take large bottle-gourds, *zaa zakiringi*,
> Your husband has killed the *kpengbere* elephant,
> *Zaa zakiringi*.'

When they returned home it flew and settled on the granary and spoke this speech. So Kpoko told it to her mother, and her mother beat her and smeared her with chicken dung and threw her into the bush. It spoke to her by herself and she understood, and she went and took her daughter again and anointed her with oil and red dye and put her on a stool. It then flew to where her husband was, and settled on a branch above him and spoke to him:

> 'I have arrived at the home, *zaa zakiringi*,
> Let them take large bottle-gourds, *zaa zakiringi*,
> Let them take large open-wove baskets, *zaa zakiringi*.'

So his wife collected bottle-gourds and open-wove baskets, and many people went to the wilderness, there where he was, and they started to decant the oil into those things they brought with them, and they were all filled. When this man returned he went to the *Atari* oracle and tapped *Atari* on the head, and when it boiled over he fell quickly and *Atari* rolled him over on the ground and it told him to make a feast for all the people so that when the people had eaten their meal his daughter would appear from the grave. So he made a feast, and when the people had eaten, Ingo changed into a butterfly and flew and settled on her mother. After that she flew as a butterfly into a hut. Then as her mother entered it she saw Ingo herself seated there. So her mother washed her well and anointed her with oil and seated her on a stool, a fine glistening-with-oil stool. Then a man whose name was Rinza married her and he went with her into the wilderness so that nobody ever saw her again.

I. *Ture and Yangaimo's feathers* (L.)

THERE was a man called Yangaimo whose father was already dead. He departed and took the plumes of his father with which his father used to dance. He built for himself a homestead and he cleared a plot of bush for his eleusine only, for these plumes of his provided him with his meats.[1]

One day Ture departed and arrived at Yangaimo's homestead, and there he saw many men. He (Yangaimo) told his wives to prepare porridge and his wives started at once to prepare it. When the porridge was ready Yangaimo went to the verandah of his hut and took his plumes and appeared with these in the courtyard, and he began to sing, saying

> '*Yu* Yangaimo, these plumes of father,
> Father gave to Yangaimo.'

The people took up this chant and indeed it was like a wailing (at a funeral). Yangaimo danced vigorously. Three times they took up this chant and then in a moment the plumes took Yangaimo up into the heavens. Birds came from all over the earth and fell to the ground. The granaries were filled with them. These birds, they cooked themselves. When they had finished (falling) Yangaimo descended and went to the meat and distributed it to all the people, and they all had their share. When Ture saw this affair folly took hold of him. He said to Yangaimo that he, his friend, would return home, and Yangaimo consented. So Ture arose and went back to his own home, and he told (his wife) Nanzagbe that he had seen a fine thing.

Ture slept two nights, and on the following morning he took the path to Yangaimo's homestead, and, as Yangaimo was out walking, when Ture appeared he did not see anyone. Ture went to the verandah of the hut and saw the plumes of Yangaimo. Some hornets were near them, real fierce hornets. Now Ture had come to steal the plumes of Yangaimo. When Ture pulled away the plumes the hornets rushed fiercely on him to sting him. But Ture paid no attention to them and clung on to

---

[1] He did not require oil-bearing plants or other vegetables to go with the eleusine porridge.

the plumes and fled away with them. But one little feather
became loosened from the hand of Ture and fell to the ground.

Now Yangaimo had a presentiment on his way to where he
was going, and he returned home in all haste. He got back and
passed at once to where his plumes had been, but he could not
see them. It seemed as though he would kill himself. He reflected and said to himself 'Who is it that has done me this great
ill?' When he looked he saw Ture's footsteps, and when he
searched the ground he saw just one little feather which had
been loosened from the hand of Ture. He took it and attached
it to a little piece of cord and put it in his hat. While he was
occupied in doing this he looked up and saw Ture with a
swarm of birds wheeling around him.

Now when Ture had taken the plumes he went home with
them and when he appeared in his homestead he told the
people to come and they came like the grains of earth in
number. Ture told his wives to make porridge without anything
more (seasoning). Ture's wives had indeed prepared this food.
Now Ture took his plumed hat and put it on his head and went
out into the open (sun) and sang a song, calling on the people
to chant the response to his name:

> '*Yu yu* Ture, these plumes of father,
> Father gave to Ture,
> *Yu yu* Ture, these plumes of father,
> Father gave to Ture.'

The people took up this chant strongly. The plumes took Ture
up in a moment into the heavens and small birds fell down and
the place was full of them. Yangaimo said to himself 'Ah, this
man! How can I deal with him?' Yangaimo got up and took
the little feather which had been loosened from the hand of
Ture and he put it (the hat) on and took up his song, saying

> '*Yu* Yangaimo, this plume of father,
> Father gave to Yangaimo.'

This feather took Yangaimo in a moment into the heavens.
Yangaimo forthwith met Ture. Yangaimo went with Ture to
seize his plumes. As Ture went towards the west Yangaimo
passed to the east. Thus Ture and Yangaimo began a violent
altercation. Now Yangaimo saw what the position was and he

said to himself 'If I continue to act thus I shall never succeed
in getting back my plumes.' Yangaimo said to Ture 'My friend,
you dance for your part below and I for my part will dance
above.' Ture agreed to this, and they both began to dance
anew. However, Yangaimo deceived Ture so that he might
take away his plumes. Thus they danced vigorously. Yangaimo
remained above and suddenly swooped down, and as Ture
went to one side Yangaimo suddenly seized his plumes from
Ture. Then as Ture detached himself from the sky he fell. At
once Yangaimo took his plumes. Ture began to die. The birds
all dispersed, and all the people also.

This is why men say that theft is bad, because it was through
theft that Ture died, on account of the plumes of Yangaimo.

J. *Ture and Yangaimo's feathers* (G.)

Now there was once a man called Yangaimo. When his father
died he arose and took his father's feathers with which his
father used to dance. There was power in these feathers. He
stuck them in his hat. These plumes were his great meat; when
he lacked meat he told his wives to sweep the courtyard, and
he took his horn of medicine (ashes) and set it up in the courtyard, and he took his plumed hat and put it on his head and
said 'My wives, you gather close-wove baskets and open-wove
baskets, and pots and bowls, and you wait right here.' He then
put his hat on his head and flew above and sang his song,
saying

'*Yuu* Yangaimo, Yangaimo,
Yangaimo, you come to take plumes.'

Yangaimo danced with vigour, these plumes took Yangaimo
straight to the sky. Birds came together from all over the
world and fell into the courtyard, and the granaries were
filled. These birds cooked themselves. When they were finished
Yangaimo came down and took the food and gave it to everybody, and all had sufficient.

Ture began to go to Yangaimo's home, and when Ture
went there Ture saw him doing this thing. Ture deceived him,

telling him that he was his mother's brother; Yangaimo accepted that, so when Yangaimo was absent Ture took his plumes and his medicine (ashes) which were in the horn and went off with them. Hornets were near them, real fierce hornets, and they made for Ture savagely and stung him many times, but Ture abandoned nothing, he fled with them (the feathers and the ashes). Just a little thing (a feather) broke off from Ture and fell to the ground.

Ture arrived at his home and said to his wives 'You burn all your sesame,[1] for we shall never more lack meat.' Only his wife Nangbafudo did not burn her sesame. Ture said 'You sweep the courtyard, my wives.' They set to, to sweep it. He said to them 'You collect close-wove baskets and open-wove baskets, and pots and bowls.' They did accordingly. He said 'You wait in the courtyard here.' Ture took those plumes which he had stolen and put them on his head and went out into the open (sun) and began to fly, and while flying he sang this song, saying

'*Yuu yu* Ture, *yu* Ture,
You come to see me with plumes, *yuu yu* Ture.'

That man whose plumes Ture had stolen had a presentiment on the way to where he was going and he began to return in haste and came and arrived at his home and looked for his plumes, but he did not see them. He reflected and said to himself 'Who is it who has done me this great ill?' When he looked around he saw Ture's tracks and when he searched the ground he saw that one little feather which had broken off from Ture. He took it and tied it to a short cord and put it in his hat. When he looked up to the sky and saw Ture, a swarm of birds circling around him, he flew and struck those birds falling into Ture's courtyard. Yangaimo then said 'So it was Ture who stole my plumes, is not Ture a thief?' Yangaimo flew after Ture on high and sang his song, though Ture did not see him coming after him. Yangaimo sang, saying

'*Yuu* Yangaimo, Yangaimo,
Yangaimo, you come to take plumes.'

[1] 'Sesame' here stands for all vegetable accompaniments which are eaten with otherwise rather stodgy porridge. They would not need them in future because they would have plenty of meat to take their place; and meat is much more tasty.

This feather took Yangaimo straight, right into the sky, and he met Ture. Yangaimo then snatched the plumes from Ture's head. Ture began to stumble on high and began to fall to earth. Yangaimo said to Ture 'Friend, you for your part dance on the earth, I for mine dance on high here.' Ture accepted that. So the Tures danced indeed on the earth here.[1]

K.   *Ture and the woman's dogs* (Zakili–E-P.)

THERE was once an old woman who trained her dogs, of which she had many, and she called one by the name of ngbanguru (lion), and the name of another was zege (hyaena), and the name of another was bahu (lion). She set out after her game to hunt it with these her dogs, and she built a great granary, and dried meat filled it. She built another granary, and dried meat filled it. Ture arose to journey and went to see this great granary and saw it, and was silent and returned and arrived at his home, and twined his cord and went and chopped down his big stake and when he came to the water he erected the stake of his snare and pegged the spring into the ground, and he then spread out the noose at the edge of the water.

At daybreak next morning he came and arrived, and when he arrived he put his foot into the noose, and it sprang and threw him to the other side (of the water). Then he took his large bag and went and arrived at the home of this woman. The woman had already taken her grindstone and placed it, which was that resounding stone, and she ground her oil seeds. It (the oil) filled the pot. Ture arrived near this meat and removed much of it in a pot, and he put it on the fire. While it was stewing he took his water for porridge and put it on the other side of the fire. When it was bubbling too he went after leaves of *dakpa* and plucked them and brought them,[2] and the water for the porridge boiled. He then went and took some flour and brought it and poured it into the pot for porridge and mixed it and broke off a lot of the porridge into a bowl and then put it

---

[1] I think that the point is missed here by the narrator. 'Above' and 'below' make more sense in the previous version.

[2] For placing on the cooked porridge and for scooping it out. The botanical name is *Pileostigma reticulata*, one of the *Combretaceae*.

in his bag. This woman was out gathering salt when Ture did this in her home. The porridge being ready, he, Ture, jumped up and went to the side of that stone and sounded it (by grinding it), and it said '*Wongo* Ture, I am Ture, I sound Nawongowongo's stone, it sounds "*Wongo* Ture".'

This woman, she cried out, saying 'Lion, hyaena, listen to my stone which sounds.' They opened their mouths to run to the home while biting off sticks (on the path) and throwing them behind them. Ture stood beside this stone, and then he made off. When Ture saw them he dashed off with all speed. They came and saw Ture and bounded after him to chase him. Ture fled hard at once. They sped after him, and Ture fled hard, and he put his foot in the trap he had prepared and it sprang him and threw him to the other side (of the water). The dogs came and stood and howled after Ture on the other side. Ture returned and arrived at his home, to his mother, and he took his dried meat and those lumps of porridge and he ate and ate and ate it all up.

Then little Leopard arose and came and appeared in Ture's home. Ture said to him 'My younger brother, I have found animal flesh belonging to a woman whom people do not go near. My friend, come let us go together.' Ture told him to twine his cord and he began to twine it. When it was ready he said 'Let us go.' They went on and on and when they reached the side of this water Ture said 'You cut your snare-stake.' He went and cut it. So he cut the stake for his snare and set it at the edge of the water like Ture's; he set his snare, and all was prepared. Ture put his foot into the noose of his and little Leopard put his foot into the noose of his, and they raised them and cast them on the other side. Ture said 'Let us go', and they went on their way for a long time and arrived at this dried meat. They took a large pot, what a big pot! And they took meat till it filled it and put it on the fire. So, when he had put it on the fire, Ture spoke to little Leopard thus: 'Comrade, while you look after the fire I will go and pluck *dakpa* leaves.' So Ture went straight to little Leopard's snare and tied up the noose completely and set his own in order, and then he plucked some *dakpa* leaves and returned with them and came to little Leopard in the homestead. He then put the pot of porridge at the side of the fire and broke off some sesame and threw it into the meat and mixed the meat with it; then when the water of the porridge bubbled, he stirred the porridge. Then he took a big bowl and broke it (the porridge) into it (in lumps) until it was full. So he broke it off and when the bowl was filled he said to little Leopard 'Get up, let us go'; and he broke off little Leopard's portion into his bag and took his own with the bowl and broke it into his own bag. So they went and appeared beside this stone. Ture said '*Wongo* Ture, I am Ture, I sound Nawongowongo's stone, it sounds "*Wongo* Ture".' She cried to her dogs, saying 'Hyaena, lion, my meat is finished in the home.' They started off with all speed and ran and ran and reached the home.

When Ture and his friend saw them thus they started off with all speed. Ture ran straight for the place of his snare and put his foot in its noose, and it sprang together with Ture and threw him to the other side. When little Leopard put his foot in his noose it was not released. The dogs caught up with little Leopard, and little Leopard abandoned everything and fell into the water, to go on until he entered into Crocodile's fish-trap. Now as he went there, Crocodile came to inspect his fish-trap, and he took hold of its cord and drew his fish-trap and it was heavy for Crocodile. Crocodile then said 'This fish-trap of mine, what is this heavy thing in it thus?' He drew it out and threw it ahead on to the ground at the river side, and he took little Leopard from this his trap and cast him back, and the fish ate him up entirely. Then he began to bring out his fish on to land, such a quantity of fish, five baskets full. He then carried them to return with them, and returned and entered his home, and then began to prepare his fish, to dry them, and they dried. Ture in the meanwhile had gone straight to his home and took his dried meat which was in the bag and ate it all up. But Leopard never came to ask Ture about his son.

L. *Ture and the woman's dogs* (Kamanga–E-P.)

A WOMAN arose and made her home and trained her dogs. Ture arose and went and took little Bushbuck. They went and arrived at the edge of water, such a great expanse of water. They set a snare and it lifted them and threw them to the other side, where her home was. She had arisen and collected her dogs to wander off into the bush to go and hunt her game. That is where she was. Ture appeared at her home, and he took her meat and cooked it, and he went to her eleusine grain and poured it on to the grinding-stone. It sounded '*Wongo* Ture.' She said thus: 'Who is sounding our *wongo wongo* stone oo?' Ture said to her 'It is I o, I Ture, I sound on the stone "*Gburugo*".[1] I sound on the stone "*Wongo* Ture".' He ground eleusine on the stone again. The stone sounded '*Wongo*.' She said 'Who sounds our *wongo wongo* stone oooo?' Her dogs started off with all speed. Ture arose and took his bag and collected dried meats and put them in the bag. Little Bushbuck cooked porridge, and he broke it into a bowl, and he cooked oil (to go with the porridge). Her dogs, the name of one was Zazabili, of another Bangbokubori, and of another Manguru. They cried 'Zazabili ooo ooo', they cried 'Bangbokubori ooo ooo', they cried 'Manguru ooo ooo.' Ture started off with all speed and reached and messed up the noose of little Bushbuck's snare completely. Ture fled with little Bushbuck; Ture then put his foot into the noose of his snare, and it lifted him above the water to the other side. Little Bushbuck fled and put his foot into his snare, but it was all messed up. Her dogs arrived and seized him; she said 'Bangbokubori, mind you catch him.' She arrived and cut him up and took him back home to eat him.

Ture went and took Grey Duiker. Duiker appeared. While Ture set his (snare), Duiker set his, and they went to the homestead. Ture kindled a fire. They searched in vain for her. Ture took meat; Ture took a pot and put it on the fire with the meat. He then told Duiker that his stomach was upset. He went and messed up Duiker's snare altogether, and just put his own in order. Then he came to sit down. Little Duiker said to him that he was going to gather leaves of *nomba*[2] and *mboyo*[3] for them to cook with them. Ture then entered the hut in the woman's home and took her salt. Duiker said he was going to draw water, and he went and messed up the noose of Ture's snare and set his own. Duiker said to himself 'So! Ture cheated, and did he not do the same to those people whom he brought here?'

She took her dogs. Ture started up quickly and took his bag

---

[1] The sound of the smaller grindstone being rubbed on the larger one.
[2] An *Hibiscus*.   [3] Also an *Hibiscus*.

and took away porridge in it, together with the meat. Duiker took away his in his bag just as Ture had done in his. The dogs arrived and started off at all speed. They fled. Duiker put his foot into his snare and it lifted him from his place to the other side. Ture put his foot into his, but it was all messed up. He took hold of a branch to get away from the dogs. She arrived and spotted him above, and said 'O Ture! you have been eating my things.' He told her to go and get a large and very sharp knife, and stand with her legs apart, and he would begin to descend to dash between her legs; and she should raise her arm high so that when he jumped down she might stab him deep with her big knife. As she made to stab him as he jumped down she cut her own thigh. He fled with all speed and climbed another tree. She came and spotted him up above. He told her to take an axe and cut down the branch above. She cut it and it broke and fell into the water. He was saved.

M. *Ture and the woman's dogs* (G.)

THERE was a woman who lived by herself; she had no husband, only her many dogs. Their names were Bangbi, Banga, Nguabakinde, Karawandokiri, and yet others. She crossed a great expanse of water and made her home beyond it, right in the wilderness, with her dogs. She was very rich, she had much of everything—eleusine, sesame, millet, and also dried meat in a separate granary. Those her dogs, she went hunting with them for all kinds of animals and they caught them—buffalo, waterbuck, hartebeeste, elephant—what big dogs, bigger than lions! She ate meat of her hunting all the time.

Ture heard about this woman and he came to the edge of this great water and asked himself how he could get to the other side. He thought about it and said to himself that he would twine some cord to set a snare. He went and twined a very long length of cord and set his snare at the edge of this great water. Then he said to himself that he would try it out and he put his foot in the noose and it lifted him and threw him to the other side, and he said 'That's fine! I will eat all this woman's things.' Ture set another snare on the far side and he put his foot in the noose and it threw him again to this side. Ture said 'All is ready.' He took his big elephant-hide bag and hung it over his shoulder, and he put his foot in the snare and it lifted him and threw him again to the far side, and he went stealthily to this woman's home, but he did not see her there, for she was out hunting with her dogs. Ture went and looked in her granaries and found ground-nuts in two granaries, sesame in three granaries, dried meat in four granaries, and eleusine in five granaries, every sort of food, for she was rich. Ture climbed up the granary and gathered up her dried meats and came and crushed them up (to cook) on the fire, and put water to cook porridge on the fire, and when the meat simmered he went and gathered up some of her sesame and cooked it with it, and when the water of the porridge simmered he mixed the porridge and then quickly scraped out the porridge from the pot and put it (into a bowl) on the ground, and when that was done he took the meat off the fire, and he went to sound on that woman's grindstone which sounded like a bell, telling her to come. Ture sounded on it and it spoke, and this woman was far away, as far as to Wau,[1] searching for her animals. When Ture sounded on it she stopped and heard it, and when she heard it she stood and asked, saying 'Who sounds on Nawongowongo's stone o?' Ture said on it thus:

'I am here, I Ture, I sound on Nawongowongo's stone,
It says "*Wongo* Ture, *wongo* Ture".'

As soon as she heard what Ture spoke on her stone she dispatched her dogs, saying 'O Bangbi, that man who sounds on my stone, you kill him.' She came with them with all speed; they rushed towards the entrance to the courtyard. Ture took the porridge as well as the meat and emptied them into his elephant-hide bag. These dogs saw Ture and they sprinted on and on. Ture took his things and ran away and trod on his noose and it threw him to the other side, and these dogs ran to the edge of this great water only to see Ture on the other side. Ture stood on the other side and spoke to this woman and her dogs thus: 'You look at your foods which I have stolen! What will you do to me?' While Ture was departing

---

[1] A great distance.

on the other side this woman collected her dogs to return to her home.

Ture ate this porridge and took some of it and went and showed it to that animal Digdig, and when he ate it it tasted fine and he said 'O friend, Ture, where did you find this excellent food?' Ture replied 'I found it with that woman who lives on the other side of that river over there.' Digdig spoke to Ture thus: 'Friend, Ture, when you next go to eat it you must tell me; I will come to you tomorrow morning.' Ture agreed to what Digdig said and replied 'All right, that is just what I would like, that we go together.' They slept and then right early in the morning Digdig arrived at Ture's home and said 'Ture let us go.' Ture arose and they went on and on and arrived at the edge of this great water. Ture spoke to Digdig thus: 'What I use to get to the other side, it is my snare.' Ture set his, and Digdig set his also, and when all was ready they put their feet in the nooses and they lifted them to the other side, and they then began to set other snares on that side so that all was ready. They entered her home and looked in vain for her, and they went to her granary and collected dried meat and came and crushed it up into a big pot and placed it on the fire, and when it was simmering they collected eleusine and pounded it, and when that was done they roasted it[1] and ground it into flour. They cooked it, and they cooked meats, and all was ready. She was not there, she was far off, as far as Wau. Her stone which sounded like a bell, Ture went and sounded on it so that it would speak and when she heard it she would come. This affair, Ture had already been deceitfully to spoil the noose of Digdig's snare. He sounded on the stone and it called out her name, 'Nawongo, *wongo, wongo.*' She asked, saying 'Who sounds Nawongowongo's stone o?' Ture said 'I am here, I Ture, I sound on it, it says "*Wongo* Ture, *wongo* Ture"!'

She sent forth her dogs and they ran forward and she called out to them saying 'Oh! Look for the man who sounds on my stone.' These dogs rushed ahead and approached Ture. They emptied porridge and meat into the bag and then they fled away, and Ture put his foot into his noose, and it threw him

---

[1] After pounding, the grain of eleusine is roasted. The women do this to soften it for grinding. They say the grain tastes better when first roasted, but the main purpose in roasting it is to make it easier to grind.

to the other side. Ture had already altogether messed up Digdig's and when Digdig put his foot in it, oh no! It did not take him to the other side, because Ture had earlier messed it up. These dogs started to pursue Digdig and chased him hotly along the river bank and caught him and killed him. Ture stood on this side to watch them, how they treated Digdig on the other side. Ture said to them 'Since you have killed Digdig on account of your food, look at your food in my hands. What will you do to kill me, as a great water is between me and you, what will you do to catch me?'

Ture ate this porridge on the other side and these dogs watched him as he ate it. He ate it till he could eat no more, so he put what was left into the bag and went and showed it again to another animal, Red Duiker. Ture took it and went and gave it to him, and he took it, and when he ate it it tasted fine to him, and he asked Ture 'Where is this thing?' Ture said 'If you like that we go together, you sleep, and just as it will be light you come and we will go together.' So, Duiker slept, and right early in the morning he arrived at Ture's home and spoke to Ture thus: 'I have come, let us go.' They arose and went on and on till they arrived at the edge of this water, and they set their snares and when they were ready they put their feet in them and they took them to the other side. They then set up other snares on the other side and they were prepared. Then Ture and his companion went to the woman's homestead but they did not see her, she was wandering. So they collected dried meat and cooked it, and they cooked porridge quickly and put it down (off the fire) and awaited the meat on the fire. Ture spoke to Duiker thus: 'I am going to the bush,[1] you stay right here.' Ture did not go to the bush, he went to spoil the noose of Duiker's snare, saying to himself that these dogs would eat this Duiker. Ture returned and went and sounded on the stone. She asked, saying 'Who sounds on Nawongowongo's stone o?' Ture replied on it

> 'I am here, I Ture, I sound on it,
> It says "*Wongo* Ture, *wongo* Ture".'

She dispatched her dogs and they came on and on, and when they got near, Ture picked up the porridge and poured it into

---

[1] The expression here means 'to excrete'.

the bag. They saw Ture and they began to chase him and Duiker. The mistress of the dogs cried out to them, saying 'Mind you catch Ture.' When they came and got near to Ture he trod on his snare and it took him from them and threw him to the other side. For his part Ture was saved. Duiker said for his part 'Oh no! Oh no!' He trod in vain. The dogs started to pursue Duiker and chased him hotly along the river bank, they chased him on and on until they caught him. This woman threatened Ture, saying 'Ture, confound you, wait till my dogs get you!' Ture replied to her from the other side thus: 'Can you cross this great water to catch me?' This woman killed Duiker and went home with him. Ture said to her from the other side 'Look at your food.'

He sat down to eat this food, and when he was satisfied he took what remained to depart with it, and he went and gave it to that little animal Grey Duiker, and when he ate it it tasted good, and he said 'Eh! My friend! Ture, where did you find this nice thing?' Ture replied 'Would you like to go with me to get it?' He said 'Yes.' Ture said 'You sleep, then right early tomorrow morning you come and we will go together.' He agreed. Very early in the morning Duiker appeared before Ture and said '(I have come for) that journey we arranged yesterday.' They went and arrived at the edge of this great water and they prepared their snares and when they were ready they took them to the other side, and they went and arrived at her home, and she was out wandering with her dogs. Ture showed Duiker around, saying 'That is the granary for sesame, that is the ground-nuts' granary, that is the one for eleusine', and he showed Duiker the dried meats' granary. They said 'Let us collect dried meat to cook it with oil.' They gathered up her flour to cook it, and as they were making porridge Ture said that he was going to the bush, but it was not to the bush he was going; it was this excuse he used to deceive the animals with, saying he was going to the bush, whereas it was a lie. Ture thought he was going to deceive Duiker with it. But Duiker was no fool. Ture went to spoil (Grey) Duiker's snare so that they would kill him, just as he had done for Digdig and they killed him, and for Red Duiker and they killed him. Ture went and messed up Duiker's snare and set his own in order, and then he returned. Duiker said to Ture that he was going to the bush for his part also. Duiker came and saw that Ture's snare was in good order whereas he had messed up his own completely. Duiker left his as it was, he did not put it in order, thinking 'No matter, since Ture has spoilt mine, later I will come and tread on the noose of his.' He went and appeared in the homestead after Ture, but he said nothing.

They cooked porridge and when it was ready Ture broke off a lump and dipped it into the broth and gave it to Duiker to eat, and he ate it and said 'It tastes fine.' He said 'Who is going to carry the bag with porridge in it?' Ture said 'I am going to carry it.' Duiker said 'No you are not, it is for me to carry it who am a child.' Ture went and sounded on her stone for her to come, he sounded on it and it spoke. She asked, saying 'Who sounds on Nawongowongo's stone?' Ture replied

'I am here, I Ture, I sound on it,
It says "*Wongo* Ture, *wongo* Ture".'

She herself heard it before her dogs heard it. Ture sounded again and her dogs heard it, and she spoke to her dogs, each by name, 'Bangbi, Banya, Karawandokiri, Nguabakinde,[1] you run, that man Ture who sticks to us, you catch him.' They came on and on and as they approached Ture they began to chase Duiker, and Duiker fled right to the place of Ture's snare, and Ture spoke to Duiker thus: 'It is not yours there, Duiker, it is not yours there.' But Duiker did not hear. Duiker had already run and arrived and put his foot into Ture's noose and it had taken him to the other side, together with the porridge. Ture looked in vain for there seemed to be no means of escape. When Ture saw Duiker on the other side he was very angry.

These dogs started to pursue Ture and chased him hotly along the river bank. Ture then did a little thing right there at once to escape from these dogs. He plucked the red fruits of the Kaffir apple and put them over his eyes and he climbed with them into a tree and took a harp to play it to deceive these dogs together with their mistress. He played on the harp singing a song, looking only upwards while singing, saying

'Looker-up, I look down,
All men die, shimmering.

[1] The names of the dogs mean 'big world', 'big animal', 'dog-call', and 'wooden porridge-stirrer'.

Looker-up, I look down,
All men die.'

This woman came and appeared with her dogs. She asked
Ture, saying 'That's fine! Man, have you seen here that man
Ture?' But Ture did not answer her. She asked him again
'*He!* Man, have you seen here that man Ture?' She did not
know that he was Ture, on account of the deception Ture
practised. She asked Ture once more, and Ture said to her
'I do not look downwards, I only look upwards, for if I look
downwards everybody will die.' Ture said to her 'You tie up
your huge dogs to a tree, if you don't tie them to a tree I will
look downwards right now and you will die.' She tied up all her
dogs to a tree; when she heard what Ture had said, she said
'O man! Let me be, I will tie them to a tree, do not look downwards.' Ture agreed, and she tied up her dogs to a tree, and
she began to depart. It was those huge dogs of hers which Ture
feared and therefore he told her to tie them to a tree. Ture then
descended from the tree and he fled and escaped from this
woman and her dogs.

N. *How Firefly cheated Ture, and Ture and Nanzagbe's termites* (T.)

TURE was there. Now the season of termites came and Ture
said that they should go to collect termites. They prepared the
ground for this and then went home. When it was evening
Ture went to inspect the termite mound and when he got to it
he saw Firefly all aglow. Ture went back home, and when it
was dusk Ture said that they should go after the termites, but
his wives need not bring fire, for he had found fire in front of
the mound. They went to collect termites. Three of his wives
did not bring fire, only Nanzagbe took fire with her, hiding it
in a pot. They went after termites. As it was the season of termites they began to come out of their mound. Nanzagbe said
'Ture, they are about to fly, bring fire.' Ture went and seized
Firefly and put him on the dry stalks and blew on him in vain.
The termites flew away.

Only Nanzagbe took her fire which she had hidden in the pot. She got it aflame. She awaited her termites with it. Ture ran about in vain and chased after Firefly in vain. The termites escaped and were finished. Ture lacked termites and so did three of his wives. They began to go home. Nanzagbe was drying her termites in the sun and went to draw water. Ture went to cheat and took the red juice of a tree and sprinkled it over the termites and said to Nanzagbe 'That brother of yours who was here, it is his blood you see.' Nanzagbe said she did not want those termites, she was going to her dead brother's home. While she was on her way to her dead brother's home Ture carried the termites into a cave and he said to Tortoise 'Let us go to eat termites in the cave.' He went with Tortoise and they arrived there. Ture then told Tortoise to go and wash his hands and then they would eat the termites. Tortoise went off to a stream and back, and while he was away Ture ate up all the termites, and Tortoise got none. That is the end of the story.

APPENDIX I

A FINAL tale, in which Ture does not appear, is given in the vernacular with a line by line translation. This is not a linguistic study, so no linguistic analysis is attempted. As has earlier been said, there is no correct way of writing Zande; and, in particular, word-division could be presented differently from what I have found to be convenient—this has always been a controversial issue in the recording of African languages. Were this a linguistic study it might be demanded that the tones, which are quite strong in Zande, be marked, but I would in any case not be capable of marking them, though presumably I was making an approximation of the tonal sounds or communication would have been more difficult than it was. I may also be excused for not attempting the task on the grounds that it has not been found necessary to mark the tones in printed Zande, which means a few school texts and translations of biblical and other religious literature, the context being a sufficient indication of meaning.

Zande is a language far from easy to learn and speak. I am well aware of my own short-comings, but the anthropologist has one great advantage. He is conversing always within the native frame of reference, about what interests them, whereas officials and missionaries, however well they may speak a language, are only too often speaking of matters which are outside the context of the native's social life and his cultural milieu. Should anyone wish to inform himself about the structure of the Zande language he can consult the books listed below.

LAGAE, C. R., and VANDEN PLAS, V. H., 1921, 1922, 1925. *La Langue des Azande*, Gand.
GORE, E. C., n.d. (1926). *A Zande Grammar*, London.
—— and GORE, Mrs. E. C., 1931 (rev. ed. 1952). *Zande and English Dictionary*, London.
'GERO' (GIORGETTI, F.), 1957. *Panorama Grammaticale Zande*.

70. *Two sisters* (R. R.)

Kumba   a   du   yo   ki   vungu   awiriko   ue   ni   adegude.   i   ki
There was a man who begot two children, both daughters. When

ta   sona   ka   da   ba   ade   nzunzu   ko   ki   ya   fu   yo   we,   kina
they had grown up and become women he told them that one man

gu kumba sa ni ka rogo yo, kina ko sa ni ka ra na yo wa
was to marry both of them, he alone was to sleep with them as his

ga   ko   ade;   ka   i   wi   nga   kura   kumba
wives; they were not to have intercourse with any other man

berewe wa sa ya. ka i wi kumba ko ki imi yo a ima
whomsoever. If they were to have intercourse with a man he would

ni   ba   sa   kindi.   i   ki   idi   e   fu   ko   wenengai.
at once kill them. They consented fully to what he said.

gu rago ki ya giri i ki ya fu ko i na kpi nyamu ka ndu
One morning they said to him that they wished to go and attend a

sa pumbo ku rogo kura ringara tuturu na ku ba yo. ko ki
feast in a district far from that of their home. He agreed to their

idi e fu yo, ono ko ki ya fu yo we, wa i a ndu ka i ti
request, but he told them that when they went they were to be sure

nga ga ko ndika wa sa ya, i tingidi gu pai ko a gumba
not to disobey his commandment, let them bear in mind what he had

fu yo mbata. i ki ya fu ko i a manga nga pai wa sa te.
told them before. They told him that they would do nothing wrong.

i ki mbembedi ga yo ime wenengai gbe, ki kakai ga yo aira
They washed themselves very well, and they rolled up their mats,

dunduko, nga gu i a ndu ka ra auru e yo. i ki ndu a ndu kindi ki da
those they were going to sleep on. They went on their way and arrived

pati gbere yo nyemu. i ki do o a do kindi, rago ki giri, uru ki ndu
at the dance in the evening. They danced till dawn, and then through

berewe ki ti. rago ki ta gira wiso i ki ni mo ka tingida pa
the day till the sun set again. When the day broke they began to

yega fuo ba yo ku kporo no.
think it was time to return to their father and home.

i ki ta guari ka mera gene yo, akumba ki mere fuo
When they arose to set forth on their way three men followed

yo biata. gu ko ki ya fu yo, 'ako adewirani oni ini
them. One of them said to them 'O our sisters, you be compassionate

pai fu rani ki idi nga fu rani ani pi nga na oni gene ere, oni ka susa.'
to us and let us lie with you on the way here, and then you can pass

i ki gi e a gia gbua ka i a karaga nga pai sa ni
on.' They just listened to what he said, saying nothing in return. He

wa sa ya. ko ki dari yo vuru, i ki ta turo gbe ko
importuned them in vain, and when they were a long way off he

ki karaga ti ko. agu yo ki ni ndu na yo kindi, ki
turned back, but the others continued to go along with them and

ni dari yo. i ki ka a ka kindi, ko ki karaga ti ko fuo
continued to press them, and they continued to refuse, and one of
gu kura ko na karaga ti ko mbata.
them turned back after the other who had earlier turned back.
gu ko ki ndu na yo kindi, ki ni dari yo. i ki ya fu
The third man continued to go along with them, and he continued
ko we, 'ani a ida nga a wa sa te, bombiko
to pester them. They said to him thus: 'We are quite unwilling, for
ba rani a kido rani a kido, ki ya ka ani mangi pai gbegbere ko
our father has threatened, saying that if we act wrongly he will kill
imi rani a ima. bombiko ko na tuka mange rani a tuka ni e; ka ani
us. For he has plaited our (pubic) hair cunningly; if we act wrongly
mangi pai no gbegbere ko ini e a ina bombiko a nga boro o sa ka tu e wa
here he will know it, for there is no one who can plait like him.' He
ko te.' ko ki zadi kpe a zada kindi, ki ya fu yo we, 'ka si
then set up a loud lamentation, saying to them thus: 'Even though he
vura du wa ko na tuko o a tuka mi a tu e kina wo a.' i ki ya fu ko we,
has plaited it, I will plait it just the same.' They said to him thus:
'ani na gunde a gunde ni lengo, bombiko ka mo tu nga a wa
'We are truly afraid, because if you don't plait it like him,
ko te, ka mo mangi gbegbere pai na ani, ko ini e a ina ni rengo.' kumba
if you do ill with us, he will know for sure.' The man
ki ka kindi, ki ya fu yo we, 'oni ini nga pai fe
persisted, saying to them thus, 'You be compassionate to
re ti e ki fu nga a fe re mi tu nga o.' i ki ya
me and let me have what I want and I will plait it as it was.' They
fu ko i a ida nga a wa sa te. ko ki ka koti yo kindi,
told him that they would not at all consent. He still stuck to them,
ki ya fu yo we, ka i a fu nga a fu ko ya ka ko a
and he said to them thus, that if they would not give him what he
karaga nga ti ko wa sa ya. si ki
wanted, still he would not turn back in any circumstances. When
ta kpakara bangiri yo, umvuru ki ya fu tame we, 'ako
it became difficult for them the elder sister said to the younger 'O my
tamere wa ani kpi be gi kumba re ani a manga ko
younger sister, since we are troubled by this man, how shall we deal
wai? si ngba ka mo ndu fuo ko, ani ga ba rani imi
with him? You had better go with him, and then we can go home
rani, na wa ani na ka fu ko vuru.' tame
and be killed by our father, for it is in vain that we refuse him.

ri   ki   idi   e   fu   ri   wo.   i   ki   ya   fu   gu
The younger sister agreed to the suggestion. They said to this man

kumba re we, 'wa mo na imi rani ti e fu barani mo tu gu
thus: 'Since you wish to make our father kill us, you plait the hair

mange re wenengai wa barani ni tu e ni ina e.' ko ki ya fu
well, just as our father plaited it, with cunning.' He said to them

yo, 'oni ongo a onga adawire, mi a tu e kina ku ba a.' i ki ni
'You be quiet my sisters, I will plait it just as it was.' They went off

kpara ti mvuo na ri. i ki ima a ima kindi ki ta da ko ki ni
into the bush. They stayed there a long time till it was finished, and

mo ka tu mange gi degude re. ono si ki gasi ko a
then he began to plait the hair of this girl. But it was too difficult for

gasa, ka ko a tu nga a wa ba yo a tu e yo wa
him. He was not able to plait it at all as their father had plaited it.

sa ya. umvurari ki ke na ni a vuru, si ki gasi ri a gasa.
Her elder sister strove with it also in vain, it was too difficult for her.

i ki ni ndu a ndu kindi ki ta kura ko yo du ba
They continued on their way and arrived at their father's home.

yo ni. ngbadu ko ki ima kita. ko ki ini ni ba sa ki ya kumba
He was already grieved. He knew at once that a man had been after

ndu sa ri. ko ki ongo a onga ni ba sa kindi, ki poi koti yo,
her. He remained completely silent for a while and then he saluted

ki sana yo tipa gu gbere i a ndu sa ni; i
them and asked them about that dance to which they had gone;

ki peke pa a fu ko dunduko, ono ka i a gumba nga gu pai
and they described it all to him, but they did not tell him anything

na mangi fu yo wa sa ya. ba yo ki ya fu yo
about what happened to them afterwards. Their father said to them

we, ko na kpi nyemu ka bi mange yo dunduko awere bombiko wa i na
that he wanted to see all their hair immediately for since they

raki ko yo ue ka i mangi gbegbere pai yo. ko
had slept two nights away they might have misbehaved there.

ki uru roko ti kina gu ri nga mvuru mbata, ko ki
He removed the barkcloth of the elder sister first, and he saw his

bi sabe ko kina ku ba a wa ko a tu e. ko ki gbisi
handiwork in proper order, just as he had plaited it. Then he moved

fuo gu ri nga tame, ki uru roko ti ri ki ya
to the younger sister and he removed her barkcloth and when he

ngere gu fuo ko ko a tu mange ri na ni mbata ka si a du nga
examined the design he had plaited her hair in, it was not the

wo wa sa ya. si ki du a du zauzau gbua. ko ki ongo kina ku kiri. ko ki
same. It was all just loose. He remained quite silent. He told their

ya fu na yo we, ri imi akondo ue, ki songo gbamu ki di
mother to kill two fowls and raise the roof of the granary and

nzeme yo ka pasa agi akondo na ni re. ri ki mangi a wa ko a gumba a;
take oil from it to cook these fowls in. She did as she was bid;

ono ka ri a ina nga gu pai na manga wa sa ya, bombiko ko a
but she had no idea of what was going to happen, for he had not

gumba nga a fu ri te. ko ki guari ki di gu wene roko nga gu boro
told her of it. He rose and took some fine barkcloth, such as no one

a bi nga a mbata ya, ki ukadi ri na ni wenengai. ko ki mai atongo
had before seen, and he decked her carefully with it. He put rings

ti wiri nzaga ri dunduko. i ki tu ri ri wenengai. ko ki yembu
on her fingers. They plaited her hair beautifully. He called for

e na bakinde fu ri. na ri ki sana ko, ki ya
porridge and meats to be brought to her. Her mother asked him,

fu ko, 'gini pai mo a manga ri na ni?' ko ki ya fu
saying 'What are you going to do to her?' He replied that he was not

ri ko a manga nga pai na ri wa sa te. ri ki ri bakinde toni
going to do anything to her. She ate only just a little porridge and

gbua ki mbu e, bombiko ngba ri a zera a zera ti ni. Ko ki
stopped eating, for she had no appetite for it. He waited for some

ni sungu a sungo kindi, ki guari ku ari ki tumba ri a tumba nibasa ki ni
time and then sprang up and picked her up suddenly and started

zubo ni oto ka ora ka ba ri ku dio. na ri ki zubo fuo ko ki ta
to run with her to throw her into the river. Her mother started off

kpara fu ko, 'mo zogo wire kina o. kumba mo
after him and cried out to him 'Put my child down, husband, why

na imo ri tipagine?' ka ko a gia nga a wa sa ya. ko
are you killing her?' But he would not listen. He ran with her at

ki oro a ora na ri nibasa ki ba ri ku di yo. fuo gure kina bakere ba tio
once and threw her into the river. Then an enormous fish came and

ki ye mbiri ri a mbira na ba ri. fuo mbira u ri ku vuru yo u ki ni
swallowed her whole. After swallowing her into its belly it went on

ndu a ndu kindi ki ta da kina pangba ime yo rogo ngume u ki kusi ri
until it reached the sandy bank of the river and it brought her up

ki mai ri auru gi ngume re. u ki ta mera, ri ki ni guari
and deposited her on the sand. When the fish went she arose and

a guari o ki ni mo ka kura ku pia yo. ri ki ndu a ndu kindi ki bi guga
emerged on to dry land. She went on and on until she saw a

na fuo aboro pati e. ri ki dakpa ku ari yo ba ri gu
water-hole with footmarks of people nearby. She climbed up above this

guga re ki sungu kina ari yo. bebere uru ki ta da gbinza de ki ni
water-hole and sat there above. At midday an old woman came to

mo ka ye ka tu ga ri ime. ri ki kuru ku pati guga, ri ki ya ngere
draw her water. She arrived at the side of the water-hole, and

ku ime yo ri ki bi kirimo boro yo nga gu wene
when she looked into the water she saw the reflection of a person

boro. ri ki bere e ti ga ri ki ya kina kirimo
there, such a fine-looking person. She thought that this fine reflection

ri du ngba were. ri ki ni mo ka tona ga ri bia ka bi e. gu bia ri a bi
was of herself. She began to sing her song. That song she sang went

e, si du re, 'atika mi ni ngba were, atika mi ni tuku ri re ureure,
thus: 'Am I not handsome? Do I not plait my hair like a mane,

mi ni uka a?' ri ki ngere ku ime yo ki bi kirimo ri ime
spilling down to the shoulders?' She looked into the water and saw

yo. ono gu degude re ri ki ongo a onga ki.
her reflection in the water. But that girl above remained absolutely

gu gbinza de re ri ki tona ka do ga ri gbere berewe,
silent. Then the old woman began to dance her dance again, for

bombiko ri a bere e ki ya kirimo ri du. fuo gure ri ki ya u
she thought it was her own reflection. Then as she looked upwards

ngere ku ari yo ri ki bi gu degude re ni ba sa. ri ki ya fu ri we, 'mo zoro
she at once saw the girl. She said to her 'You come down here,

ko no dia wire.' ri ki zoro fuo ri, i ki ga ku kporo yo.
wife of my son.' She came down to her, and they went to her home.

gu gbinza de re, wiri ni ki du o na kungu ti ko, ono ka gi degude a ina
This old woman had a son who was a leper, but the girl did not

nga a re ya. rago ki ta bira i ki mbakadi ba fu ri kina ti
know this. When dusk came on they prepared a bed in the hut

gu bambu gi ira kungu a du ti e yo re, i ki vagadi ko na kina akoro.
where this leper was, and they covered him with a pot. They all

i ki rimi ku dimo yo dunduko ka ndu ka ra rame. gu degude re ri ki da du kina
went indoors to sleep. When the girl was fast asleep the leper came

ku rame yo gi ira kungu re, ko ki kuru ti akoro yo ki ye ki pi pati gi degude re,
forth from beneath the pot and lay down beside the girl without

ka ri a ina nga ya. ko ki ni wi ri a wi ki ni ga ku ba
her knowing it. He had intercourse with her and then went back

ko yo ti akoro yo, ono ka gi degude a ina nga a re wa sa ya.
to his place beneath the pot, but the girl knew nothing about it.

rago ki ya giri kpoto ri ki du a du na kina togoro na kure na kpanda.
In the morning her skin was covered in sap and blood and pus.
ri ki ya fu gu gbinza de re gini pai du were, gine ni mangi kpoto
She asked the old woman what was the matter, what had happened
re were yuru? ri ki ya fu ri we, 'ka ti ngia kina gu boko
to her skin during the night? She replied 'Perhaps it was that
mo a sari ru gba ku wio, u du tomeru a zi ro.' gu
pumpkin you cut open yesterday to cook it, it is its sap which has
degude re, ri ki ongo kina ku o, ka ri a karaga nga pai
taken hold of you.' At that the girl was silent, she said no more to the
fu ri berewe ya. gu kura rago ki ya biri si ki du kina wo wa si a du
old woman. The next night it was the same as it had been the night
gba. gu degude re ri ki ini a ina ni ba sa ki ya wiri
before. The girl then realized at once that there was something
pai kina o i a manga ri na ni. ri ki ongo a onga, ka ri
happening, something they were doing to her. She kept silence and
a karaga nga pai wa sa ya. uru ki ta da sa bawe i ki ndu ku ati
said nothing. When it was about ten o'clock in the morning they
yo, ono i ki ya fu gu degude re we, ri sungu
went to the cultivations, but they told this girl to remain in the
kina kporo no ka ra fogo boko fu yo. ri ki idi e fu yo. i ki
homestead to cook fresh gourds for them. She agreed to do this. They
guari na baira kporo na gu gbinza dia ko re du na rukutu
all arose, the master of the home and that old wife of his and his
awiri ko a, i ki ndu sa bino du ki e kina gu degude
little children also, and they all went to cultivate, leaving this girl
sa re kporo no tipa manga riae. ono gu wiri yo nga
by herself in the homestead to prepare food. But that son of theirs
ira kungu ko i na oka ko ku dimo yo ku ti akoro yo.
who was a leper, him they hid in the hut under an upside-down pot.
i ki ta mera, gu degude re, ri ki ndu ki kati boko ki
When they had left, the girl went to pick a gourd and brought it
ye na u ka ra ru fu yo. ri ki gumba pai ni sa ri ku kpoto ri yo, ki ya gu pai
back to cook it for them. She said to herself inside herself, that thing
ni na manga ri yuru gini pai nga a? ri ki rimi ku
which kept on happening to her in the night, what thing was it? She
dimo yo ki ngereke ku ti ba yo dunduko, ka ri a bi
entered the hut and searched carefully under the bed, but she saw
nga e wa sa ya ri ki ya u tumba akoro ku ari ri ki bi gu
nothing. When she lifted up the pot and saw the leper she put the

ira kungu re. ri ki vagadi akoro berewe kina ku ba a. ri ki kuru ku zegi yo,
pot down again in its place. She came out of the hut, and she made

ki gindo we ti baramai yo, ki gbisi ga ri bakere akoro
a fire in the kitchen-hut, and she shoved her large pot to one side

ki uka ime ko yo si ki hi e, ri ki moi e ku we
and she poured water into it till it was full, and then she put it on the

yo. ri ki guari ki kati boko a kata ni dungu ru gbe ki ye na u ku
fire. Then she went to pick many gourds and brought them to the

pati gi bakere akoro re. ime ki ta ba puyepuye wenengai,
side of the big pot. The water was nicely boiling bubblingly, and she

ri ki sapu boko dunduko, ki e ru mbata ime ba
sliced all the gourds and put them on one side for the water to boil

wenengai. ri ki rimi ku dimo yo ki tumba akoro ki gbe gu kumba
hard. Then she entered the hut and lifted up the pot, dragging the

ti e yo re. ri ki ba ko ku sande ki ni mo ka yera
man beneath it. She then threw him to the ground and cut his throat

goko na ga ri sape. ko ki ta kpi ri ki mbakadi ko dunduko ku rogo gu
with her knife. When he was dead she cut him up and put his flesh

bakere ba akoro re, ri ki mai boko ku auru pasio gu irakungu re,
in the big pot, and then she put the gourds on top of the flesh of this

ki vagadi ngba akoro na kpe dunduko. ri ki ni
leper and covered well the mouth of the pot with leaves. Then she

guari ka mera. agu aboro na ndu ka sopa bino, i ki yega ku
walked off. Those people who went to hoe their cultivations returned

kporo no, i ki yembu ri vuru, ka ri a hi nga wa sa ya.
home and called out to her in vain, for she did not answer at all.

i ki rimi ku dimo yo, ki ya ngere i ki bi kina kure
They entered the hut and when they looked around they saw blood

vuru bombu, i ki ya u ndu ku ti baramai yo ki bi
in the hut; and when they went to the kitchen-hut they saw the

boko we yo. i ki zogo boko we yo ki rogo gu ru na du
gourds cooking on the fire. They took the gourds off the fire and took

auru ki ni ri ru a ri. i ki rogo gu ru berewe ki ya
the top ones and ate them. They took others and then, when they

u ngere ku sande yo i ki bi kina pasio gume yo. ba gi kumba
looked beneath them, they saw the flesh of their kinsman. The father

re, ko ki ni mo ka ora ka do fuo ri, ono ko ki do fuo ri vuru, ka ko a bi
of this man began to run after her, but he did so in vain because he

nga ri wa sa ya; ko ki ni mo ka karaga ti ko ku sa yo. gi degude re,
did not see her at all, so he turned back again. The girl continued

ri ki ndu a ndu kindi ki kuru ku ba ri yo. o i a bi ri ni
on her way and arrived at her father's home. When they saw her

ka i a ina nga ri ni ipo ya, i ki ni sana ri vuru,
they did not at once recognize her, and they questioned her in vain,

ka ri a karaga nga pai wa sa ya. ba ri ki ini ri a ina dunduko,
for she did not answer a word. Her father recognized her completely,

ono ka i a gia nga fugo ri wa sa ya. ko ki ndu ko yo du atari
but they did not hear her speech at all. He went to where the *Atari*

ni, ki sana ra, ami ki ya fu ko we, ko ndu a ndu ki sungu kina
(oracle) was and questioned it, and it told him to go and seat himself

pati we yuru, ko ki zo kina ga ko roko na we ti ngba a,
beside the fire at night and arrange to set light to the edge of his bark-

ko a gia fugo ri a gia. ko ki ndu ki sungu pati we
cloth, and then he would hear her speak. He went and sat by the fire

yuru, awiri ko ki ye ki sungu pati ko; ko ki zo ngba ga
at night, and his children sat beside him, and he burnt the edge of his

ko roko ni we, si ki ni gbi ki ni fu a fu gbe. kina gi
barkcloth in the fire, and it burnt and made a great stink. Then this

degude re, ri ki ya fu ko, 'buba ga mo roko na gbi.' ko ki ya fu ri,
girl said to him 'Father, your barkcloth is burning.' He asked her

'si wari?' ri ki ya fu ko, 'si na gbi ti ndu ro yo.'
'Burning where?' She replied to him 'It is burning on your leg.'

fuo gure i ki ni mo ka tona fugo na ba ri ka fu wenengai.
After that she and her father began to converse and to talk well.

si ki ni mo ka nyesa ni ba sa kindi. i ki sungu wenengai.
And so all was finished right away and for good. And they lived
together happily.

'si du mi ni ndu a ndu ti ni kindi ki kuru ku
'So it was that I went for a long way and arrived at the home of

tukure yo, mi ki bi ko ko ni ta dia ko. mi ki ya mi ya fu ko
Tukure and found him beating his wife. When I was trying to ask

we, "ako gbia, gine mo a ta dia ro ti ni?" ko ki ni mo ka
him "O master, why do you beat your wife?" he began to get

zinga a zinga fe re ki ni kpi nyemu ka ta kpata a ta na mi. si du mi
angry with me and wanted to pick a quarrel with me. That being so,

ni ya fu ko we, ko ta dia ko a ta. ko ki ya fe re we,
I said to him, let him go on beating his wife. He said to me then

"ka mi zingi nga ya", *ko ki fu kondo fe re, mi ki mai ru auru ngbadimo*
"Don't lose your temper", and he gave me a fowl, and I put it on
ku kandisi yo. gu boro ka kpi nyemu ka ri kondo ni
the lintel of Kandisi's doorway. Anyone who wants to eat the fowl,
ndu ka ri ru.'
let him go and eat it.'

APPENDIX II

An index is given below to all Ture stories (including the one of Appendix I) which have previously appeared in print or are about to do so. The numbers are those of the tales as listed in this book, which correspond up to no. 50 to those of G.1.

Several versions of a tale may be found under a single entry. The titles of the stories to which the index refers are not always exactly the same as those of this volume. The privately printed Oxonian Press texts have been presented to the Royal Anthropological Institute. The key to the entries is as follows:

G.1   GORE, Mrs. E. C., 1951. *Sangba Ture* (revised by G. Riley), London.

G.2   GORE, The Revd. Canon E. C., n.d. (1926). *A Zande Grammar*, London, pp. 121–33.

L   LAGAE, C. R., 1921. *La Langue des Azande* ('Introduction Historico-Géographique' par V. H. Vanden Plas), Gand, pp. 183–236.

S.1   EVANS-PRITCHARD, E. E., 1963. 'Some Zande Folk-Tales, I', *Sudan Notes and Records* 44, pp. 43–66.

S.2   —— 1964. 'Some Zande Folk-Tales, II', *Sudan Notes and Records* 45, pp. 59–78.

S.3   —— 1965. 'Some Zande Folk-Tales, III', *Sudan Notes and Records* 46, pp. 50–66.

K.1   —— 1964. 'Some Zande Texts—Part 3', *KUSH* 12, pp. 251–81.

K.2   —— 1965. 'Some Zande Texts—Part 4', *KUSH*, 13, pp. 213–40.

K.3   —— (in press). 'Some Zande Texts—Part 5', *KUSH*, 14.

J   —— 1965. 'Four Zande Tales', *The Journal of the Royal Anthropological Institute* 95, i, pp. 44–74.

J.L.1 —— 1964. 'Variations in a Zande Folk-Tale', *Journal of African Languages* 3, pp. 103–34.

J.L.2 —— 1966. 'Zande Trickster and other Tales', *Journal of African Languages* 5, pp. 128–60.

M   —— 1964. 'Two Zande Tales', *Man* 64, no. 132.

A.Q.1 EVANS-PRITCHARD, E. E., 1964. 'Four Zande Tales', *Anthropological Quarterly* 37, no. 4, pp. 157–74.

A.Q.2 —— 1966. 'Some Zande Folk-Tales from the Gore Collection', *Anthropological Quarterly* 39, no. 4, pp. 265–87.

O.1 —— 1964. *Zande Texts*, Part 4, 34 pages, Oxonian Press (privately printed).

O.2 —— 1965. *Zande Texts*, Part 5, 32 pages, Oxonian Press (privately printed).

F.G. GIORGETTI, F. Not yet published.

v Vernacular.

t Translation.

1. G.1 (v); L (v, t); K.1 (v, t).
2. G.1 (v); L (v, t); K.1 (v, t).
3. G.1 (v); K.2 (t).
4. G.1 (v); S.1 (v, t); S.3 (v, t); J.L.2 (v, t).
5. G.1 (v); G.2 (v, t); S.1 (v, t); O.1 (v, t).
6. G.1 (v); J (v, t).
7. G.1 (v); L (v, t); O.2 (v, t).
8. G.1 (v); S.1 (t).
9. G.1 (v); J (v, t).
10. G.1 (v); A.Q.2 (t).
11. G.1 (v); K.1 (v, t).
12. G.1 (v).
13. G.1 (v); S.2 (v, t); A.Q.2 (t); J.L.2 (v, t).
14. G.1 (v); A.Q.2 (t).
15. G.1 (v); S.1 (v, t).
16. G.1 (v); L (v, t); J (v, t).
17. G.1 (v); S.2 (v, t); K.2 (t).
18. G.1 (v); S.3 (t).
19. G.1 (v); S.3 (t).
20. G.1 (v); S.3 (t).
21. G.1 (v); S.3 (t); A.Q.1 (v, t).
22. G.1 (v); S.2 (v, t); S.3 (t).
23. G.1 (v); L (v, t); K.3 (v, t).
24. G.1 (v); S.2 (v, t).
25. G.1 (v); K.3 (v, t).
26. G.1 (v); S.2 (v, t); S.3 (v, t); J.L.2 (t).
27. G.1 (v).
28. G.1 (v); M (v, t).
29. G.1 (v); K.2 (v, t).
30. G.1 (v); K.3 (v, t).
31. G.1 (v).

32. G.1 (v); K.2 (v, t).
33. G.1 (v); G.2 (v, t); K.1 (v, t); J.L.2 (t).
34. G.1 (v); O.1 (v, t); A.Q.2 (t).
35. G.1 (v); A.Q.2 (t).
36. G.1 (v); A.Q.2 (t).
37. G.1 (v); K.2 (v, t).
38. G.1 (v); G.2 (v, t); J.L.1 (v, t).
39. G.1 (v); K.3 (v, t).
40. G.1 (v); O.1 (v, t); O.2 (v, t).
41. G.1 (v); A.Q.2 (t).
42. G.1 (v); L (v, t); M (v, t).
43. G.1 (v); L (v, t); K.3 (v, t); A.Q.2 (t).
44. G.1 (v); L (v, t); S.2 (v, t); A.Q.2 (t).
45. G.1 (v); A.Q.2 (t); O.1 (v, t).
46. G.1 (v); A.Q.2 (t).
47. G.1 (v); A.Q.1 (v, t); A.Q.2 (t).
48. G.1 (v); K.2 (v, t); J.L.2 (v, t).
49. G.1 (v); K.3 (v, t); A.Q.2 (t).
50. G.1 (v); A.Q.1 (v, t); A.Q.2 (t).
51. A.Q.1 (v, t).
52. S.2 (v, t); J.L.2 (v, t).
53. K.1 (v, t).
54. K.1 (v, t).
55. O.1 (v, t).
56. S.3 (v, t); O.1 (v, t).
57. O.1 (v, t).
58. O.2 (v, t).
59. S.3 (v, t).
60. K.2 (v, t).
61. S.3 (v, t).
62. L (v, t); O.2 (t).
63. S.3 (v, t).
64. S.3 (v, t).
65. G.2 (v, t).
66. Not published.
67. J.L.2 (v, t).
68. J.L.2 (v, t).
69. K.3 (v, t).
70. J (v, t).
H. J.L.1 (v, t).
N. J.L.2 (v, t).

INDEX

ant, 120.

Atari (oracle), 36, 49, 53, 90, 95, 125, 131, 133, 142, 151, 176, 179, 206, 207, 208, 233.

banana, 164, 186.
barkcloth, 1, 7, 39–40, 44–45, 68, 94, 97, 104, 107, 116, 117, 134, 145, 178, 205, 228, 229, 233.
bat, 27, 84–86, 93.
bees, 10, 73, 134; eye-bees, 59–60, 135.
blood-brother, 6, 37–38, 46, 53, 54, 60, 151.
bread-fruit, 84–86, 93–95.
buffalo, 9, 89, 107, 119–20, 121, 124, 125, 126, 141, 142, 168–70, 193, 198, 217.
bulbul, 101, 192, 201.
bushbuck, 64–66, 76, 158–60, 177, 180, 215, 216.
butterfly, 208.

caterpillar, 8, 51.
chicken (*also* cock, fowl), 7, 8, 10, 45, 46, 47, 52, 53, 119, 120, 121, 141, 147, 148, 173, 184, 203, 205, 206, 208, 229, 234.
cicada, 27, 28, 95–96.
cistola warbler, 201.
civet cat, 149–50.
crab, 135.
cricetus, 152–3, 156–8.
crocodile, 95, 215.
cuckoo, 115, 194, 201.

digdig, 66, 219, 220, 221.
dog, 7, 8, 56, 57, 58, 61, 62, 63–67, 80, 155–6, 196, 213, 214, 215, 216–23.
dove (laughing, and long-tailed), 115, 191, 201.
duiker (grey and red), 66, 84–87, 97–99, 131, 179, 216, 217, 220, 221, 222.

egg, 8, 48, 60, 69–71, 119, 120, 121, 146, 169.
elephant, 9, 79–80, 97, 107, 113–17, 132, 185, 190–205, 207, 208, 217.

eleusine, 7, 10, 37, 63, 64, 65, 75, 172, 173, 192, 205, 206, 209, 216, 217, 218, 219, 221.

firefly, 137–9, 223–4.
fish, 10, 40–41, 54, 67, 68, 100–1, 102–3, 111, 117–18, 121, 122, 215, 229.
flies, 183, 184.
francolin, 194, 201, 206.
frog, 8, 109–10.

gourd (bottle-, cup-, *also* pumpkin), 38, 231, 232.
grasshopper, 164, 172.
ground-fruit (*nonga*), 90–91, 179.
ground-nut, 7, 10, 63, 65, 99, 100, 107, 108, 127, 128, 218, 221.
guinea-fowl, 71, 72, 115, 128, 129, 130, 162, 192, 201.

hammerhead stork, 115–16, 202; *see also under* mocking-bird (*zakiringi*).
hare, 146.
hartebeeste, 217.
honey, 1, 10, 11, 21, 45–46, 73, 78, 120, 121, 123, 134, 156.
honey-bird (-sucker), 45–46, 179.
hornet, 209, 212.
hyaena, 213, 214, 215.

iguana, 152, 160.
in-laws, 6, 44–46, 59, 60–71, 77, 99, 144–6, 147, 168, 169, 177–80, 183.

kaffir (custard-) apple, 66, 135, 222.
kite, 83–84.
kpikoro (insect), 27, 75, 160–2, 183.

leopard, 130–3, 152, 156–60, 177–80, 214–15.
lice, 90.
lion, 130, 213, 214, 215, 217.
lizard, 42, 106, 119.

mahogany tree, 153.
maize, 7, 10, 75.
manioc, 7, 10, 37, 45, 100, 129, 130, 137, 175.

maternal uncle (mother's brother, *also*
sister's son), 6, 22, 47, 68, 69, 127,
132, 154, 155, 161, 168, 169, 182,
183, 212.
millet, 217.
millipede, 48–49.
mimosa tree, 73, 74.
mocking-bird (Ethiopian thrush, *zakiringi*), 192, 195, 202, 203, 207, 208.
monkey, 77–78, 94.
mushroom, 1, 5, 10, 21, 135–7, 150–1.

Nangbafudo (Ture's second wife), 28,
41, 43–44, 53, 59, 79, 80, 86, 99, 103,
107, 136, 137, 138, 139, 147, 148,
178, 182, 212.
Nanzagbe (Ture's first wife), 28, 40–43,
46, 51, 59, 71–73, 76–77, 78, 79, 81–
82, 95, 96, 97, 103, 119, 122, 131–2,
135, 136, 137, 138, 139, 141, 144,
145, 146, 147, 148, 151, 161, 162,
163, 165–7, 178, 182, 183–4, 190,
192, 193, 195, 196, 197, 198, 203,
209, 223–4.
Natagbinda (one of Ture's wives), 178.
Nawondiga (one of Ture's wives), 182.
Nzagbe (Ture's daughter), 190, 192,
195.

owl, 153.

partridge, 192.
pigeon, 179.

rat, 37, 67–68, 102, 103–4, 130, 131,
146, 183, 190–1, 193, 196–8, 203.

rubber-vine, 57–58, 63.

salt, 1, 10, 41, 90–91, 153, 158, 171,
180, 193, 214, 216.
sesame, 7, 10, 63, 64, 91, 92, 107, 108,
144, 146, 171, 172, 176, 212, 214,
217, 218, 221.
snake, 8, 47.
spider, 20, 23; *see also under* Ture.
squirrel, 152.
stone outcrops (-flats), 1, 38, 41, 48, 49,
81, 82, 146, 147.
swallow, 201.
sweet potato, 7, 100, 175.

termites (and their mounds), 1, 5, 9, 10,
11, 21, 27, 40–42, 43–44, 50, 51, 55,
58–59, 66, 67, 73, 74, 76–77, 79–80,
81–83, 97–99, 102, 120, 136, 137,
138, 144, 145, 146, 149, 150, 159–61,
165–7, 168, 170, 178, 223–4.
thunder, 27, 141–2, 164.
toad, 8, 30, 146–8.
tortoise, 81–83, 160, 224.
Ture, *passim*; *see also under* spider.

vogo tree, 153–5.
vulture, 62, 163–4, 195, 201.

wagtail, 27, 81–83.
waterbuck, 107, 198, 217.
weaver-bird, 28, 75, 201.
woodpecker, 120, 121.

yam, 1, 7, 10, 11, 38–39, 95–96, 147,
163–4, 185, 186, 187, 188, 189.